I'M ALIVE

The Bishop Michael Reid Story

JAMES PETER JANDU

INDIA • SINGAPORE • MALAYSIA

ISBN 979-8-89322-657-7

Disclaimer: This book contains direct quotations and statements attributed to individuals as recounted by them or documented in writing. These are presented to provide a faithful representation of their perspectives and experiences at the time these statements were made. The inclusion of these quotations is intended for the purpose of discussion and analysis within the context of this book. It does not imply the author's endorsement of every view or detail contained therein. The statements are reproduced here to offer a comprehensive narrative and are meant to reflect the views of the individuals who made them, not necessarily those of the author. While efforts have been made to present these statements accurately and within context, the interpretation of such material may vary among readers.

The opinions, beliefs, and viewpoints expressed by the author in this book do not necessarily reflect the opinions, beliefs, and viewpoints of any affiliated institutions or individuals. This narrative is intended to provide a personal perspective on the author's life experiences and is not intended to defame, purge, or malign any entity, individual, or group. The conversations, thoughts, and emotions detailed herein are represented to the best of the author's memory and have been reconstructed for narrative purposes. Some dialogues and events have been compressed, expanded, or otherwise modified to fit the coherence and structure of the book.

This work is presented as a recounting of personal experiences and is not intended as a comprehensive historical documentation. The author acknowledges that other participants in these events may have different recollections and interpretations.

By proceeding beyond this point, the reader acknowledges this disclaimer and accepts that the author and publisher are not liable for any misunderstandings, offences, or damages perceived to have been caused by the content of this book.

Honouring the cherished memory of Bishop Michael Reid
(15 May 1943 – 13 January 2023) and Dr Ruth Reid
(1945 – December 2011) for their many years of
dedication to the Gospel of Christ.

Contents

Contents

Preface

*"The story of his conversion and subsequent
global ministry is truly unique."*

T.L. Osborn, Osborn Ministries International

Prepare to be astonished by this story that undoubtedly bears the fingerprints of God. Throughout my writing experience, this piece stands unquestionably out as the most unforgettable. While crafting this book, I had to pause and blink away tears of joy and sadness. Undeniably, this is a genuine account of a triumph of Biblical proportions.

This book is for anyone seeking to understand the ways of God. Ministers especially ought to thoroughly read this from beginning to end, ensuring not to overlook a single word. It offers exclusive, undisclosed insights from the life of Bishop Michael Reid, revealing how God calls and accomplishes His work through earthly vessels.

This writing, spanning over three decades, began as a gift idea in the 1990s by Dr Reid for her husband's fiftieth birthday. Bishop Reid added his version, and in 2010 they invited me to provide an updated perspective. The project was on hold until 2023 when I decided to complete it as a tribute to this extraordinary couple. Their story must be told, and it cannot be forgotten - the half has not been told. I was determined not to let Bishop Reid's life and my experiences with him vanish in the grave. Hence, I wove these stories into the book you are now reading, preserving his memory for future generations.

I recall that whenever I or someone else asked Bishop Reid how he was, he'd answer vociferously, "I'm alive!"

Introduction

Bishop Michael Reid was celebrated by many. To truly comprehend him, one must delve into factors shaping his identity—encompassing God, interpersonal relationships, inherent traits, and beyond. My collaboration with him shaped my view of who he is, influencing this book's perspective. It presents the narrative from Bishop Reid's viewpoint, making it biased in that regard.

Indeed, a story has two sides, but the other side has been widely shared. A key lesson emerges in this story: refrain from hasty judgements fuelled by gossip; grudge holders tend to depict a distorted reality. As the adage goes: 'A lie can travel halfway around the world while the truth is still putting on its shoes.'

Nonetheless, this account emphasises compassion, avoiding belittlement of anyone's experiences, and acknowledging our shared human fallibility. We are all like roses with thorns. I aim to provide accurate information; therefore, I use legal documents, emails, and letters whenever possible. Any misinformation is unintentional. Repetition and discrepancies may arise due to limited sources and multiple authors writing across three decades.

Chapter 1 by James Jandu summarises Bishop Michael Reid's life history, commencing with a prophecy from 1855.

Chapters 2 to 4 are authored by Bishop Michael Reid: a living testimony of a living God working in a living ministry and an example of how God builds His Church and prepares a ministry as a gift to it.

Chapters 5 to 16, penned by Dr Ruth Reid, guide us through the formative years, her meeting with her husband, the birth of the Church, and the trials and adventures of their ministry life. Parts of this chapter were written in the 1990s, so they read in the present tense.

Chapters 17 to 25, authored by James Jandu, cover Bishop Reid's ministry accomplishments, the circumstances leading to his dismissal and my introduction to him. I outline how my journey to be with him was part of God's plan, and the purpose behind it was unveiled in due time in a private message he and Dr Reid conveyed to my wife and me.

In conclusion, the final chapter summarises valuable lessons from the life of Bishop Reid, aiming to glorify God through these accounts of a contemporary Apostle of Jesus Christ.

Chapter 1
Michael Reid

A Brief History
By James Peter Jandu
1855 Supernatural Visitation

"The time has come! Now is the time to leave this country! We must flee to America. All who remain here will perish."

This remarkable 19th-century prophecy led to an intricate series of events that ultimately gave rise to the ministry of Bishop Michael Reid—a story of love, dedication, and betrayal.

In 1855, Efim Gerasemovitch Klubniken, an Armenian boy from Kara Kala, became renowned as the 'Boy Prophet.' At age eleven, he received a vision. Efim prophesied an imminent era of unspeakable tragedy in the region. He warned of a time when they must flee to a land across the sea.

In the early 1900s, the Lord directed Efim to warn Armenians of an imminent prophecy. Accepting the message, believers sold everything and migrated to America. Among the first to leave were

Efim and his family. Demos Shakarian Sr., who relocated from Armenia to America in 1905, is the forebear of Demos Shakarian.

The prophecy came true, resulting in a tragic loss of over a million lives and the destruction of Kara Kala. [See Appendix for full story]

Demos Shakarian had a vision of ordinary Christians gathering, so in 1952, he founded the Full Gospel Business Men's Fellowship International (F.G.B.M.F.I.). The inaugural guest speaker for F.G.B.M.F.I. was Oral Roberts. It spread into over 80 nations - meeting in thousands of chapters.

In 1965, an airlift of 375 Americans, led by Demos Shakarian, arrived in England.

In a crowd of around 4,000, Demos Shakarian singled out Michael Reid, then an atheist, and heard God saying, "Go get that man. I have a work for him to do."

In a crowd of around 4,000, Demos Shakarian singled out Michael Reid, then an atheist, and heard God saying, "Go get that man. I have a work for him to do."

Michael Stafford Baines Reid

Michael Stafford Baines Reid was a Christian leader based in Essex, England, widely recognised as Bishop Michael Reid and the visionary behind the Peniel Pentecostal Church, later known as Michael Reid Ministries. His life was guided by an invisible divine hand, including a ministry spanning over three decades.

He was born in Beckenham, Kent, on May 15th, 1943, amidst a world at war. Meanwhile, significant figures were emerging across different corners of the world, each destined for their unique paths that would cross with his. Oral Roberts was pastoring a small Church in Shawnee, Oklahoma. At the same time, T.L. Osborn

                    I'M ALIVE

embarked on his first pastorate in Portland, Oregon. In Nigeria, Benson Idahosa played under the scorching Sun. At the same time, a young Judson Cornwall, only 19 years old, completed Bible School and got married, while a three-and-a-half-year-old Nicky Cruz grew up on the witchcraft-infested island of Puerto Rico.

In this remarkable year, Michael Reid came into the world, weighing 10 pounds 12 ounces, amidst an air raid. A joyous and responsive baby, he had an older brother, John, just 13 months ahead of him, whose mission in life seemed to be brushing Michael's hair.

Yet, the shadow of war loomed over Michael's life. When he was a mere few months old, his mother's quick actions saved him from a Luftwaffe attack at Biggin Hill airfield, pulling him from his pram just moments before a German Messerschmitt aimed its cannons at it, becoming trapped in the trees—had it shifted just two inches further, he would have perished. This incident underscored the protective hand of Almighty in his life. However, this was not the only time Michael defied death.

When Michael was at the tender age of two, Barbara McCartney, whom God had destined to be his wife, was born in Uganda. Christian influence touched Michael's life early on, with his paternal step-grandmother teaching him to pray at four. Remarkably, by five, his gift for debating was already well-developed, impressing a barrister friend of his father, who foresaw a future for Michael in Parliament, the law, or the pulpit. Possessing an exceptional memory, Michael could recite extensive passages from Henry Wadsworth Longfellow's epic poem, "Hiawatha."

The family eventually settled in Westgate, Kent, where Michael found delight in spending joyful hours playing in rock pools on the beach. However, one eventful day, a near-drowning incident brought him face-to-face with fear as a wave swept him into the sea. He felt a sudden connection to God's presence in that moment of distress, and he was miraculously rescued by a woman sitting on the promenade.

As Michael's life unfolded, he encountered challenges and blessings, leading him on a path of faith and service. Along the way, his journey intertwined with significant figures and events that would shape his destiny.

God was diligently working on developing Judson Cornwall, a 25-year-old pastor at a small Church in Kennewick, Washington, while in the same year, 1951, T.L. Osborn's influential book, "Healing the Sick," was published, playing an indirect but impactful role in Michael's life from the late 1960s onwards. Also, in that eventful year, God inspired Demos Shakarian, a 38-year-old dairy farmer from Los Angeles, to establish the Full Gospel Businessmen Fellowship International (F.G.B.F.I.), thousands of miles away from Kent. Little did anyone know that 14 years later, Demos Shakarian would play an unforeseen role in Michael's life.

The timing seemed divinely orchestrated when, just ten weeks after Michael's ninth birthday, 33-year-old Oral Roberts delivered the inaugural message of the F.G.B.F.I on July 27th, 1952. Tragedy struck Michael's life as he lost his father at just 39 years old, succumbing to a heart attack exacerbated by his past wartime experiences. His death left the family facing financial struggles, compounded by his mother's pregnancy with their fourth child, leading to the foreclosure of their home by the bank.

Due to his father's affiliation with Freemasonry, Michael and his brother John received education at Masonic boarding schools, with Michael residing at the Royal Masonic School in Bushey, Hertfordshire, for several years. During this time, his passion for sports blossomed, dreaming of becoming a professional athlete and admiring cricket legends such as Godfrey Evans, Dennis Compton, Len Hutton, Frank Typhoon Tyson, and Jim Laker.

Throughout ages nine to eighteen, Michael's life revolved around boarding school routines, occasional visits home and to Ireland during holidays, moments of mischief, and aspirations of athletic glory. The Anglican services at the school didn't resonate with him, leading to a period of cynicism towards religion due to perceived hypocrisy among the clergy. However, this journey of scepticism would eventually pave the way for his return to God.

At the age of 12, while Michael was on his path, 15-year-old Nicky Cruz was sent from Puerto Rico to live with his brother in New York City, leading him down a different, tumultuous path into gang life in the Bronx for the next three years. Just eight weeks after Michael's 15th birthday in July 1958, Nicky Cruz, who had recently found salvation, began attending Bible School in California.

God continued to work out His plan, and in 1960, during Michael's final year at school, Benson Idahosa experienced a life-changing encounter with God in Nigeria. This event birthed a ministry that not only impacted the nation's Christian population within 30 years but also, 35 years later, forged connections between Michael's ministry and those of Oral and Richard Roberts and T.L. Osborn.

Before becoming a pastor, Michael Reid was a Metropolitan police officer and an insurance salesman. A 35-year-old Judson Cornwall began constructing a Church in Eugene, Oregon. At the same time, at 37 years old, T.L. Osborn returned to India after 14 years.

At 18, Michael entered local government and excelled, passing the Royal Institute of Chartered Surveyors exams in estate management. However, after only 18 months in this career, his hunger for something more challenging and thrilling led him to join the police force. After training at Hendon Police College, he served in the Metropolitan Police Force, starting as a traffic officer and later joining the C.I.D., patrolling Mayfair and Soho. His dedication to rid society of criminals led to numerous arrests and convictions, surpassing the accomplishments of many in their lifetime. His bravery and commitment led to commendations and a reputation for fearlessly apprehending criminals.

Despite his outwardly unshakeable atheism, Michael was nicknamed "Tiger" for fearlessly engaging in debates with fervent Christians while serving as a police officer. However, Michael's soul was troubled beneath this strong facade, often contemplating life's purpose during sleepless nights. Despite internal promptings to pray, he ignored them.

In 1965, divine timing intervened as God began to weave together the threads He had carefully prepared for generations. American Church leaders, including Demos Shakarian and Oral Roberts, arrived in England, and two police colleagues invited Michael to attend their meeting. Initially sceptical, he sought to debunk God's existence but was profoundly moved by testimonies of transformation through Jesus, especially from a 25-year-old Nicky Cruz.

Demos Shakarian singled out Michael and invited him to another meeting to discuss drug addiction. A decisive moment unfolded when an African American lady sang "The Old Rugged Cross" with tears running down her cheeks, followed by singing in tongues. Touched by this experience, Michael realised God's reality. At his conversion, he heard what seemed to him to be an audible voice telling him, *"Give all you have, and I will provide."* He promptly emptied his wallet into the donation bowl and has stuck to this principle ever since. This marked the beginning of his obedient journey in service to God's calling.

 I'M ALIVE

The following day, Michael spent time with Nicky Cruz, further intertwining their lives. 1965 also saw the official opening of Oral Roberts University, which significantly impacted Michael's later ministry. Discovering his spiritual gifts, he realised he could no longer continue as a police officer. Thus, he transitioned to a new path, praying for the sick, preaching, and eventually working in a home for rehabilitating drug addicts and alcoholics.

Regrettably, an incident at the home led to Michael suffering a fractured spine. Miraculously, healing evangelist Richard Balter prayed over the telephone, and the fractures reunited after the cast was removed.

Starting from the instant of his spiritual rebirth, Bishop Reid was instilled with a deep yearning for the knowledge of God. He ardently immersed himself in the Bible and the works of divinely influenced individuals, including George Whitefield, George Fox, Charles Spurgeon, and Smith Wigglesworth. His commitment to growing in Christ was steadfast: *"When I first became a Christian, I couldn't find people who knew what I experienced. I went to Church after Church...I found a place where there was life. I'll tell you every weekend on a Friday when I got out of work, I drove 250 miles to go where there was life and drive back overnight on the Sunday to get back to work on the Monday."* He continued: *"...When I went into business... God came first.... because the Word of God was the most precious thing in my life...I never missed a weekend..."*

Starting from the instant of his spiritual rebirth, Bishop Reid was instilled with a deep yearning for the knowledge of God. He ardently immersed himself in the Bible and the works of divinely influenced individuals, including George Whitefield, George Fox, Charles Spurgeon, and Smith Wigglesworth.

In 1968, God's plan entered the next phase as He spoke to Michael again, directing him to find a "Paul" to sit under. Obediently, Michael moved to the north of England and spent two years under the ministry of Pastor G.W. (Wally) North, witnessing the Church's growth to around 250 members.

However, conflict arose due to jealousy and political manoeuvring, leading Michael to clash with the Church elders, who eventually turned against him. Disillusioned, he vowed never to preach again, opting for a career in selling printing machines. Although he excelled in this field, it was a challenging time for Michael.

Unbeknownst to Michael, significant events unfolded in the lives of individuals who would later play pivotal roles in his journey. Benson Idahosa married Margaret in Nigeria. T.L. and Daisy Osborn held their monumental Congo campaign in February 1970, and Oral Roberts fought for his university's accreditation.

On May 8th, 1970, Michael attended a meeting in Liverpool, unaware that Barbara McCartney, a 24-year-old woman, was also present. God spoke to her, revealing that he was the man she would marry. Introduced by mutual friend Roy Cossack, they quickly connected and went out for coffee with a group. Within seven weeks, they were engaged, and on October 10th, 1970, they exchanged vows in Liverpool, adding another significant thread to the tapestry of their lives.

Just two weeks before, Benson Idahosa acquired his first plot of land for a Church. Concurrently, Oral Roberts opened the Mabee Centre in Tulsa, achieving unanimous full accreditation in July 1972. Around the same time, Benson Idahosa held his inaugural evangelistic campaign in Benin City. At the same time, Michael achieved accolades in his sales career. Their second child, Matthew, was born, and life seemed to be on an upward trajectory.

Michael initially stopped preaching due to negative Church experiences. His path changed when his company pressured him to compromise his integrity, prompting a job search. Despite an appealing sales position in South England, Michael prioritised his values over wealth. He answered his calling, founding a Christian bookshop and printing business in Ripon, Yorkshire, marking a new chapter in his life.

As he engaged with customers in the bookshop, Michael openly discussed matters of faith and prayed with them, yet he hesitated to step into preaching. Across thousands of miles in Nigeria, Benson Idahosa had completed his new Church and started broadcasting the Redemption Hour on national T.V. The influence of T.L. Osborn on Michael's life was apparent as he shared reel-to-reel footage of T.L. Osborn's Crusades in churches and gatherings throughout the early 1970s.

During this time, Michael's life took various twists and turns. He joined the Christian community of Turner's Hall in Essex, where he encountered individuals who would later form the Onger Christian Fellowship. Amidst financial struggles, illnesses, and emotional hardships, Michael and his family faced a trying period. However, divine intervention brought about a miraculous improvement in the health of his youngest daughter, Sarah, reigniting Michael's commitment to his calling.

Bishop Reid's 1989 Interview with Demos Shakarian: *"…my third child…was six months old. And I began to notice something was wrong with her. We took her to the hospital, and she had tests. And the specialist said, Whatever you do, put this daughter of yours into a home. She'll be a vegetable. She'll never move. She'll never talk. She'll never do anything." [Holds back tears] And it was a sad time.*

And I cried to God, and I said, "Lord, it can't be that way." I prayed many prayers that he'd take her home because I couldn't bear it. And one day, in a meeting, God came and spoke, and he asked me whether I loved her. And I said, "Father, you know I love her."

And he came again and said, "Do you love your daughter?" And I said, "You know I love her."

Then, the third time, he came and asked me the same question. He said, "Do you love your daughter?" And I said, "You know I love her." And then he said the most wonderful words to me. He said, "Well, if you love her as an earthly father, how much more do you think I love her as a heavenly father?" And at that moment, I knew he'd heal her. And we watched from that day on. Everything changed. And within six months, we took her back to the same specialist, and she's perfectly healed... she's fourteen now, and when she runs towards me with her arms outstretched, saying, "Daddy, Daddy, I remember there's a God of grace and love who heals, who delivers, who makes whole. And God used it to turn my heart again to the call that was put there all those years ago when you first met me."

Amid these challenges, Michael's career took an unexpected turn as he found a new job with Save and Prosper. His exceptional performance led to him being promoted to President of the Sales Force, overseeing two hundred and fifty men. He was recognised with numerous awards and even addressed the entire company during a luxurious trip to Rome, receiving the prestigious Ian Gibson trophy.

Unknown to Michael, God orchestrated events globally, aligning everything in Benin City. Benson Idahosa's completion of the impressive Miracle Centre set the stage for an unexpected adventure in Michael's life.

Rev. Trevor Dearing relayed a message from God to Michael Reid, stating that if he didn't resume preaching immediately, he never would. Despite initial reluctance, Michael received a divine directive to commence preaching. His mother's reaction to his ministry calling was severe: *"I lost my father when I was nine, but I remember my mother when I got a good job, and I was prospering and doing well and when I told her I was giving it all up to follow the Lord she went bananas. 'How can you do that?'...in fact, for four years, she didn't speak to me, wouldn't write to me, wouldn't communicate with me."*[1]

In 1976, Bishop Reid started a Bible Study in his home in Bowes Drive, Ongar, Essex, with three people - the Church's birth. On November 14th, 1976, Ongar Christian Fellowship held its inaugural service at a spacious home in Fyfield, Essex. Rev. Trevor Dearing delivered an inspiring sermon and offered prayers for the sick to a congregation of around thirty individuals. Following this service, the congregation continued to meet at his house or another location called Ashlings in Moreton, Essex, as both places could accommodate the growing number of attendees. As Bishop Michael Reid preached, taught, and conducted healing ministry, the Church attracted an ever-increasing number of people. He balanced his marketing career over the next three years while gradually transitioning into full-time ministry.

In the late '70s, Bishop Reid attended a meeting where missionary R. Edward Miller, originally from Oregon, was preaching. Ed Miller had collaborated with Tommy Hicks in Argentina, where crusade attendance reached between 200,000 to 500,000 people. God instructed Bishop Reid to have this man speak in his Church, though he initially resisted for about twenty minutes. Remarkably, Ed Miller had only one evening available during his stay in England. Within two minutes of driving Ed to the meeting, Bishop Reid recognised him as a man sent by God. Astonishingly, 18 years prior, during the revival in Argentina, Ed had a vision of a man in England whom he would meet, and that man turned out to be Bishop Reid.

---

1 Sermon, June 16th, 1985

Before Michaels conversion, God had already foretold this encounter to Ed. Ed cancelled his itinerary and stayed with the Reids for a fortnight. They would talk from 6 a.m. until 3 a.m. the following day. Michael had finally found someone who understood his deepest desires.

Two or three months later, the Church had a visitation from God, during which He instructed Michael to stack the chairs. The Church increased rapidly, outgrowing its premises several times, and by 1981, the largest publicly available hall in Ongar could no longer accommodate it.

God had challenged Michael to build a Church according to how he wanted it to operate, as he was very sceptical about what he had seen in many churches throughout the country. Despite facing accusations of control, he never pursued ministry aggressively. He says: *"I find so many people they're looking for ministry they're looking for gifts, they're looking to do something. Hey, the source is God himself."* In a sermon around June 16th, 1985, he details his preaching struggle: *"I've never found it easy being a pastor...I find it very difficult because it goes against my natural nature. Naturally speaking, I'm a very shy, inhibitive person. No one believes that, but it's true. In my nature, that's in my inner nature, ... I've always found it very hard to stand up in front of people and speak...I always was very embarrassed. I grew up very shy, introverted...I find sometimes...when I see the things that [...] I want to run."* Only those indeed called by God comprehend the challenges of leading a ministry.

During a sermon titled Christian Diligence, he clarified: *"You know, being a preacher is the most dastardly thing in life because you get up every week and you preach what God gives you to preach and... it's the foolishness of preaching that saves people, and you know that at least two-thirds...that sit in front of you.....are going sit there, listen and do nothing about it...no matter what you say to them. ...and you think, 'My God, there's better ways to earn a living.' ...Paul said, 'Woe be me if I don't preach the Gospel.' The love of Christ constrains me. The only reason I'm here is because I love Christ. If you think you drew me here, think again honey, they're better things to do with life...this isn't an easy job..."*

Despite challenges, he persisted as a resilient leader, and God established a significant ministry through him. In its early expansion, the Church encountered numerous adventures and incidents.

National Exposure:
False Accusations against His Ministry

In 1982, the Church changed its name to Peniel Pentecostal Church after relocating from Ongar. Peniel was the place where Jacob met face-to-face with God (Genesis 32:30). Michael Reid's ministry was far from dull, brimming with divine escapades as he encountered God face-to-face.

In 1981, News of the World tabloid approached Bishop Reid, alleging that he was a cult leader running hostels with 18-year-old girls. In response, Bishop Reid requested to visit the alleged hostels to verify the situation, offering his Church members' details for verification if the accusers disclosed their names. He also cautioned against publishing such a story, threatening legal action for libel.

Later, it appeared that an organisation linked to a Church member's mother orchestrated false accusations. The Assemblies of God issued a favourable report on Peniel Academy. However, the organisation, led by F.A. Allen, sent a letter claiming Peniel Church was a cult. Bishop Reid contacted the leader, and the Chairman admitted the letter was baseless, leading to an unexpected twist in the plot.

One morning, a man named Brown called at 7 a.m., wanting to meet and share helpful information. Bishop Reid agreed, but before proceeding, he consulted with his solicitor, who advised caution, warning that this might be a newspaper trap.

On the scheduled day, Dr Ruth Reid, Meidre Cleminson, and Bishop Reid met at the agreed-upon location outside C.L.C. While Bishop and Dr Reid waited at a nearby restaurant, Meidre patrolled the street. After a long wait with no one showing up, Bishop Reid took the initiative and found a man wearing a red scarf and trench coat in a shop. They brought him to a restaurant, where he mistakenly believed Japanese tourists were involved in a plot to trap him. Bishop Reid had to reassure him that the tourists were unrelated. This meeting sparked significant suspicions: Who was this man, and what was his motive?

During the discussions, it was revealed that Special Branch had infiltrated a particular organisation, and the person was their operative. He presented a significant document at the meeting. Special Branch later sent Bishop Reid the organisation's meeting minutes, which mentioned that prophets of God were aware of their conversations. Bishop Reid pursued legal action and won the lawsuit.

Global Media Attention

The Peniel Pentecostal Church was part of the International Communion of Charismatic Churches (I.C.C.C.), a coalition of national and international ministries. At the time, the I.C.C.C. included over 6,000 leaders in Africa, Australia, Europe, North, Central and South America, and Asia. These leaders represented over 10 million people. After years of resistance, Archbishop Benson Idahosa eventually convinced Pastor Reid to undergo consecration, and in 1997, he was bestowed with the title of Bishop by the I.C.C.C. in Benin City, Nigeria.

In 1999, the Church gained worldwide media attention with an ad featuring David Gregg's miraculous healing from sciatica. This led to a dispute with the Advertising Standards Association

     I'M ALIVE

regarding miracles, resulting in coverage by major media outlets like CNN, U.K. national newspapers, T.V. news stations, and the BBC World Service.

The ministry later became known as Michael Reid Ministries while preserving the Peniel name for its college, school, and choir. Between 2003 and 2006, Michael Reid Ministries experienced unprecedented growth as it approached its 30ᵗʰ anniversary.

Bishop Reid consistently invited top Christian speakers, including Dr T.L. Osborn, Archbishop Benson Idahosa, Dr Judson Cornwall, Dr Marilyn Hickey, Dr Richard Roberts, Archbishop Silas Owiti, Bishop Robert Kayanja, Dr Terry Law, Rev. Bill Wilson, and Rev. Melvin Banks, among others, making the ministry a host to some of the finest ministry gifts in the Christian Church.

Worldwide mission trips from North America to the Middle East, Africa, and Australia increased significantly, with thousands of healing and salvation miracles. Peniel Academy, now ten times larger, consistently achieved the top ten national examination rankings. Peniel College of Higher Education rapidly expanded, offering O.R.U. bachelor's degrees, bachelor's, master's, and Ph.D. degrees from University of Wales, and a Bible diploma for distance learners.

In 2005, Bishop Reid and other notable figures founded the Christian Congress for Traditional Values (CCTV), which gained widespread exposure through live national television and radio appearances. CCTV's mission of addressing moral and legislative challenges to the Christian voice has had a significant national impact. This significantly impacted later events, resulting in a ministry takeover.

Over three decades, Bishop Michael Reid and Dr Ruth Reid established a remarkable ministry that included an internationally renowned Church, the largest charismatic Bible College in the U.K., and a prestigious school that was one of the top schools in the U.K.

Global Ministry

Michael and his wife Ruth journeyed across the globe, spreading the message of miracles, healing, and faith, and serving the Church. At a graduation ceremony, Dr Richard Roberts, President of Oral Roberts University, introduced Bishop Reid to a crowd of approximately 10,000. He thought it was appropriate for Bishop Reid to be awarded an honorary degree for his lifelong service to global Christianity, considering he had earned a master's degree in practical theology in 1998 and a Doctor of Ministry degree in 2002.

Bishop Reid dedicated the degree to those who greatly influenced his life: Demos Shakarian, and his late friends Archbishop Benson Idahosa, Dr T. L. Osborn, and Chancellor Oral Roberts.

He played a notable role in the Pentecostal landscape, participating in events like the Society for Pentecostal Studies. Established in 1970, the society offers a platform for interpreting the Pentecostal Movement for the broader Church community. The 32nd annual gathering was the largest of thought leaders from the Wesleyan and Pentecostal charismatic spheres. At this event, Bishop Reid, representing the I.C.C.C., presented his doctoral thesis on the unbiblical nature of Strategic Level Spiritual Warfare.

Guided and Protected by God

Several times, his life was divinely shielded to fulfil his calling.

"One day, I was going to Upminster with my wife to catch the underground train. However, I felt something was wrong, so I decided not to go to London. I didn't like the idea, so we returned home. It turns out that the train we decided not to board was the one where three

I'm Alive

Muslims with kit bags carried out an explosion...Thankfully, we never got on that train. Thank God." [Referencing the 7 July 2005 London bombings, also known as 7/7]

"When I was in Israel years ago with my wife...in Jerusalem, and... we wanted to go out and get coffee...so we went out to look at a coffee shop...with friends. We came to a place where there was a coffee shop, and there were tables by the window. Ruth and I walked in there with our friends. And we were going to sit down, and I just said, 'No, I don't want to drink coffee in this place. I just don't like it. Come on, we'll go back to the hotel.'

"We went back to the hotel...10...15 minutes from the coffee shop...We got coffee with a little harassment... So they bought us coffee with some biscuits."

As we sat down, we heard a big explosion. Five minutes later, the police came to the hotel. At the very coffee shop we'd gone to sit in by the window, an Arab, a Palestinian...put his bicycle...full of Semtex, in the frame of it...just outside the window.... there were women and children...it would have been us killed. I think they killed about 20...I saw these poor people running around...thank God, when we walked into that coffee shop, I just had a feeling, 'No, we don't want to be here.' Fortunately, I did, or I wouldn't be here now."[2]

Guided by God, he built a tremendous ministry, recognising God as the source but understanding that it required more than a divine call: *"Do you know what makes this Church what it is? Faithful people. People who have given their lives to be faithful. I'll tell you what makes the school the most successful in the country: faithful people. I'll tell you what makes the Church what it is: faithful people."* Indeed, like every God-established ministry, the wheat and the tares grew together.

---

2 May 12th, 2016

Chapter 2
Saved for a Purpose

By Michael Reid

It happened on a sunny day in August. I was only six years old; my brother John was thirteen months older than me. Our family had gone down to the beach to enjoy the Sun and the sea near our home at Westgate, Kent. Just before our picnic lunch, the pair of us ran down the slipway from the promenade to play in the sea. It was high tide, and the waves were washing up the slipway. My parents were preparing the picnic on the promenade, and it seemed such an idyllic day.

At that time, I had not learnt to swim, but the slipway was very wide, and we felt quite safe playing there. John and I began to play underwater, holding our breath to see who could stay under the longest. Suddenly, a strong wave washed me away, and with my outstretched foot, I felt the edge of the slipway. All of a sudden, that idyllic day turned into one of panic. The sea was over 12 feet deep. I could not swim, and I could not get back to the safety of the slipway. I had my eyes open and saw bubbles of air going up and knew I was drowning, and there was no one to help. With seeming resignation, I remember thinking, "O God, here I come," as I lost consciousness.

It was a busy weekend at the beach, and as it was lunchtime, many of the families were driven to the promenade by the high tides and were busy preparing their meals. Others were sunbathing and enjoying a beautiful day. There was one woman eating her lunch and looking out to sea. Suddenly, she just about noticed a little hand break the surface of the water between the waves. She leapt up and dived off the promenade, fully clothed, and swam quickly to where she had seen the hand. She plucked my unconscious body from the sea and brought me back to the slipway and out of the sea. Very quickly, a doctor friend who was there helped to revive me. To this day, I thank God for that woman who rescued me.

I was not a Christian at the time and had never heard the Gospel, but somehow, deep inside, I knew I belonged to God. It was a child-like simple faith, born from a grandmother who had taught John and me to pray when I was four years old. When she came to visit, she taught us simple prayers to say every night and John. Her influence put within my life a seed that would, in years to come, bear fruit. In a very simple way, I was plucked from the deep with a heart that was committed to God.

I was not a Christian at the time and had never heard the Gospel, but somehow, deep inside, I knew I belonged to God.

As years have gone by, I realise how Almighty God has everything under His control. A woman, on a promenade on a day out, was observant enough to see a child in distress and act as a guardian angel. So many times, I meet people who recount how God has intervened to save them supernaturally from the most terrifying circumstances, and their realisation that they always belonged to God. It is a revelation to which every true child of God comes. We were in Him before the foundation of the world. Everything in our lives proves it. Once we are born again and filled with His Spirit, everything in life begins to make sense, and we understand how the hand of God has worked out every detail. The negatives of life become positives when we see His hand protecting us, keeping us, and drawing us to Himself.

Many times in life, we experience ups and downs as circumstances seem to conspire to rob us of what we feel we have. From that moment when I knew God had plucked me from the deep, I began a quest to find the reality of who God was and what He was really like. My parents were not churchgoers, far from it. They were turned off by Church and religion, except for baptisms, marriages, and funerals. Yet, somehow inside of me, I knew there was a God who was real.

When I was eight years old, another strange thing happened. At two o'clock in the morning, I was awakened by a neighbour. I was surprised to find him in our house. My brother and I did not know what was going on when he told us, "Your mother needs you both to be brave." We did not know what he meant, and then he revealed that my father had died of a heart attack just an hour before, and my mother was really in shock. Everything became a blur. As a youngster, I did not know what to think, but I remember the next morning when I was in our garden, after breakfast, I saw a hearse come and take away a coffin with my father inside, and the strangest thing happened. Within myself, I thought, "If Jesus had been here, my father wouldn't have died. He would have raised him up." Deep inside of me, I had a strange faith and a comfort that took away grief and pain. It was not something I could explain to anyone, but it was so real to me. In my teenage years, I went to a public school where we had chapel every morning. There came a time when I wanted to meet with God.

                    I'M ALIVE

There was a longing in my heart to find the reality of His life. It was hard to explain to people what it was that worked within me, but somehow, I felt that God had to be more real than He was portrayed in the chapels. I tried to reach out to Him. How disillusioned I was, talking to clergy who only had the concept of religion, without the living encounter with Christ. I am sad to say that I got completely turned off from the things of God when I saw the hypocrisy. It just made me angry realising they did not know any better than me.

When I left school, I joined the police. I believed I could make a difference in society and do something to correct the wrongs that I saw so patently obvious. I dedicated myself to really working for what was right. Once again, I found scepticism and corruption were everywhere. People's motives were far removed from what I expected. It was a political minefield, and it was not long before I saw the absurdity of our legal system, our prison system, and the uselessness of an individual trying to make a difference by putting people behind bars. The frustration of everything got me down. Many a night, when I got home to my section house in the early hours of the morning, I heard a still small voice saying, "Why don't you pray?" and I would turn over in my bed and go to sleep, angry that such a thought had come to my mind. But grandmother's influence wouldn't die. There was a seed that had been planted, and it resolutely worked towards fruit.

It was just a few inconsequential happenings that changed a seed that seemed so dead into a blossoming harvest. A moment I shall never forget when a man filled with the Holy Spirit asked me the most important question of my life, "Do you believe that Jesus died on Calvary's tree and took all your sins into His own body, that He took the power and the punishment of it for you?"

I said, "I've always believed it," but for the first time in my life, I knew it inside.

"Do you believe," he asked, "That Jesus Christ was raised from the dead by the glory of God the Father?"

My answer was simple, "I've always believed it," but for the first time in my life, I knew it was true inside.

Faith was born in my heart at that moment, so different from the child-like belief and yet so similar. The seed that had fallen into the ground and died suddenly burst forth into new life. From that moment, it was as though I had never sinned in my life. I did not have a past, I had a future. Everything made sense. This God who had sought me out had finally burst into my soul. I was alive; alive in God and He lived in me. All the scepticism, all the fears, and all the rejection vanished in a second, and love enveloped my heart and soul. The God of whom my grandmother had spoken became my God, my Lord, and my King. Everything in the world was different. Everything I saw and thought was transformed the moment I confessed the truth of who Jesus is and what He had done for me. I had been born from above by a sovereign work of the living God and would never be the same again. What a God we serve.

The Early Years

When I was first converted and baptised in the Spirit, I was so full of joy that it was like walking on air. The Bible became so alive to me. I loved to read it. I just praised God for who He was and what He had done. Some months later, I met a Pentecostal pastor who was shocked to find my freedom in Christ. "Goodness me," he said. "You have to have a disciplined life to be a Christian," and proceeded to explain to me all the rituals I must go through to walk with God. Firstly, a quiet time of at least an hour every morning before I went to work. Secondly, I must read ten chapters of the Bible every day. Thirdly, every night examine my day and confess all my sins to

God. Then I had to examine my relationships with people and put them right daily, speak in tongues a minimum of an hour a day, and so on and so on.

I tried his ritualistic approach to Christianity and soon realised he had brought me under law, and I was no longer living under grace. If I failed in any of the tasks he had set me, I felt I was losing my relationship with God. I had been bewitched by legalism. I shook off his whole ritualistic way like a bad dream.

When I was a young man and newly born again, I just overflowed with joy. There was nothing that God had not done for me. Why, He became everything to me. He changed my mind, my heart, my soul, and my spirit and gave me rest for my soul. It was like walking on air. It was a carefree life because it was His life. I went to stay in a home in the north of England. One of the guests in the house was an ex-missionary from India. She was in her 50s and exuded every attribute of religion that anyone could imagine – she was utterly, totally, and inconsolably miserable. I felt so sorry for her when I realised she had spent years on the mission field and ended up in total frustration. I could not help singing and laughing. I was alive.

I shall never forget, that after a couple of days, she caught hold of my arm and said to me, "Young man, it's not natural to be happy all the time."

Throughout my life, I have found two types of ministers: those who seek to restore and lift up, and those who judge and condemn. Really, it is the seed of the bond versus the seed of the free. The seed of the bond are the religious people (the modern-day Pharisees and Sadducees) who always look for faults and condemn anyone who does not live by their standards. They have an austere legalistic system and woe betide you if you do not conform to their rules. That is exactly the problem that Jesus faced when He walked the Earth. The Pharisees and scribes could not allow Him to walk in liberty and were always looking to catch Him out in word or deed. I know Christian leaders who have that 'gift' and many so-called Christians who have been brought up with the misery of religion.

Throughout my life, I have found two types of ministers: those who seek to restore and lift up, and those who judge and condemn. Really, it is the seed of the bond versus the seed of the free.

When I was a young man, I was really enjoying a conference I was attending. The weather was beautiful, and during a lunch break, the young men went out onto the lawns and played football. We had a great game and went back to the afternoon meeting. We were greeted with frosty faces by old grouches. Our crime? We had kicked a football on a Sunday! How dare we desecrate 'The Lord's Day!' I remember some of the young men apologised to these miserable people who could not bear to see a man smile. I did not apologise. I was not going to bow to their religious spirit. I thoroughly enjoyed my game of football and thought how unwelcoming they made the Church of Jesus Christ. For them, it must be a place of no joy, no fun, and no laughter – let us just be serious and sad. Little wonder few young people wanted to be part of it.

Chapter 3
Ministry

By Michael Reid

When God first saved me, He spoke to me and said that if I gave everything, He would provide. It was an unconditional promise from a loving, heavenly father. For over 40 years, He has kept His word and never deprived me of one thing that I needed. When we started the Church 30 years ago, He spoke to me and said, "You know what you don't want, now build what you do want." I did not want anything that I saw others had built. I wanted a family, a group of people who would love one another, care for one another, and live in unity with one another. I also wanted to see the Church based, not on the "Enticing words of man's wisdom, but in demonstration of the Spirit and of power" (1 Cor. 2:4). I wanted the Church's faith to stand in the power of God, not the wisdom of man. From the earliest meetings, God did such beautiful miracles because wherever the Gospel is preached, miracles happen. No miracles, no Jesus! I realised I had to move out of the concepts of religion and live in the reality of God's life.

A fine example of what I am talking about occurred in the early days of our Church. At one meeting, a woman that I had never seen before arrived and sat in the front row. She looked very depressed and smelt like a stale ashtray. She listened to the simple Gospel message that was preached and responded to the altar call at the end of the service. I found out after the meeting that she had been a 'wino,' who could not start the day without at least a half bottle of wine. She was also a chain smoker (some sixty cigarettes a day). Her home situation was terrible, and her children were very maladjusted. Drunkenness was her way of coping with life.

Her second marriage was a disaster. She and her husband screamed at each other most of the time, and the neighbours got a running commentary of their battles, whether they wanted to hear them or not. That night, God sovereignly met her and totally delivered her from her drink habit, and the very desire to smoke vanished. Inside, her life changed. She went home from the meeting a new woman.

Her husband felt unable to cope with such a drastic transformation and, in a rage, smashed all the china in the house and threw a saucepan of boiling water through the kitchen window. He was out of control. So his dear wife decided, God had changed her so he could also change her husband! She brought him along to the next meeting, and they sat on the front row. He laughed the whole meeting long and ridiculed all the truths of God; yet, he had to admit that his wife was totally changed. He knew something had happened to her, but he could not explain it.

At the next meeting, she brought her husband again, and this time, there was a totally different reaction. He cried the whole meeting long, and at the end, he came forward and asked Jesus to save him. What a transformation! Everything changed in his life. A couple of days later, a neighbour confided to his wife that she was sorry her husband had walked out on her. She could not understand how the neighbour could have gotten such a strange idea, until the neighbour explained, "I haven't heard him shouting and throwing things, so I thought he'd left." She shared how Jesus had totally transformed their lives and set them free in a very sovereign way.

About two months after this woman had come to Church and been transformed, she brought her son, who was having terrible nightmares and was extremely violent. Truthfully, he had become this way by seeing the violence in his own home and living in an atmosphere of hatred and animosity. Now, everything had changed, and he could not cope with the transformation and became more disturbed than ever. I prayed for him, and immediately the nightmares stopped. His temper tantrums ceased, and he became calm and rational. Jesus Christ is the answer to every need. He meets us in our innermost beings and transforms our lives. There is no one like Him. He is the Saviour of the whole world.

One thing I would like to point out is that 30 years later the family is still going on with Christ and never once did they backslide or have problems with their previous bondages.

I remember well my first trip to Africa to visit the work of the late Archbishop Benson Idahosa at the Church of God Mission in Benin City, Nigeria. Archbishop Idahosa was a very good friend of mine and had told me that if I did not visit Benin City with him, he would not visit us in Brentwood anymore! He felt I needed to see what God had done in Nigeria and enlarge my vision.

It is so necessary to see success and allow it to inspire you to take on the challenge. Such was my experience in Nigeria. I saw over 40,000 pastors and elders from over 18 countries around Africa come to join in open-air meetings in Benin City for one week. I was amazed at the 1,500 people in the choir, the professionalism of the music in the Church, and the crowds that flocked on Sunday to hear the Word of God. My response to what I saw was to say, "If God can do it here in Africa, surely He can do it in England, or anywhere in the world?"

During his lifetime, Archbishop Benson Idahosa established over 6,000 churches with 7.5 million members in Nigeria. He was used by God to raise fourteen people from the dead and had a miraculous ministry that no one could deny. He visited over 149 different nations to preach the Gospel and poured out his life for the ministry. He was one of the most gentlemen I have ever known and yet strong in the power of God's Spirit. I shall never forget seeing him sitting in his office in Benin City with over 200 people waiting to see him. He spent time talking to each one, praying with them, and often reaching into his pocket to give them money to help them. He had time for the lowliest and cared about each individual. What made him so different from so many modern-day evangelists was that he would go amongst the crowd and talk to each one of them. He was accessible, available, and full of love for the individual. For me, he was closer than a brother, and I thank God that He brought Benson into my life.

Let me tell you what happened at one conference I attended in Benin City. The 30,000-capacity Faith Miracle Centre was packed; the gangways full. No one else could get into the building that afternoon. Everyone had come to hear the Word of God. In the midst of the excitement, there was a disturbance at the back of the hall. Someone was trying to push in but there was no way

     I'm Alive

to get inside the building. The Archbishop noticed the disturbance and stopped the meeting to ask what was going on. The report that came back was that a woman had brought her four-year-old son from the hospital. He had died of an asthmatic attack some four hours earlier and she had brought the corpse to ask the Archbishop to pray for him.

There was no way to pass through the crowds, so the little boy was passed over the heads of the people up to the platform. The Archbishop took the lifeless corpse into his arms, blew in his face three times, and then stood him up on the pulpit. To the amazement and joy of all present, life came back into the little boy, and he was totally healed and returned to his joyful mother. Three doctors had been unable to help with his asthma and he had died in the hospital emergency room. Yet three times the Archbishop blew in his face and life returned. It is little wonder that his ministry was so successful. I know I was there, along with some thirty people from my Church when it happened.

Archbishop Benson Idahosa was an unusual man, respected by all, misunderstood by many and feared by the government of Nigeria. I think my good friend, T.L. Osborn, described the Archbishop best when he said, "Truly, he was like an Old Testament prophet with a New Testament faith and understanding." Presidents shook in his presence and when he spoke, he spoke as a man with authority. He had an amazing ability to control large crowds and minister the Word of God with such power, demonstrating it with miracles following.

Over the years, some 40 years now, since I became a Christian, I have been amazed at the advent and demise of error. One moment a 'new truth' suddenly appears on the horizon and, due to worldwide media attention, Christendom gets hurtled into the latest fad. Christian books, magazines, and television programmes become obsessed with the 'new truth' and spread it across the world. The propagators become the people of the moment and race from platform to platform to speak in churches and at conferences. Usually, they talk of a 'new tide' sweeping Christendom, which will be the answer to all the Church's needs. Yet it is not long before people realise it was a mere doctrine of men and the wave turns into a stagnant pool.

I remember well going to the Albert Hall and listening to self-appointed apostles vowing to work together 'for the Kingdom's sake.' It was in the 1970s. Apparently, this was going to be the move to restore the 'Apostolic and Prophetic Movement.' Great swelling words of commitment, loyalty, and humility came from these so-called 'leaders.' No longer was there going to be competition; they were going to submit to each other. As I listened to what they were saying, I turned and said to my wife, "Give them six months, they'll be at each other's throats like dogs." I was totally wrong. It only took three months!

More recently, a 'prophet' (so-called) prophesied in Ghana that there would be a terrible drought and people would die on the streets. When I arrived for a mission in Ghana, I was confronted about this prophecy by the national television and asked what I thought they should do. The prophet had returned to Nigeria, where he came from.

I said, "This man is a liar. I come to bring you good news, of a good God, who has come to bless this nation, heal the sick, deliver the captive, and lift people up. This is the God I know." I told them there would be no drought and no starvation – and there wasn't.

I could list hundreds of examples of scaremongering and prophecies that people speak out of their own hearts. Often, I think they are trying to be fortune-tellers rather than prophets of God.

 I'M ALIVE

When I was a young Christian, I found so many people who were looking for 'the Holy Grail;' the secret that would bring the return of the Lord. In the early '60s,' they looked into past revivals and read books like 'The Welsh Revival' and 'War on the Saints,' trying to replicate what other people had done. I remember a dear Scottish Christian man with flaming red hair who read about Reece Howell's experiences and decided that God had told him to become a Nazarene and not to cut his hair.

The dear lad was in his late twenties and grew long hair and a big red beard. He used to walk about Liverpool 8 [a district of Liverpool] and the children in the streets would shout after him, "Hey, Noah, what's happening?" He became a source of ridicule, poor man because he tried to replicate someone else's experience. Tragically, the sin of emulation [that means copying what others have done] has become so prevalent in today's Church. It does not produce reality. Only the Lord can do that!

Since we have become an international ministry, reaching out to many nations in Africa, Asia, South America, North America, and Australia, we have come into contact with so many ministers of all denominations. The thing that probably shocks me most is how many pastors feel they must stand aloof from their people and clothe themselves with what one would call 'an air of mysticism.' They don't open their homes, nor their hearts to the common people. Somehow the teaching of ministry has come down to manifesting gifts of the Spirit, preaching and prophesying, without true compassion and identification with the people.

I remember well when I was first confronted with the Gospel by Demos Shakarian, he took time with me; even though hundreds of people were in the hall wanting to talk to him, he became totally involved with me. God had spoken to him and told him to "Go get that man. I have a work for him to do." He had the sensitivity of

Spirit to leave everyone and obey God and devote his time to God's purpose. For the next four days, he had time to help, encourage, and guide me, even though he had some 350 Full Gospel Businessmen and preachers, who had come to London with him. Demos and his dear wife, Rose, planted a seed within my heart in those days that transformed my life and moulded my future. I just thank God that they were so unlike much modern ministry that fails to have time for the individual.

I was in Houston, Texas, over 20 years ago at a large meeting surrounded by some 8,000 people. I was shocked to see how the men on the platform were surrounded by bodyguards. One of the preachers, after he had preached a sermon and made an altar call, to which hundreds responded, just coldly announced, "You're healed," walked off the platform and was ushered out of the back.

A dear lady in a wheelchair was at the end of our row, and I heard her husband lean over and say to her, "Just say you're healed." She was crying, and so was he. I got so angry that the ministers just dumped everyone and left. I couldn't believe their lack of compassion and care. Afterwards, I went with friends to an Italian restaurant for lunch, but I could not eat. I was just so grieved at the way the poor people had been treated. Jesus Christ had time for the multitudes. He healed everyone. He took time from morning to night, praying with them, teaching them, and caring for them. He identified with them because He had compassion on them. My question that lunchtime was, "Where is the compassion of Christ in all of this?" For two days after that meeting, I found it impossible to get my mind off the lack of care. I felt the ministers had become professionals and lost sight of the hurting people. That experience changed my life.

"The trouble with you, Michael, is you get too involved with people and their needs. You respond too easily. If you really want

  I'M ALIVE

people to respect you, you and your wife have got to withdraw from your people and live privately. It's important they don't know how you live. You have your people in and out of your home and you're too familiar with them. To succeed in ministry you have to be separate from your people; otherwise, they'll despise you when they realise, you're just as human as them," so said a well-known minister to me.

I responded, "But I'm a people-person. I can't help feeling their hurts and wanting to spend time with them. They need someone who cares and will sacrifice his time to help them. I am what I am, whether I'm in the pulpit or outside of it. What you see is what you get. Our Church has thrived on fellowship, companionship, and the compassion of Christ. We need to bring that back into churches and restore ministers who are true servants, not lording their position over the flock of God."

He replied, "I can tell you, it's totally against the teachings of Bible School. Ministers need to distance themselves from the people; otherwise, they'll lose their authority."

My reply was, "I disagree. If I have to separate myself from the people I love and care for, I'd rather not be a minister. Jesus Christ was always in the midst of the multitude and was always moved with compassion, to heal the sick, deliver the captive, and encourage the downcast. I want to be like Him."

Some 30 years ago, God told me to build a Church. His command to me was simple, "You know what you don't want, now build what you do want." I had seen the tyranny of the 'Heavy Shepherding Movement,' and the extremes of the old Pentecostals and realised that what I wanted most of all was for our Church to be a family, a caring people where each loved one another. I wanted people who were available for each other and who laid down their lives for their friends. For many years we had no elders, no deacons, and incidentally no problems. It is amazing how quickly a man changes when he is given a title. Position inflates, and it is not long before they forget they are to be the servants of all and begin to expect everyone to serve them.

During the early days of the Church, I kept my job so that I was not chargeable to anyone. In fact, once the Church moved to a small hall, I paid the rent out of my pocket. I had to get there early in the evening to sweep the floor and put out the chairs before the folks arrived. I considered it the right way to lead. As the Church grew, miracles happened, and people came from far and wide just to receive a miracle. Finally, the Church grew too big for me to hold down a job as well, and for the sake of my health, I became the full-time pastor.

Over the years, thousands have come to the Church in desperate need of help. Often all they need is someone to take the time to listen to them and love them. They do not need cold religious dogma. They do not need formulated solutions to their problems. They do not need self-righteous religious fanatics trying to cast demons out of them. What they need is someone with the love of God shed abroad in their heart by the Holy Ghost. I have found the greatest need in most people's lives is to be 'accepted in the beloved.' They need to find a God who is not angry with them, not condemning them but has compassion that lifts them and transforms their lives and circumstances.

The Church of Jesus Christ needs to return to the simplicity of loving people and caring for them as Christ cares for the Church. What we don't need are social workers. We need to hear the Word of God, not only in word but in demonstration of power and the Spirit.

     I'm Alive

Chapter 4
The Formative Years

By Ruth Reid

This is the first attempt ever that I have made in venturing into the world of writing. It has been with trepidation as I have no formal training in this area of expertise. The first thing that prompted me to start was about eight years ago when Dr Judson Cornwall suggested that I should write an "Ebenezer" book to keep track of all the wonderful things that God has done in the Church. What caused me to finish the book is that it is Michael's 50th birthday in May 1993, and I suddenly felt inspired to complete it for that event. I also had to transcribe what I had already done from one computer to another, so it was an excellent opportunity to revamp and update what I had previously done.

As his wife, I am completely prejudiced in his favour so you will not get a totally unbiased picture. I have so enjoyed our 22 years together-life has never been dull! There have been times when others have encouraged me to try to change him or tame him. I am glad to say that he has never been deterred from anything that he has felt that God wanted him to do, despite any method I may have tried to influence him. I have come to deeply respect his absolute determination to follow the injunction that Mary told the servants at the wedding feast, "Whatsoever he saith unto you, do it." His heart is sold out to his Lord and Savior. Anyone who has heard him preach about the love and grace of God could not doubt this.

I hope that what comes through to the reader is the wonderful way in which God has led us, as a family as well as a Church. I have wanted to show how the excellency of the power is of God in a very human vessel. I hope that it is an encouragement to others in the ministry to let go of the heavy burden of the Church, which I have observed many carry, and realise that it is Christ who builds his Church, and He does an excellent job. I hope that no one tries to take this story as a blueprint because that is not my purpose. One thing we have learnt along the way is that God never repeats himself, so it is always exciting not knowing how He will instruct us to solve each challenge as we face it. Many talk about the cost or price to pay for following Jesus, but I can only say that I have never really paid any price at all. I have just been on the receiving end of a wonderful heavenly father who has given and given and given!

Let's Begin at the Beginning!

If you are someone who knows you are a child of God and chosen for a specific purpose by the Lord of all glory, you will be able to look back at your life thus far and marvel at how God has orchestrated all the circumstances of your earthly pilgrimage. I find that there is nothing more reassuring and mind-blowing at the same time than God, the God of all creation, caring so much about EVERY detail of my life! God as the master potter prepares a life for His use long before that person is born! We were in Him before the foundation of the world (Rev 13:8). King David describes the process beautifully in Psalm 139:13-16. I will just quote verse 16 from the New Living Translation as it describes exactly what I have been trying to say...

   I'm Alive

"You saw me before I was born, every day of my life was recorded in your book, every moment was laid out before a single day had passed."

With this thought in mind, I have approached the task of telling the story of the life of Michael Stafford Baynes Reid, my husband, companion, lover, and best friend of forty years of marriage on 10/10/10. I not only tell his life story but also describe how God prepares a ministry as a gift to His Church, marveling with awe and wonder at God's immense faithfulness. He is the one who has done everything from start to finish - He is the author and finisher of our faith! (Heb 12:2). Am I biased? Yes. Will this book be an impartial record like a biography should be? No. Is my husband unusual and controversial? Yes. Will I tell it the way it is, warts and all? No, we have this treasure in an earthen vessel so that the excellency of the power might be of God and not of us (2 Cor 4:7). I intend to highlight the excellency of the power of God and how He forms the earthen vessel. Am I excusing sin? I would not dare to insult my saviour by denying what has happened. Have there been any negatives or trials in our lives? Plenty, but GOD...

Michael Stafford Baynes Reid was born in Beckenham in Kent, May 15th, 1943. His mother, Ann Reid, was only eighteen years old when he was born, so she had her hands full as she already had an eleven-month-old baby John. John was born two months premature after his mother fell down the stairs. It was most unusual for a baby to survive in those wartime conditions being so premature. As they grew up together, they were constant companions in mischief and arguing with each other. The stories they tell of their escapades would have turned any mother's hair grey at a very early age!

His father, John, was born in Allahabad, India, the son of a military surgeon who spent most of his life there. John grew up in India but came to England to join the R.A.F. where he became a fighter pilot as the Second World War was in full swing. His station was Biggin Hill in Kent, which was a constant target for German activity, so they were all in real danger. Once, a German plane flew very low down, machine-gunning the prams in the gardens—Michael had only just been removed from the pram! A shell went through the pram—what an amazing escape! Again, when he was older, a land mine was dropped and landed in their garden but was caught in a tree by the kind of parachute that went with it—it was swinging a few inches from the ground. They all hid under the dining room table until the bomb disposal unit removed it!

His father had been a great sceptic about anything to do with 'religion,' having been brought up a Roman Catholic and rejecting it at an early age because of the hypocrisy that he saw. His mother visited the Anglican Church on occasions, but it did not figure as a matter of great importance in her life. (That is not how it remained; in the latter years of her life, she became a Christian and even moved to be near the Church that we pastored.) However, there was one member of the family who was very devout—his paternal step-grandmother. After her husband died, she came to stay with them. She used to sneak into the children's bedroom and teach them how to pray. It made a vivid impression on his childish mind, and Jesus became very real to him.

At the age of six, he was at the seaside at Westgate on Sea with the rest of his family. He nearly drowned when he fell off a breakwater into deep water below. As he sank beneath the surface for the second or third time, he stopped panicking. He suddenly realised that he belonged to God and if he died, he would go to be with Jesus. Fortunately, his hand broke the surface again, and a woman dived in fully clothed to save him.

The danger from the war had far-reaching effects in that his father's plane was shot down over the English Channel by a German fighter plane. He spent 14 hours in the freezing cold water before he was rescued. It weakened his heart, so he died in 1952 aged 39. LIFE WAS NEVER THE SAME FOR MICHAEL! His hero, provider, and champion were gone forever! He and John were not allowed to go to the funeral, but he remembers watching the funeral procession drive away from the house. He recalls thinking to himself if Jesus had been here my dad would not have died. He would have raised him from the dead! Where did that thought come from? His family certainly did not believe in miracles! Our wonderful Lord was at work even then.

His mother was four months pregnant when the tragedy hit the family. Her circumstances changed so radically! From being the wife of a successful businessman with a very large house in four acres of garden, she had to live with her parents in one room with her baby daughter and two sons when they were home from school. They moved from Kent where they lived by the sea to Essex where his mother had grown up.

Michael and his elder brother were sent to boarding school courtesy of the Freemasons. His father and grandfather were both Masons. He was eight years old when he was sent to the Royal Masonic School in Bushey, Hertfordshire. Michael rarely talks about this experience, other than to say that he hated the bullying that was endemic in those types of schools. As he reached higher up in the school, he made every effort to rid the school of bullying, including nearly being expelled for attacking his housemaster for bullying. Fortunately, his headmaster intervened and moved him from that house to reduce the tension. However, he succeeded in achieving his goal so that bullying was practically stamped out in the whole school. He enjoyed their excellent sporting facilities, spending as much time away from the classroom as he could, playing cricket, basketball, rugby, hockey, water polo, and tennis!

He says that they taught him to live like a gentleman but never how to earn enough money to maintain the lifestyle of one. He did not do well in his A-levels just because there was no one who he would listen to, to guide him as to the importance of achieving good marks to succeed in life.

At the age of eleven, he read a book about becoming a Christian which profoundly affected him, so he gave his life to Christ in the best way he knew how at the time. However, when he discovered that the school chaplain was a homosexual who took advantage of his position of trust, he completely turned against Christianity as embodied by the hypocrisy that he had been exposed to. He studied to make himself a 'good' atheist and loved to argue with anyone, knowing that he could usually completely confound them all.

After leaving school, he started in local government, studying estate management to become a chartered surveyor. He only survived the boredom and lack of opportunity for advancement for about a year when he began to look for something with more challenge and excitement. His next choice of career alighted on the Metropolitan Police Force, where he found plenty of the latter. It only took him six months of being in uniform before he joined a crime squad in 'plain clothes,' stationed in West-End Central, with his beat being Mayfair and Soho. He says that he took up his cause of ridding society of criminals and was so diligent that he arrested far more people in his two and a half years as a policeman than many who make it a lifetime career.

Once the excitement and thrill of the chase began to wear off, he became more and more sceptical and disillusioned with this type of life. He began to wonder if everybody was warped and twisted like the majority of people that he met in the course of his duty. Inside, he did not care whether he lived or died and would take on dangerous assignments just for 'the hell of it.' His nickname

I'm Alive

was 'Tiger' both to the police and criminals because he managed to pounce on so many; often they would come his way without him trying.

One incident he remembers well was when a message came over the car radio of his patrol calling them to a murder at a pub. When they arrived, they found that the barman had been held up at gunpoint by a young soldier demanding he open the till. The barman refused, so the soldier took fright and shot him as he ran off.

As Paddy, the barman, staggered around the bar and fell dead, the people in the pub thought that he was joking around as usual, so it took them a while for the horror of the reality of the situation to sink in. After dealing with the situation as best they could when they arrived and taking statements, Michael and his fellow policeman had to wait for the ballistics squad to arrive to search for the bullet. He sat looking at the body with the owner of the pub wandering up and down, wringing her hands worrying about how she was going to get the blood out of the carpet by the next time the pub opened. Questions began to bombard his mind as to the purpose and meaning of life. Here was a man so suddenly to lose his life—what was it all for? Now and then after this, he would feel a prompting inside as he lay in bed suggesting that he should pray. He would turn over in disgust, trying to ignore it and fall asleep.

Chapter 5
Another Beginning

– The Real Thing

Acouple of policemen from his section house invited him to a meeting where they claimed that God spoke. He laughed at their claim and told them they had been conned as the meeting was run by Americans; there was no God who spoke. He told them that he would go with them and search the hall for hidden microphones and loudspeakers from which he imagined a booming voice would come declaring "This is God." Accordingly, he went early to search but found nothing. Instead, he was approached by the organisers of the meeting and asked if he would give his word not to arrest anyone, as all the drug addicts, etc. who were coming to the meeting began to leave as soon as they saw him. He gave his word, not intending to keep it, and sat down to listen to the proceedings.

Despite his prejudices, he began to be interested as he heard drug addicts and prostitutes get up and testify to the delivering power of Jesus Christ. How many he had seen locked away in a prison cell, only to return to the habit when they were released? How was it these people could kick the habit and stay delivered? True to form, he had to satisfy his scepticism by inspecting the arms of the ex-drug addicts afterwards to make sure that they were not shamming. The strange thing was that the two other policemen who accompanied him to the meeting remained unimpressed by the proceedings and just thought that it was boring. For him life-changing—for them, death. "To the one we are a savour of death unto death; and to the other a savour of life unto life." 2 Corinthians 2v16.

A large American approached him with other people and asked him if he would go to another meeting and talk about drug addiction in London. This large American was none other than Demos Shakarian, founder of the Full Gospel Businessmen's Association. He had come over to England with about 400 other businessmen in an 'airlift' to take meetings that were arranged for them all over the country in churches to tell about the wonderful things that were happening at the beginning of the Charismatic Move of God. He had the wisdom to mention nothing about God to Michael. Instead, he asked him to come to another meeting to talk to a group of people about drug addiction in London. This group was hoping to set up a home for drug addicts and alcoholics like Teen Challenge. One of the other men asked him if he was a Christian. There was a deathly hush until the man remarked that that was the fifty-thousand-dollar question, and Michael abruptly answered that it was his business.

A large American approached him with other people and asked him if he would go to another meeting and talk about drug addiction in London. This large American was none other than Demos Shakarian, founder of the Full Gospel Businessmen's Association.

The next meeting he had been invited to was in Spurgeon's Tabernacle at the Elephant and Castle, where there were about four thousand people. Michael sat about forty rows back and listened once again to people getting up to testify as to the delivering power of Jesus Christ. An African American lady, Mrs. Simpson, got up to sing as a solo the hymn 'The Old Rugged Cross' with tears coursing down her cheeks. Then she began to sing in what he thought was her native language, which he later discovered was the gift of tongues. At that moment, he knew deep inside that God was real. Paul writes that speaking in tongues is a sign for the unbeliever.

The next thing to happen was the collection—a bad time for him, BUT...A voice spoke so loudly to him that he looked round to see who was talking to him. As no one had spoken, he realised that the voice came from within. God spoke to him, telling him that if he gave everything, He would provide. He put his hands in his pockets and put all the money he had on him into the collection plate, only realising what he had done when it had gone too far!

A voice spoke so loudly to him that he looked round to see who was talking to him. As no one had spoken, he realised that the voice came from within. God spoke to him, telling him that if he gave everything, He would provide.

At the end of the meeting, Demos made a beeline for him, neglecting all the other dignitaries on the platform—because as he told him years later, God had spoken to him as well. He told him "To go get that man as I have a work for him to do." He invited him back to his hotel for coffee, but as they made their way down the auditorium, Michael tugged Demos' arm and told him that he knew that he was more hooked than the drug addicts that had spoken. He was on the respectable side of the law, but he would tread on anyone to get on in life. Demos smiled encouragingly and told him to come along with him. As they arrived at the front near the platform, he had to gingerly step around a lady who had just been prayed for and fallen under the Spirit. Demos laughed and remarked that this religion was strong stuff! Michael offered to take Demos and Rose his wife back to their hotel in his car with another couple. As they laughed and joked in the car, he realised that the only jokes he knew were dirty ones. Arriving at the hotel, Demos suddenly suggested that he would take them all to the Steak House next door and treat them to a meal. As he was eating, that voice inside reminded him that God had already provided because he had no way of paying for his meal. He had put all his money in the collection.

In-room 1105 of the Hilton Hotel, Park Lane, the most important event of his life took place. Demos explained to him that Jesus died for him and rose again, at which he declared that he had always known it, but this time he knew it inside. They began to pray and sing, and to his horror, a great desire to laugh welled up inside as a great weight seemed to roll off his shoulders as he asked Jesus to come into his life. He did not want to laugh in case of offending these lovely people, but he had to screw himself up in desperation and prayed that they would stop. At last, they did, which caused him to breathe a sigh of relief. He danced and sang at the top of his voice back to the police section house; he did not care who heard him, there was such joy coursing through his being. He could not go to sleep that night, so he ran a hot bath, which he kept topping up as necessary, and read the New Testament that they had given him until the morning. What a contrast to other times when he had rolled in late to the section house having drunk at least half a bottle of whisky!

He could not bear to be away from the fellowship of his newfound friends, so he returned to their hotel and was introduced to Nicky Cruz and others with whom he spent the next two days. Earl Pickett told him of his need to be baptised in the Holy Ghost, whom he had never heard of before. His attitude was that whatever God had for him he wanted, having been told that Jesus would baptise him in the Holy Ghost. He shouted, in case He could not hear, asking Him to baptise him, and found that the tremendous joy of the day before welled up inside again together with the laughter. This time he just let go and laughed and laughed, then found himself speaking in a strange language that he had never learnt, which he later found out was speaking in tongues. He tried it from every corner of the room, fast and slow, loud, and soft, and then checked out of the window to see if the traffic was still passing down below. It was such an unusual experience that he wanted to check if he was still on planet Earth! It is amusing to speculate if the angels had a good laugh too at Michael's expense as they rejoiced over the sinner that was saved. To see how God in His mercy and grace caught him out while he was trying to prove that He did not exist and how his prejudices came tumbling down under the wonderful power of God's love and forgiveness.

He knew that he could not continue in the police as he describes his work which dealt with 'brothels, ponces, and other undesirables.' He told his superintendent what had happened to him in graphic detail until he noticed that his eyes had got as round as saucers. He was so shocked that he declared that Michael would never go on the streets again. One of the commanders who knew him very well rang him up and demanded to know what kind of joke he was pulling as he of all people would never be caught up in 'religion.'

There were other incredulous policemen—this time three Christians. They had set themselves a year previously to test to see if God answered prayer. To REALLY prove Him, they chose the most corrupt and unlikely policeman that they worked with, to pray for to get saved. You can guess who they chose!!! He would have bashed their heads in if he had known what they had done at the time as they undertook to pray for him every day for a year. When God answered their prayers, they were astonished. One of them, who had moved away, even had to drive back to see if it was true. As he recounted his

I'M ALIVE

story, they interspersed it with hallelujahs until the point where he mentioned that he had spoken in tongues then there was a deathly hush. God had gone too far beyond their rigid parameters of religion! They told him speaking in tongues was of the devil! However, it did not deter Michael as he was only too delighted with what God had done in his life and he only felt sorry for them.

Chapter 6
God's Leadings

As Demos and the others prepared to go back to America, Michael wept as he said goodbye to his newfound friends. He felt like an orphan! Demos had introduced Michael to a man who was going to open a home for the rehabilitation of drug addicts and alcoholics run along the same lines as Teen Challenge, so he decided to go and work there. Very early on in his Christian experience when he prayed for people strange things happened. Like when he prayed for a very large Irishman who fell to the floor and started wriggling to the other end of the room on his belly like a snake. He reached the fireplace, picked up the poker and rushed at Michael intending to hit him. The only thing he could think of doing in the split second was to cry "Lord" in desperation. God came to his rescue as the man crashed to the floor as the demons departed.

He discovered that most Christians did not see what he saw, which was a matter of puzzlement to him until he realised that it was another gift of the Spirit given to him at birth. Being very inexperienced in Christian life, he would tell people what he knew about them from God, and it caused great fear and hatred at times as well as bringing great liberty. People would call him the man with the eyes and think that he could see everything, but the truth was he could not see anything unless God showed him. Nowadays, he very rarely uses that gift to avoid causing fear. He believes that knowledge, when kept, becomes wisdom. He may wait many years before telling someone what he knows, choosing the right time when it will be positive and constructive.

On one occasion, a demented alcoholic stole two carving knives from the kitchen intending to kill him. As he approached him, God warned him that he had the carving knives hidden—the only way of escape was to jump from a first-floor window, but he landed awkwardly on the concrete path below, jarring himself badly. He ran to his car and drove to the police station to warn them of the crazy man because there was no knowing what he would do next. He went to walk out of the station only to find that he completely collapsed and could not move. X-rays at the hospital revealed that his spine had been fractured in two places, and they could not imagine how he got to the police station at all. He was encased in plaster from the neck downwards and told that it would be several weeks before the fractures would mend, and he would be lucky if he ever walked again properly.

With this cheerful news, he had only one person to turn to in prayer whose answer came a few days later. An evangelist with a gift of healing rang him up and prayed for him over the phone. He knew that God had answered his prayer, but it was quite another thing to persuade the medical staff that he was healed. After much argument, they agreed to cut off the plaster and X-ray him again just to keep him quiet. To their amazement, they could see where the two fractures had been, but the bones were neatly knitted together!

God spoke to him again in that clear, audible voice after a couple of years and told him, "Timothy, find a Paul to sit under."

He knew exactly what and who God meant, so he packed all his belongings into his car and moved to the north of England. This 'Paul' was the only man he had ever met who had seen revival in his Church years before, so he spent the next two years ministering with him and learning from him as much as he could. He moved to Liverpool to help with a new fellowship that was just starting with Norman Meeton. It began to grow around his ministry of healing and miracles, and in a short space of time, the numbers had grown to about 250.

'Paul' left the area to go down south, and once he left, the political infighting began. The elders were jealous of the gifting that Michael had been given because it meant that the people turned to him for help, and he would not keep his mouth shut about things he thought were wrong. As an example of the problems, he was passing an open door where some of the elders and others were praying for a girl who wanted to be baptised in the Holy Ghost. It was obvious that they were not having much success, so he walked into the room asking her what the matter was. The difficulty was explained to him, and he reached over to her, touching her on the head, telling her that there was no problem with her request and immediately she was baptised in the Spirit and spoke in tongues. The lady who manipulated for power with her money was heard slamming the door and shouting, "Why does it work for him and not for us?"

Somehow, they had to silence him, so they got together and summoned him to speak with them. They laid before him several charges of things that he was supposed to have said and done, some of which he did, but not in the context in which they took them. They read him out his judgement that they were going to excommunicate him and commit him to the devil. They forbade him to enter the Church premises again, and he was not allowed to speak to anyone in the Church. Overnight, no one would speak to him or his friends and the people whom he had led into the things of God.

He found this such a shock, and for several days, he had the most terrible temptation to return their curse on their heads, but God told him that if he did, it would work, unlike their curse on him. He told him that he was called to bless and not to curse, so he listened to the Lord and let the matter drop. Looking back now, he can truly say like Joseph to his brothers, "You meant it for evil to me, but God intended it for good." A friend of his remarked some months later that if ever he wanted to be blessed like Michael, he would ask the elders from that Church to curse him as well. It was a real blessing because he needed to get out of that group of churches whose teachings had gone into error. Today, those churches are hardly in existence, having collapsed one by one.

Michael handed in his resignation to God, telling Him that he would never preach again after what had happened. His analysis of the situation now is that he knew that he was called by God, but he went out before he was sent and consequently landed up in a mess. The wonderful thing is that God does not listen to our words but the intentions of the heart. He gave Michael valuable breathing space and time to mature in life before He challenged him to pick up the mantle again. It was not a question of God abandoning him to his own devices; He continued to intervene in miraculous ways as the story goes on to tell. There is such security in knowing that God never lets go.

He decided to train as a teacher, starting the course at Edge Hill Training College, Liverpool. He passed all his first-year exams with distinction but became disillusioned with teaching as he realised that the government of the day was training far too many teachers so that there was very little hope of him getting a job at the end of his four years of college. It might have seemed a waste of time, but in light of future events, God knew what he was doing.

The teacher training became invaluable as he contemplated setting up a Christian School. His training in chartered surveying stood him in good stead with all the building work that was undertaken at Peniel. He jokingly remarks that he could have no better training as a pastor than being a policeman; very little shocks him. Of course, his business experience proved such a help to the Church without the support of which many of the projects could never have been undertaken. People know that he has been out in the real world and will be able to help them with many aspects of their lives. A lawyer friend of his remarked that it must be so helpful for the people to have a "street-wise" pastor when so many pastors have never worked in the world or made things so complicated with their intellect. Nothing is ever wasted in God!

As has been already mentioned, his next venture was into the business world. He went for a job at Fisher Bendix, and at the interview, he realised that one of the secretaries was taking more than the usual interest in his answers. She spoke to him afterwards and told him that he would not be interested in the job that he had applied for; her husband was looking for an assistant to work with him. Would he be willing to wait until she had finished work and follow her home to meet her husband? All sorts of possibilities as to her motive flooded through his mind, but in the end, he decided to take her at face value, and she did indeed do as she promised. Her husband took Michael on as his assistant salesman in an international firm, Addressograph Multigraph, which sold printing machines and copiers. He discovered that he had a tremendous ability in selling, even though the training manager informed his boss that he would never make a salesman! God prospered him in such a way that he was earning more than the Prime Minister of the day.

     I'M ALIVE

Chapter 7
He That Findeth a Wife

God was meanwhile at work in another person's life completely separately until the time when He saw fit to bring them together. Barbara Macartney, as she was then, was the youngest daughter of C.M.S. missionaries. She had two sisters and a brother who were all born in Uganda. She was born there too, which was her parent's field of work and left at the age of four when her parents returned to the U.K. They lived in New Kent Rd in southeast London—what a contrast after Uganda! She remembers going to the local primary school past the bombed-out Church next door. When she was seven years old, her father became a vicar of two parishes, Upavon and Rushall, deep in the heart of the Wiltshire countryside. She loved growing up with their pet cows, hens, bees, and the occasional goose to be fattened for Christmas. Her senior schooling was all done at Devizes Grammar School. Her A-level results were not spectacular, but university was a must in her family who worshipped education.

She discovered very little reality in her parent's religion and only went to Church as a matter of duty because her father was the vicar, and she sang in the choir. However, she went to a young people's camp at 18 years of age at Lee Abbey in Devon and discovered that there was more to Christianity than she had thought—she realised that these people had a joy and vitality that she had not seen before. At the end of the camp, she went forward to ask God for what she had seen in them - the joy. Her life did change somewhat, and the Bible became interesting and alive for the first time. However, the joy gradually vanished in about three months as she went to university and decided to taste some of the side of life from which she had previously been protected.

She got a university place at Leeds university to study Chinese and Sociology. She had a romantic idea of going to China as a missionary and becoming the second Gladys Aylwood! The sociology was to fall back on if this did not come to pass. It was a four-year course, but she struggled with the language, reading, and writing, and it never became a living language like others she had learnt by going to the country and having to speak the language so that communication became vital. It was very difficult to go to China at that time.

Her life vacillated between the world and Christianity for the next few years. She went to study for a year of training as a Child Care Officer at Cardiff University paid for by Lancashire County Council as part of a training scheme. She started going to a Baptist Church there which she enjoyed and felt convicted that she should get baptised. Her father was horrified, but she decided to go ahead when she reached the age of majority at 21 years. However, she realised that something was not quite right because after the baptism she was supposed to give her 'testimony,' and to her consternation, she had nothing to say. She heard about the baptism in the Spirit and sought the experience without any success, even going to a little Pentecostal Church in London where the pastor told her that if she repeated the words "The blood of Jesus" over and over again she would begin to speak in tongues. His words came to pass—she spoke in tongues—but was very disappointed in the whole experience, it was not at all what she had expected.

After Cardiff University, she returned to Liverpool to continue her training as a Child Care Officer. Her parents had left the country again to return to Uganda as missionaries. She remembers thinking indignantly that children leave their parents; parents don't leave children! God had his reasons for disturbing her nest, and Liverpool was quite near some of her relatives and friends. In a series of three meetings at the little Pentecostal Church she attended, God stepped into her life in an unforgettable way and changed everything for her. She was expecting to enjoy these special meetings but found to her annoyance that the more she heard, the more uncomfortable she became. She did not realise this uncomfortable feeling was the conviction of sin as the preacher expounded the verse from Proverbs - as a man thinketh in his heart, so is he.

In the third service, the preacher was talking about the Church being like a darkened glass with black spots in it when God spoke to her inside and told her that she was one of those black spots! Alongside this bombshell came a vision of hell which was so real that she felt the flames and saw the smoke and heard people screaming as they fell into the pit. Next, to her horror, she felt that she was falling into hell! Any residue of Anglican reserve went out of the window, and she yelled at the top of her voice, "Lord Jesus, save me!" bursting into tears. She sobbed until the end of the sermon.

After the meeting, she went to the preacher to ask him what he felt had happened to her. He replied that he only had two words from God to her which were, "Humble yourself." She hadn't a clue what he meant but did not dare to ask for an explanation. She went home to her flat (apartment) and realised the only person she could ask was God. She knelt by her bed and asked God what it meant to humble herself. God began to unfold to her the meaning of the experience that she had had. He showed her life like a book—we will all face that book one day. It is better to allow God to refine us now than to wait till judgement day when it will be too late to change! As He turned the pages, each one showed her what her true motives were for what she did and how she thought inside. She began to realise that God looked at the true motive of the heart, and what He saw in her life, He did not like.

As He opened the first page, she saw that she had been brought up to think that education was the 'God' and despised anyone who did not have a university education, especially preachers! The next page showed her that she only did social work to make her feel good rather than to help the people that she worked with. She could compare her life with theirs and think that she was far superior to them. The next page revealed that she thought she was doing God a favour to believe in Him considering the intellectual stable from which she came. Who with her intellect could believe in fairy tales like Adam and Eve? How the mask of religion completely blinded her to the truth of God that was on the next page.

Had anyone suggested to her that these were her motives the day before, she would have been horrified, as the cloak of religion that shrouded her mind made her think that she was a very nice person. God had to shock her into realising that she was headed for hell with those attitudes. Jesus died to deal with our sin nature, not just our sins. Once she accepted God's opinion of her and admitted it was all true like the Syrophonecian woman whom Jesus called a dog, everything changed! She lay on her bed as God filled her over and over again with His wonderful love and forgiveness. She was enraptured with joy for a very long time! She began to speak in tongues—this time the real thing! She heard God calling her His child, and she knew that He was her heavenly father.[3]

---

3 (Romans 8:15)

                    I'M ALIVE

Another area of her life that needed sorting out was that of the matter of a husband. She had tried in her own strength to find one and only ended up being really hurt. God spoke to her one day through the verse from Proverbs that "he that findeth a wife findeth a good thing." It dawned on her that she did not have to go looking for a husband; the husband would look for her. Faith came to her heart, and with great relief, she made a covenant with God that she would not look for a husband but leave Him to choose. She would not go out with any other man until the Lord said so! A few months later, she attended a meeting where Pastor Wumbrant from Romania, who wrote the book 'Tortured for Christ,' was speaking to several thousand people. She saw Michael in the crowd a good way off, but God spoke clearly inside telling her that he was the man she was going to marry. She was amazed as she had no idea who he was and how she was going to get to know him. Had she heard from God, or was it her foolish imagination again? However, a mutual friend introduced them at the end of the meeting, and they went out for coffee with a group of other young people. At least she knew his name, but nothing else!

Six weeks passed, and she was sure by that time that she had just been stupid, which was 'confirmed totally,' she thought when she met him at a friend's house with what looked like his girlfriend. The following week, she visited these friends again as she always did to find that he was there again, but this time on his own. As she sat and listened to him talking to her friends, she found that she fell deeply in love with him that evening. When it was time to leave, he offered to help with her car which was playing up. He used the excuse of the car to come and see her the next evening, and three days later, he asked her to marry him. She had no doubt as to her answer! Three months later, they were married.

How was Michael so sure that she was the right girl for him? He sat outside her apartment in his car, talking to his Heavenly Father.

He told the Lord that his emotions were too involved so that he could not hear Him if he tried. However, he needed to know if this was the girl God wanted him to marry. He apologised for asking the Lord for a sign, but it was the only way he could be sure. So he told Him that he needed a sign on the next vehicle that passed his car. A lorry drove by - he looked at the front, the sides, and the back - NOTHING! Then he noticed the number plate WED, and he knew that was the answer for him. He went straight up to her apartment, only to find he had to wait until some relatives had gone, and then he popped the question. She had no doubt what to answer because God had already told her he was the man she was going to marry. They often wonder how long the poor lorry driver had to drive around Liverpool until that very moment.

Looking back over the years, Ruth is convinced that these words are some of the most vital words God has ever spoken to her. Their marriage has been under attack in so many ways throughout their walk together. Before she ever got married, different pastors and other Christians warned her not to marry Michael. After their marriage, other 'very helpful' people tried to persuade her at different times that she had made a big mistake. What they did not understand was the calling of God on his life, and they objected to God's choice of the vessel. In recent times, those words resonated in her being to help her stand strong under the most sustained onslaught against the marriage. They have been the solid rock on which she has withstood every force set to destroy it.

...then he popped the question. She had no doubt what to answer because God had already told her he was the man she was going to marry.

 I'M ALIVE

God had started the preparation work for their life together long before Ruth met Michael with her dramatic conversion that changed all her attitudes to the work of God. She had always told God that she would NEVER marry a minister. Having grown up in a minister's household, she was determined that she was never going to be so poor again. There was never enough money even for the necessities of life, so the only arguments she remembers between her parents were over money. She was determined never to suffer like that again. Our loving Heavenly Father took her at her word, and she married a businessman who was earning plenty of money! However, by that time she knew he had the call of God on his life, and she would have married him however much money he earned!

The Lord dealt with her need for financial security with the next challenge in her life. She worked as a Child Care Officer for Lancs County Council. They had paid for her training and the salary was comfortable enough for her to live on. However, she had given an undertaking when they had employed her that she would never impose her 'Christian beliefs' on her clients. After her encounter with God, she felt uncomfortable about this undertaking, as she knew that she would share her faith in Jesus if she had the opportunity. She explained to her employers how her circumstances had changed. They tried to persuade her not to be too radical in her religion, but ultimately told her she could give in her notice. She thoroughly enjoyed working her notice for the next two months, sharing with all and sundry her newfound faith. She had launched herself into complete financial insecurity without giving it a second thought! She was determined to be obedient to God and there was no marriage or man in sight at that time.

The problem was, what was she to do next? As she asked God, she felt that He was calling her to go into full-time work as a missionary and began to make enquiries with missionary societies. The obvious choice was China, so she made inquiries with Brother Andrew who was just venturing into China at that time. Little did she realise what kind of full-time work God had in store for her! It all became clear a few weeks later when God's plans for her marriage unfolded.

She never worked in a secular setting again, and God has always provided for her in so many ways that she never has suffered again from the problems of lack like she did in her childhood.

Little did she realise what kind of full-time work God had in store for her! It all became clear a few weeks later when God's plans for her marriage unfolded.

After marriage, they bought a home outside Liverpool in a place called Burscough. Michael continued to work in business, and Ruth had two children, Rachel, and Matthew. Occasionally, they would have friends to stay, and it usually turned out that Michael would pray for them, and they would go away really blessed, but he was true to his vow with God that he would not preach again.

They got to know a couple who lived in the same town and used to come to their house for fellowship. One day the wife told them that she was suffering great pain from a cyst on her ovary that had been diagnosed to be as big as an orange. Michael prayed for her, and instantly the pain left so she no longer went ahead with the operation that was booked. About a year later, they saw this couple again who had by that time moved away from the area, and they recounted how she had just come out of the hospital. On enquiries being made as to the reason for her hospitalisation, she became very embarrassed, so her husband explained that a few months after

Michael had prayed for her, the pain had returned. Consequently, she went back to the original hospital where she was again booked for an operation to remove the cyst. Upon opening her up, the surgeon could find no trace of the cyst and was quite annoyed with her for wasting his time! God gave her encouragement to believe that she had been healed even if she had to be opened up to prove it to her!

Chapter 8
Both to Abound And Suffer Need

After Michael had been married for about two years, the company for which he worked began to require him to tell lies to his customers about a very basic mistake that they had made. He refused to do so, and as the situation became more untenable, he began to look for another job. There was no lack of opportunities as he had been the second-best salesman in Europe for his company for some time. He was able to land a 'cushy number' down in the south of England with all the trappings that money could buy as an incentive. However, our faithful God thought otherwise and began to speak to him while he was in bed for two months with a virus that he had caught in Africa. The only other alternative which uncomfortably presented itself was to go over to Ripon in Yorkshire and start a Christian bookshop and printing business. It meant that he would have to sell his house and use the capital to start the business and move into rented accommodation. He was not at all enamoured with this alternative and tried his best to get God to change his mind, but no matter how much he argued, he remained sick unable to go to the job down south. God got the last word in a very amusing way.

As Michael was sitting in a very boring meeting, he made up his mind to challenge God with something that he thought would be impossible. His bargain was that if God could make the preacher get up on his chair and shout "Hallelujah," he would go to Yorkshire. He reckoned that he was quite safe as the preacher was most uninspired and uninspiring. Towards the end of his preaching, he suddenly stopped and said he felt like getting on his chair and shouting "Hallelujah." Michael immediately reminded God that their bargain had been ON the chair. Of course, in the next minute, he did exactly as he had challenged. Afterwards, when Michael told him what he had done, the preacher remarked that he was glad that Michael had not asked for him to stand on his head! Accordingly, he moved his family over to Yorkshire and opened a bookshop and printing business.

In his years of ministry in Liverpool, he had also started another Church with some friends of his in the home of a local farmer in Ripon. They would travel over to Yorkshire once a week, and God began to build a congregation together. The first meeting that Michael ever attended to preach was somewhat remarkable. He sat down at a most enormous tea table laden with all kinds of goodies only to find that the congregation had been waiting for him behind a screen onto the lounge. He sat down and began to chat casually as it was his first meeting with them, but only five minutes into his talk, a man suddenly got up from the other side of the room. He began to come towards Michael shouting "Young man, I demand you tell me whether I am a Christian or not." His reply was rather noncommittal in that he told him that the witness of God's Spirit within would tell him. He shouted again, this time standing right over Michael demanding the same question to be answered, and once again, he answered in like fashion. It only made him angrier, so he started to wave his fist in his face demanding an answer, to which Michael replied that he would think he was not a Christian by the manner of spirit he was manifesting at the moment. His wife got up from the other side of the room and marched out of the room shouting "He stinks" followed by a couple of others. As soon as they left the room, an army captain fell to his knees and said that he was sure this was of God, and he wanted it. He immediately got baptised in the Spirit along with every other person in the room. What a glorious outpouring they had there and then!

It was this Church that they went to a few years later in Ripon. As people came into the bookshop, Michael would talk to them about the things of God, and gradually more and more people were added to the Church that he attended. Sometimes he would pray for them in the back of the shop, but he still refrained from preaching. The pastor of the Church was a personal friend, but he began to be attracted to the discipleship movement. He became very influenced by Bryn Jones as the 'answers' of discipleship seemed to be the solution to the problems in the Church.

The situation became untenable, so Michael and Ruth decided to part ways, but he had to leave the printing business and bookshop behind as they were inextricably entangled with the discipleship movement by then. His workers would have all left upon instruction from the pastor, which meant that he had no way of continuing. This decision involved losing a lot of money, but God repaid with interest a few years later - He is never our debtor! A job opportunity opened up in the south of England with a Christian publishing company, so he moved his family down to Essex to stay in a 'Christian Community' while he looked for a house, etc.

Unfortunately, he discovered that the Chairman of the company he had joined was embezzling money, and as he was on the Board of Directors and would have been jointly liable, he resigned. The situation began to look worse and worse. With no job, he could not

 I'M ALIVE

continue with the purchase of the house that he had found. He was stuck with three children and his wife in one room with all his furniture, a full-sized billiard table, a grand piano, and a dog! Ruth needed to have her eyes opened as she had swallowed the teaching of the discipleship movement to the extent that if the word of an elder overrode the inner witness, then she would follow it. Living in the same environment as the leaders of this movement opened her eyes to the way that they lived, which was so far removed from normal Christian morality. They also tried to exercise control of Michael through Ruth, suggesting that she should use the threat of leaving him as the ultimate weapon.

With the stress of the whole situation, she became very ill with myxedema, which meant that she did not have enough energy for the simplest household tasks. All three children had whooping cough, which compounded the problem with disturbed nights and very little sleep. She visited the doctor one day in desperation, not for herself but for the children to get some relief from the coughing. The doctor took one look at her and told her he was not so much concerned about the children, but her. He explained that he thought that her thyroid gland had stopped functioning, which proved to be true upon investigation. As soon as the doctor spoke to her, she knew inside that he would have God's answer for her - with the proper medication, her health began to improve.

They began to notice that things were not right with their youngest daughter. She was not developing properly and reaching milestones like smiling and sitting up, which are expected around certain ages for babies. They were referred to a paediatric specialist who told them that she had a chromosome deficiency, a bit like Down's Syndrome, and that she would most likely be a vegetable for the rest of her life. Everything looked dark for Michael - no home, no job, no support from the Church, only accusations, and a very sick wife and child. There was no one to turn to except his heavenly father who spoke to him in a meeting while he was communing with Him. He asked him if he loved his daughter, to which he replied that of course he did. Again, the same question came and the same reply, but the third time God asked the same question, Michael became indignant - but then the answer was different. It lifted his heart right into faith, "How much more do you think that I love her as her heavenly father." He knew that she would be alright, and sure enough, God changed every chromosome in her body so much so that in a year she caught up two years of her life. The specialist declared her perfectly normal at the age of two after a battery of tests. The 'vegetable' has an undergraduate degree in history from Middlesex university and a master's degree in practical theology from Oral Roberts University.

As soon as he resigned from his job, he began looking for another one and within a short space of time, he was offered several. He was employed by a firm aptly named Save and Prosper! He sold investments and insurance. He was able to earn very good money again, so he was able to remove his family from the cramped conditions into their own home. It seemed like a dream as God untangled the horror of the last few months. There was an answer for Sarah and Ruth; they had their own home at last, and he had a secure job with great earning potential. The crowning blessing was that within fourteen months of starting work, he was made President of the Sales Force of 250 men with a trip to Rome thrown in. Somehow it was very important in restoring self-esteem after the seeming failure of the last two ventures in his life.

Most importantly, God intervened to completely change his direction and spoke to Michael concerning his resignation from preaching. He used an evangelist called Trevor Dearing to speak to him and tell him that God was telling him HE MUST BEGIN TO

     I'M ALIVE

PREACH AGAIN, or he never would. As he spoke, Michael knew that it was a word from God. He had not rejected him but wanted him to pick up the mantle again! He had felt that he was on God's scrap heap and that he was disqualified from ministry, but the truth is that God does not have a scrap heap for discarded ministry; his gifts and callings are without repentance. God only has a gallery full of beautifully restored masterpieces!

Chapter 9
The Birth of The Church

The leaders of the fellowship he attended went on an extended summer holiday, leaving no arrangements for meetings, etc. Michael took the opportunity to preach in their absence, and God was faithful in confirming his word with signs following. You can imagine their annoyance when they returned to find that there had been great blessings while they were gone. Michael also confronted one of the leaders about his immorality and wrong doctrine. The situation became rather heated, so the 'apostle' was dispatched to come and sort out the group and, in particular, Michael. He tried in vain to provoke Michael to some response so that he could have some excuse to throw him out of the Church, but he would not be drawn.

Frustrated with his purpose, he asked the group who would submit to the leader in question, and only about five agreed. The rest were left without leadership as they were informed that they had become 'persona non-gratis.' God had begun to open the hearts of some of these people in the preceding months through the summer meetings and a Bible Study that Michael had held each week with four of them. The Bible Study was rather amusing as he would sometimes have to get the somewhat unwilling participants out of bed at seven o'clock in the morning before he went to work. Also, one of the four so violently disagreed with him that he would end up shouting at him, with the others joining in. God had spoken to Michael to start preaching again, so he knew it was very important, and he did not give up no matter what the opposition!

Events were taken out of his hands as God intervened in the affairs of the little group most unforgettably and dramatically. The man who violently disagreed in the Bible Study also took exception to the breakup of the other fellowship and blamed Michael. He was completely against the idea of a new fellowship forming. He came to see him one Monday evening in a fury, pacing up and down the room, threatening to do everything in his power to destroy his reputation in Christian circles and make sure that he would never preach again anywhere. What he did not realise was that by that time Michael had no reputation to preserve in any Christian circle. However, HE WAS INTERFERING WITH THE PURPOSES OF GOD, which was altogether another matter! Michael and Ruth have grown to recognise the activity of a demon spirit that has attended his ministry all through. This spirit has systematically tried to destroy him and his ministry throughout their lives and at times seemed to succeed, but it never has!

Ruth was praying on Wednesday, two days later, horrified at the turn of events with such horrible opposition. She saw a vision of this man being eaten by worms like Herod in Acts — she was horrified and thought that she must be mistaken. She certainly had no desire for this man to die. At midnight on Saturday, the phone rang waking them up, but there was no answer on the other end of the line except for gasping breath, a sickening thud as he fell to the ground, and a woman screaming in the background. They recognised his wife's voice screaming hysterically because he had collapsed.

Michael jumped in the car and raced through the night, but he was already dead on his arrival at their home. Apparently, he had wanted to apologise for his earlier outburst, but he never got the words out. It came as a terrible shock to the group but made them have a healthy fear of God.

Ruth understood for the first time in her life that God would directly intervene in the affairs of men if His purposes were in danger of not being fulfilled. It gave her a real sense of security that she and Michael were not setting out on their own idea to start a Church—IT WAS GOD'S PURPOSE! His wife, and subsequently five of his children all joined the Church.

Despite all the suspicion and lies that had been sown about him through the previous leadership, they decided to form a fellowship with three elders, Michael being one of them. The other two were supposed to keep an eye on him, although they agreed that he should do the preaching, and one of the others should be the pastor. The pastor came to Michael a few months later and told him that he wanted to end the farce of his being called the pastor. All the people came to Michael with their problems and when he prayed for them the solutions were found, and things happened. So, somewhat unwillingly, he was landed with the job.

It was a problem for Michael as he felt he did not have the personality to be a pastor—sweet and kind and gentle as was expected, and there were plenty of people who were only too willing to endorse this view. He certainly does not fit the mould of a pastor, as he is very straightforward and direct, not caring who he upsets if he thinks something is wrong. He laughingly says that God takes the things that are not and makes them as though they were so that the excellency of the power might be of God. He knew he could not pastor in the conventional fashion, so he had to rely on God to do it, as He chose him for the job.

     I'm Alive

On November 14th, 1976, a well-known evangelist was invited to preach at the first official meeting of the Ongar Christian Fellowship, to which about thirty people came. It was held in the house of one of the elders which continued to be used for some of the meetings until the numbers got too great. The evangelist prayed for the sick at the end of the meeting and one woman became very demonstrative and noisy. The cat, who had strayed into the room, got such a fright that it tore across several laps in its efforts to escape. Afterwards, they discovered that the cat was not the only terrified one; a blind boy thought that a hairy demon had run across his lap!

It was a problem for Michael as he felt he did not have the personality to be a pastor—sweet and kind and gentle as was expected, and there were plenty of people who were only too willing to endorse this view.

At last, things were underway for the Church to begin and although there have been varying degrees of opposition, it has never floundered from the day it started until March 2008, when everything was turned upside down and has never recovered. (The Reids left the Church at the behest of the leadership which will be explained in a later chapter.) The local Anglican clergy found it a great threat at first and did everything to try and stop it, but after a while, they seemed to realise that it was there to stay. Two 'apostles' came by at different times, one demanding that Michael move off his patch as God had made him the apostle for the area, and the other demanded preaching rights in the Church for the same reason. Michael's answer to them both was that God had neglected to inform him of their apostleship.

Gill Green has some interesting comments to make about the early days of the Church. "I would like to go back to the first time that Michael came to my house as it was such a revolutionary start to things." Michael arrived on the doorstep to do business with my husband, who was out at the time, but he proceeded to tell me all that I had ever done, it seemed. I was amazed but managed to ask him where he had got his information, to which he pointed upwards and said 'Him.' It was as though I was the Samaritan woman at the well, and I knew without a doubt that this was God's intervention in my life. I decided to heed what was said and not reject God's way for me.

It gave me great confidence for the future after all the years of unhappiness and struggle—at last, I had met someone who spoke the Word of God to me with such authority. The only way was to face up to things as they really were, to make no pretence and to put things right. David, my husband, was delighted with the change as I had been pulling in the opposite direction to him in everything, but particularly concerning the things of God. We were at such loggerheads that we were going to different churches, and I refused to change at all. Help had come, and I desperately needed the encouragement and guidance to put into practice a way of life that was based on God's principles, not mine. The early meetings were such a help as Michael expounded the precepts of God in such a clear way that we could not fail to understand. Compared with people in my previous Church experience, he spoke with such authority that imparted faith; I could not help but accept what he said as it worked in my life.

As a group of people at that time, I felt that many of us had been so hurt and wounded by our previous Church experiences that it was such a good thing in itself as we met together on a social level as well, to eat chocolate cake and learn to laugh again. We enjoyed each other's company as we got to know one another, sharing what God was doing in our lives as we watched Him at work. God's love

     I'M ALIVE

and faithfulness became so real to me that I found it easy to do what I had previously found so hard. I learnt that the Christian walk was very natural when based on the right foundation; it was such a relief to have all the struggle taken away. I could be me—God did the changing as long as I did the responding!"

As the numbers grew, they found a small hall to hire belonging to the local community association in Ongar, a small town in Essex. It has very precious memories associated with it as it was the place where God first visited the Church. It could hold about seventy people comfortably and had a grand piano—what a step up from the little jumbo keyboard they had purchased at first. The pedal for the volume control did not work, so they had to place more books over the speaker if quieter music was required. The only key they could sing in was C as it was the only one the organist could play! Their singing was so bad that they started singing practices on a Sunday evening for people to learn some of the songs. Michael preached and God confirmed the word with signs following.

In September 1977, a most amazing event took place which Michael says was the birth of the Church. The group can be described as a formal Pentecostal Church, singing out of the Redemption Hymn Book. Michael thought that a tambourine was an instrument of the devil! All of a sudden, God intervened to completely disturb their ritual. He spoke to Michael during the service and told him to stop the proceedings and get the people to stack up the chairs. He told God he could not disturb events as the service was in progress! The next service, God spoke the same thing to him, and again he refused to cooperate. However, when God spoke to him for the THIRD TIME at the beginning of the next service, he reluctantly agreed to do what God said. He stopped the pianist from playing and singing and told the people to stack the chairs around the hall. They looked at him as though he had gone completely mad! It took a lot of persuasion to get them to obey.

Once they had stacked the chairs, they clung to them as if they were their eternal security.

What was he to do next? God had only told him to stack up the chairs. He thought he ought to have an answer as the people were all staring at him, convinced by this time that their suspicions were true—he was completely mad!! He closed his eyes, lifted his hands to heaven, and told them that they were going to praise God. His eyes flew open again as complete bedlam broke loose as he watched God take a meeting. He did nothing except stand and observe for the next two hours. This was uncharted waters—he did not have a clue what to do! Some of the people crashed to the floor and saw visions of heaven, others shouted, praised God, and danced, others saw angels join them dancing in the midst. The Church was never the same again—they became a dancing, praising people. The presence of God would just descend at the beginning of the services, and they never knew what would happen. It was so exciting to be part of a move of God. Many wonderful miracles happened of healing, but the main transformation was in the people—they were bonded together in a unity that can only be formed by the presence of God.

All of a sudden, God intervened to completely disturb their ritual. He spoke to Michael during the service and told him to stop the proceedings and get the people to stack up the chairs. He told God he could not disturb events as the service was in progress!

Michael's preaching was transformed as well. He was always interesting and challenging with miracles attending his ministry, but this was different. He did a series on the Tabernacle of Moses where the truths of God became so precious that the people did not want to go home. The services lasted into the early hours of the morning; they were riveted by the amazing truths of God as he unfolded the 'pattern of how Moses saw it on the mountain.' The

 I'M ALIVE

heavenly vision became so real as it applied to their lives, and they saw how the Church should be. (There are still over forty tapes in the archives from this series.)

Some relatives came of a man who was dying of cancer and requested prayer for him. As he was too sick to come to the Church, Michael agreed to go to his home to pray. Sure enough, the man was in the last stages of cancer and in great pain. He was not a churchgoer, so Michael began by explaining the Gospel to him. His wife tried to interrupt, saying that he had always been a good person, but he told her to be quiet as Michael knew him better inside than she did. He repented of his sin with tears rolling down his cheeks as he told him how much God loved him, and as he did so, he suddenly exclaimed that all his pain had gone! Life came back into his body, and his colouring returned to normal.

A few weeks later, his relatives returned to the Church, and when enquiries were made about his state of health, Michael was astonished to hear that he had just died. The relatives were very quick to reassure him that they were thrilled with what God had done in his life, as the last few weeks were the happiest of his life and he had no more pain at all. When the post-mortem was done, it was discovered that he had not died of cancer but of a heart attack. It must have been his time to go anyway, but God in His mercy intervened in a miraculous way for all to know that He saves and heals.

Michael met regularly with the other ministers in the town, so he suggested to them that they hold a mission with the evangelist already mentioned. To his surprise, they were quite enthusiastic about the idea, so the mission was held in the main Anglican Church in the town as it was the biggest and most central place of worship. Nothing of that nature has ever happened in that Church before or since! Many of the O.C.F. trained as counsellors and all the participating ministers were invited to pray for the sick at the end of each service. The prayer lines for the other ministers became embarrassingly short as the people realised that God was meeting those in Michael's and the evangelist's line. Several people were added to the Church as a result. Ruth remembers seeing one tall lady in the congregation; she stood out as having a deep depression cloud hanging around her. She prayed a desperate prayer asking God not to let her have that lady for counselling at the end of the service. God took no notice and lo and behold who did she have to counsel?! She has been in the Church ever since, and here is her story:

I had been interested in healing for some time and had crossed swords on that subject with the assistant minister at the URC Church that I attended. I could not understand why they talked about healing instead of getting on with the job like Jesus. I saw an advert in the local paper, which I rarely read, for the mission in Ongar and read a book written by the evangelist. It awakened a hunger in me as I heard about the baptism in the spirit and wondered if God would do anything for me. My Church knew nothing of these things so, when they pressed me to represent the Church on a rebuilding committee on the night that I intended to go to the mission, I refused, even though I was an elder. I would normally have dropped everything and gone, but something was drawing me to the mission.

I arrived early to get a strategic seat to observe what went on as I still had many doubts in my heart as to the validity of these things. I was disgusted to watch the evangelist pretend to heal someone for the press photographers. I took an instant dislike to a friendly deaf lady seated in the row in front as she insisted on talking to me while I was wishing that she would shut up. I was not in a very good frame of mind to hear the preaching; however, when

     I'M ALIVE

the evangelist appealed for people to go forward after he preached, I went forward, thinking that I would be praying for the baptism in the Holy Spirit. I was horrified when I got to the front and realised it had been a call for salvation and me an elder in my Church! I had already committed my life to God long ago, I thought.

The worst was yet to come as a vicar tried his best to pray for me, and I just became more and more embarrassed. All I wanted to do was to find an escape route but instead was ushered into a side room for counselling where I was allotted to Ruth as my counsellor. If I had a few words with her to humour her, then I would be able to make my exit fast! To my surprise, I found myself telling her details of my private life that I never intended to tell anyone. She invited me to coffee at her house after the mission, and I could not think of an excuse to say no. Later on in the service, there was a call for the baptism in the spirit, but I realised that I could not go forward as my life was in such a mess.

For the next two days, I found myself weeping on and off, which was very unlike me. I made a bargain with God that if Ruth rang me inviting me to go and see her, it would have to be on my only afternoon off or I would not go at all. Of course, she did exactly that, so I was stuck; I felt I had to go. At their home, I met Michael for the first time and knew almost straight away that there was a man with authority. He knew about the things of God in a way that I had always wanted to know—I had battled with bitterness and resentment most of my life with no answers. I had tried repenting of it many times, but this time it was different! I turned from it inside while Michael prayed for me, and Jesus set me totally free. I also had tremendous mental problems with my thought life but found that I could control it from that day forward. At the last service of the mission, I felt able to go forward for the baptism in the spirit and found a deep joy welling up in my heart so much so that I laughed all the way home in the car with a friend.

The following week I attended the O.C.F.; the two things that impressed me were the love from the people and that the Word of God was preached. I could not get enough of either as my life had been bereft of both. The decision to leave my Church was forced on me after I had invited several members to this new Church, and once they had tasted the life they could not bear to go back to the other. I decided to leave to end the conflict, although I had hoped at first to bring this wonderful new life to my Church. It was a matter of great puzzlement to me why they did not want to be revived with the life of God, but I realised that many preferred to stay with what they had always had as it was much more comfortable.

At first, my children did not understand either, even though they both desperately needed God. My daughter was the first one to start coming to Church a couple of years later, but she was very hesitant and fearful to begin with. She describes how the crunch came… "I had known for some time that God was calling me, but I was scared to commit my life to him. At one meeting, Pastor Reid told a story of a singer who had failed to give her life to God when the opportunity presented itself, which made me realise that I had better stop messing about. He asked me when I went up for prayer what I wanted from God, and I told him I wanted the fear which ruled my life to be taken away. He prayed for me, and the fear instantly left so that I found myself able to respond to God's love for me and to love him in return. Not long after this, God showed me my sin as it really was, I turned from my old life and found a wonderful faith, and joy filled me through and through. Instead of the crippling doubts, I knew that there was nothing that God could not free me from in my life."

She got married to one of the young men in the Church and had three lovely children who grew up in an environment so different from her childhood. I am so grateful to God for his provision for my grandchildren of a happy balanced home life with the school to attend as well. My son came in at a much later date having made a real mess of his life. Michael prayed for him in a Church in London where he had been invited to preach; he was knocked off his feet by God, but He met him, and he came back to the Bible School in Peniel to straighten out his life. How faithful God has been to my family in fulfilling his promise "It shall be to you, and your children, and to all who are afar off, even to as many as the Lord our God shall call." Acts 2 v 39.

Chapter 10
"Timothy, Find a Paul"

Throughout his life, God has brought across Michael's path different 'Pauls' who have helped to encourage and influence for good the ministry that He was developing. No one man could fulfil this role as they were all so different, but each had their part to play. A couple of them tried to become his sole mentors, but he discovered the richness in the diversity of gifts of men given to the Church so that he realised that exclusivity was wrong and dangerous. The first two 'Pauls' have been already mentioned, Demos Shakarian and the 'Paul' in the north of England.

In the early years of his marriage, God sent a dear man called Alf Schulters who did much to encourage him through his friendship and restore his faith in Christians after his treatment by them. He spoke of an inner walk with God that he had developed during the years he spent in a Nazi Concentration Camp. It was obvious that he still experienced a unique walk with God. Friends helped him escape from Germany in 1938 to England. He was declared a stateless person by the government of the day. They allowed him to travel the country ever since, going wherever he was invited to speak about this wonderful relationship with God.

He had a special place in his heart for prisoners and would spend a week at a time in a prison cell ready to listen to and talk to any who wanted help and counsel and lead them to Christ. Ruth had met him at a university Christian union house party when he was the main speaker. She had avoided him as much as possible because she felt uncomfortable in his presence and felt that he knew everything that was going on inside her. So she was most surprised when he phoned her a few years later after she was married asking to stay with them, as he was in the area. He later revealed that his curiosity had gotten the better of him as mutual friends had told him who she had married, so he wanted to meet her husband. As soon as they met, he and Michael got on like a house on fire and discovered many things in common including a great love of filter coffee and the books written by the wonderful men of God from previous moves of God. Michael had already collected quite a library of old books of the first generations in the various moves of God and Alf helped to widen his understanding and appreciation of others. Whenever he was in the area after that, he would come and stay as they enjoyed wonderful fellowship together. He was one of the few who understood the depths of feeling that Michael had about the things of God, and they felt that it was such a privilege to have known him. He died in about 1974.

The next 'Paul' came soon after the Church first started in the form of a missionary from Argentina who took the Reids under his wing, so to speak. Michael felt that God had told him to have him speak in the Church and he was a real blessing to them in the first few years that he came. However, gradually his wings became shackles to such an extent that it took Michael several years to extract the Church from their influence which threatened to split it into pieces. They had perfected the art of manipulation by prophecy whispered in people's ears as they tried to steal the hearts of the people in this way. Always there was a higher realm that no one could attain except the chosen few which led to such condemnation. It was so important to be a 'worshipper' which involved much weeping and seeking for such an experience. As he sought to withdraw the Church from their influence, God came to the rescue once again and gave Michael the information that he needed to show them up for what they were. What could have been devastation turned into triumph, where only one family was lost in the extraction process.

It proved to be a very valuable learning experience which he has been able to pass on to others similarly trapped but not necessarily by the same people. He has become very wary of any type of 'heavy shepherding,' or control exercised from outside the local Church, and within the Church context, he has tried to make sure that he never does to others what had been done to him. He has real compassion for those in ministry who have suffered rejection and been cast aside by their denomination or group and will go to any lengths to try and help restore them. That religious spirit that has at times in the history of this land caused men to think that they were doing God a service by burning people at the stake is still alive today, although it does not have the same freedom of expression due to the laws of our land.

The whole episode became an important learning curve for Ruth as well. As they began to part ways with this group, she found it hard to understand why complete separation was necessary. She became really upset over it so one night she went downstairs to ask God what the problem was. She was shocked to hear God tell her that she had made an idol of the leader of the group. She took his word above God's Word and put him in the place of God. She was horrified at what she had done and asked the Lord what she could do to remedy the situation. He reminded her that in the

                    I'm Alive

Old Testament, they smashed the idols and destroyed them. So she smashed the idol of him in her heart and was completely set free. She has learnt her lesson and never allowed any idol to come between her relationship with God again.

A few years ago Michael and Ruth were visiting Liverpool and heard news of a pastor friend of theirs who had first introduced them to each other. He had left his Church because he could not make ends meet with the salary that his denomination was paying him. When they met him, his wife and children had stopped going to Church altogether and he only went occasionally when he was invited to preach somewhere. They invited him and his wife out for a meal and in the process of conversation, it was revealed that not one local pastor or anyone from their denomination had tried to help them or made any efforts to speak to his wife. A couple of years later, he moved down to the Church with his wife and children who were in desperate need of some Christian input in their lives as they were approaching their teenage years with no live Church to attend. All the children attended Peniel school and were able to get good training for their future careers.

Two other 'Pauls' were a tremendous blessing to both Michael and Ruth and the Church. They never tried to control in any way. Dr Judson Cornwall had been over sixty years in the ministry and was an excellent teacher of the word. Also in the last few years, he helped Michael write three books by using his writing talents to transpose his sermons into books. The combination of the two ministries was excellent as they found that their discussions stimulated each other into a deeper understanding of God's purposes and ways. When he visited for the last time, he mentioned to Ruth that he felt that they did not need him anymore, which is probably true in the sense of someone to lean on, but they still found his fellowship invaluable.

Archbishop Benson Idahosa, the other 'Paul,' could not have been more different from Dr Judson Cornwall. God has infinite variety in the ministry that He chooses for His Church! T L Osborn says that Archbishop Idahosa was the nearest to an Old Testament prophet he had ever met. Michael and Ruth cannot begin to enumerate the wonderful influence that he had upon their lives. God spoke to him early in their relationship with him and told him to take Michael as a son. He was puzzled by this instruction and explained his hesitation to the Lord. He told God that he had heard of a white man taking a black man for his son, but he had never heard of a black man taking a white man for his son. God's reply was, 'I did not know you were black, and I did not know he was white!' That settled his doubts, and he remained a wonderful father in the faith until the day he died in 1998.

Michael met Archbishop Idahosa at a conference at Minehead Butlins Camp. It was the annual conference of one of the major Pentecostal denominations. He walked up to the Archbishop after he had finished preaching, pushed through the crowd that was surrounding him, and introduced himself. The Archbishop looked at him intently and remarked that he did not belong there; Michael responded that he thought that he did not belong there either. They both laughed, and the Reids were invited back to his chalet where Michael begged him to come to speak in the Church. He told him that he did not have any spare time because his itinerary was full. However, he managed to squeeze one evening in for them. They were thrilled when he came to the Church, and he was amazed to find a singing, dancing, predominantly white Church. He kicked his shoes off and joined in with the praises of the people!

A few days later, he phoned to say that he had cancelled the rest of his itinerary and was coming back to the Church for the rest of his time in England. They could hardly believe that God had answered their prayers more than they could ask or think! As he entered the Church for the first service instead of following Michael up to the platform, he seemed to have frozen to the spot at the back of the Church in mid-stride. He stayed there for at least ten minutes, which seemed like an eternity to Michael because he was wondering what on Earth had happened to him. He was suddenly released and walked up to the platform. The Holy Spirit had frozen him to the spot and showed him a vision of what would happen in the Church. He showed him the amazing number of signs, wonders, and miracles that would be done in the Church and how people would come from the north, south, east, and west from all over the world. Of course, this vision came to pass over the years that followed. Thousands came every year to receive a miracle, and the Church grew and grew.

The Holy Spirit had frozen him to the spot and showed him a vision of what would happen in the Church. He showed him the amazing number of signs, wonders, and miracles that would be done in the Church and how people would come from the north, south, east, and west from all over the world.

It was not without cost to him to have a relationship with the Reids. The executive councils of two main Pentecostal denominations called him in to see them and demanded that he have no more contact with Michael, or they would not invite him to their platforms anymore. He was very disturbed by their attitude, so he asked them to allow him to consult God as to his answer. He knelt by his bed and explained the situation to God and how he would upset these denominations by continuing his friendship with Michael. God spoke to him and told him that He would be upset if he did not continue his friendship with Michael! So he told the executive councils that it was no deal! His analysis of the situation was that they preach love and practice hate.

The Reids found him such an inspiration to faith, and visiting his work in Nigeria certainly helped to broaden their vision to see what one man can do for a nation. They came home from Benin where they had seen the schools, the Church to seat thousands, designed like the Albert Hall, the hospital, and Bible College. They felt like the Queen of Sheba after she had visited Solomon's Kingdom - she reported that the half had not been told. They took groups of people from the Church to the two major annual conferences of the Church of God in Benin, exposing them to the same stimulus to faith that had so deeply affected them.

In the last ten years of his life, The Reids had the privilege of travelling with him, and many times Dr Margaret as well, all over the world. They went to every continent and were exposed to such a variety of situations where God moved in such miraculous ways—it was the best Bible School that they could ever have had. After all, that was the way that Jesus trained His disciples. Many people would tell the Archbishop that they wanted to come with him, but very few came more than once. Ruth used to ask her husband why they spent so much time travelling with him instead of doing their own thing. Now she understands that it was the most wonderful privilege to learn from such a man of God.

In 1989 they had the great pleasure of meeting Demos Shakarian again. They spent three days with him and Rose in Los Angeles where they lived. Demos had suffered a major stroke a few years before, and although he was able to drive and walk, there were still some effects left from the stroke. His spirit was not affected at all—he was the same wonderful loving, cuddly teddy bear that he always had been. Dear Rose, was not so good but for a completely different reason. They had suffered the most complete betrayal at the hands of those who were closest to them in the F.G.B.M.F.I. Rose had not recovered from it and could not bring herself to open up to anyone again. She was very polite, but her open warmth of love was not there in the same way as it was before.

     I'm Alive

When Demos had the stroke and lay helpless in hospital unable to speak, there was a take over from the executive of the F.G.B.M.F.I. claiming that Demos had fiddled his expenses and thus committed fraud. They threw him out of the organisation that he had founded and given his life for. Rose was helpless to do anything as she was completely concerned with Demos' health, and to cope with this betrayal on top of all her other worries was just too much. But God intervened amazingly!

This is the way Demos described what happened. After being in the hospital for several weeks, Demos was scheduled for physiotherapy along with several other hopeless stroke cases. They all sat strapped into wheelchairs and looked to be very sorry cases of humanity. The physiotherapist in charge was despairing as to what she should do with these people, so she cried out, 'O God, can't someone do something.' At that moment, a lady strapped in her wheelchair, who had never spoken again after her stroke, began to sing that famous Gospel song, "He Touched Me." The power of God fell on Demos, he stood up, despite being strapped to the wheelchair, and raised his left hand to heaven and began to sing with her. He was speaking for the first time since the stroke! The paralysis almost completely disappeared, and he was able to be discharged from the hospital almost immediately!

What could he do to clear his name? He was banned from the F.G.B.M.F.I. headquarters; he did not have access to any records. Once again, our marvellous God intervened. A prophetess came to see him and told him that she had had a vision of the exact place in the F.G.B.M.F.I. building where all the American Express receipts were kept that would prove his innocence. She described the number of the room, the storage furniture, and the exact drawer in which they could be found. There was one lady who still supported Demos in that building and had made her disgust known to him at the way he had been treated. He asked her to help him, which she was very willing to do. She found the American Express receipts in the exact place the prophetess had described! What a miracle!

She brought them to Demos who was delighted to have such evidence in his hands which was all that was needed to clear his name. He attended the next annual conference of the F.G.B.M.F.I. and asked to be able to speak in one of the plenary sessions. He was refused permission because he was no longer on the executive council. However, he still had the title of founding President who in the by-laws was allowed to speak in the sessions if he so wished, according to the constitution. He produced an overhead projector with slides of all the receipts proving that he had spent every penny on legitimate expenses. They voted there and then to dismiss the whole board and re-elect a board that would be supportive of Demos. Of course, they reinstated Demos as President and gave him back every privilege. God is so Good!

Demos asked Michael if he would come to the F.G.B.M.F.I. headquarters and record an interview with him, telling all about his conversion, etc. Demos was thrilled to hear the story again and his testimony was written up in the Voice magazine titled London Bobby Finds Christ! Ruth and Michael came away from this encounter amazed at the goodness of God in sorting out the whole situation for Demos. They were also bewildered by the behaviour of the people who had been so cruel to Demos and Rose. Michael had already encountered such rejection himself. How is it that 'Christians' are the only ones who kill their wounded? How did the people that they loved and cared for over so many years and had been through so much together, turn on them and create so many lies about them? The only answer they could come up with was that the people did the same to Jesus. The ones who had received the miracles cried out for Him to be crucified!

Chapter 11

Jesus Builds His Church

God brought the Church into a wonderful realm of liberty and praise; they would dance and sing till all hours, so much so that the lights in the room downstairs would rattle and shake. The model railway club, who met in the room next door, complained that their model railway trains would jump off the track! They looked forward to every meeting with anticipation as they never knew what was going to happen next. If strangers came into the room, they would watch with knowing smiles on their faces and wait for the fireworks to begin. They knew that it would not be long before the newcomer would either hit the floor as God felled them or they would make a very hasty exit through the door, nearly taking it with them as they ran out. They loved the preaching, which was so revelatory and challenging.

One young man made the mistake of coming back to Church after a period of absence only to find that he got more than he bargained for! The Church had changed somewhat dramatically since his last visit, and his sin could be no longer hidden! As they began to praise God, down on the floor he went, roaring like a bull. Since they had no clue what to do with him, they ignored him and carried on praising God until he had finished about twenty minutes later. He got up a changed man—God did the work so much better in people's lives than many hours of counselling would ever have achieved.

A young woman who only spoke French was invited to one of the meetings. She sat in the service not understanding what was going on. She spoke to Ruth afterward in French and explained what happened. She prayed and said that if God was real, she wanted the man (Michael) at the front of the meeting to come down to her and pray for her. The Lord spoke to Michael and told him to pray for her in the middle of his preaching. She shot off her chair and proceeded to wriggle along the floor like a snake. She was wearing all white, so her clothing became very dirty after writhing on the floor. She did not realise what she was doing but just felt a tremendous pressure in her head, which suddenly disappeared, and she felt totally free. She accepted Jesus as her saviour!

As God added to the Church, Michael found that he became ill every two or three weeks with the weight of the workload of continuing his normal job while running the Church. God had been most faithful so that he was bringing in as much business working one day a week as when he was working five. He could do this without any problem from his work as he was self-employed and lived on commission only. He was very reluctant to give up his job as he informed God that he could afford to pay a pastor with his income. He decided to make a bargain with God, challenging Him that he would not leave his work unless He caused him to get the sack from his work. As the top salesman for the whole company, he knew that they would never be in a hurry to sack him.

The following week, he was surprised to find that his manager had changed, and the new manager did not like his mode of operation. He demanded that he work five days a week and bring in much more business. Michael refused to do this, explaining the reasons why, and asked to be kept on the same arrangements as with his previous boss. To his amazement, a telegram arrived the following day accepting his resignation! As soon as the Chairman of the company heard what had happened, he instantly summoned him to come and see him to try to rectify what was, for him, a disastrous mistake. He offered to sack the manager and asked him to name his price to be enticed back to work for them—was it a five-bedroomed house with a swimming pool and a new Jaguar every year? All this he refused, knowing that God had answered his challenge and told them that he had been bought with the highest price that could ever be paid—that of the blood of Jesus.

God's first promise of providing had never been withdrawn, so from that day to this, he and Ruth have never lacked anything that they need. The Church's giving doubled in size as soon as he left the job to cater for his income! He had also begun a very small business with a fellow salesman from his company which he continued to operate as best he could with the increasing demands of the Church. His co-founder of the business sold half of the company to him when he moved to California.

This provision of God with the business was such a blessing through the years as Michael always refused to be solely dependent upon the Church for his income in the early years. In this way, the Church never felt cheated in any way as his business paid many of his expenses which should normally fall on them. Also, money was never able to influence his decisions, so he felt free to do exactly what he felt God had instructed without fear of upsetting anyone. God prospered the business greatly, and all the profits are ploughed back into the work of God both at home and abroad. He gave the business to a man he trusted at the time, to run it on a daily basis. This situation was the envy of many visiting ministries as they observed the wisdom of God in His provision in this manner.

Events took another strange turn when the leader of the community association where they held their meetings came to Michael and asked if they would be willing to help him run the management committee. The ruling committee had been disbanded upon a vote of no confidence as the association was badly in debt, and they were allowing very questionable activities to go on in the buildings. As it was most important to keep the buildings open for their meetings, he agreed that they would help. Some Church members were duly elected to the committee. This meant that they were responsible for running the bar among other things. They ran the bar most efficiently by cutting down the drinking to a minimum, raising the prices and yet increasing the profits greatly! All their contributions were voluntarily given, so by the time they left, the whole place had been refurbished, and a thriving coffee bar helped to change the financial fortunes round to a healthy profit.

It was a very good vehicle for the Church to give towards the community and was an excellent training ground for what God had in store for later years. The whole town was divided in opinion as to whether they appreciated what was being done or resented the change in the 'status quo.' The elections were very lively events as certain sections tried to unseat them, and arguments between the factions would almost come to fisticuffs as the O.C.F. looked on. In all this time, God provided them with a secure place to meet with larger facilities into which to expand as the need arose. The ballroom with the only sprung dance floor in Essex provided excellent facilities for their joyful appreciation of their God!

One of the couples drawn to the Church in the expansion came as they needed help to rescue them from a desperate situation. Michael had employed a man to decorate his home, and he had not thought of him again until a year later as he recounts. "Until the time when my wife got taken into the hospital with a blood clot on

   I'm Alive

the brain, we had never had many problems in our lives, and we had certainly never considered that God would be concerned with them. Ten weeks went by with no improvement in my wife's condition; the doctors told me that there was very little hope of recovery for her. I was at my wit's end not knowing which way to turn for help when I suddenly remembered a conversation that I had had with a customer of mine. Mrs Ried had told me about miracle healings and the wonderful things that happen when you pray in 'Jesus' name. At the time, I was not very interested but NOW!!! I phoned the Reids, and Michael invited me along to the Sunday morning service where he promised to pray for my wife. As I sat listening to the preaching and was prayed for, I felt as though a tonne of weight was lifted off my shoulders. That afternoon I visited my wife in the hospital, I could see the difference in her straight away, and she continued to improve in health from that day on.

At first, I found it very hard to tell my wife that I had been going to Church and that I had asked for prayer for her. When she came out of the hospital, it became impossible to hide it from her any longer as she wondered why I got up earlier than usual every morning and where I went on Sunday mornings. Finally, I plucked up the courage to tell her what had happened to me at the service, how God had met me and that I was reading my Bible every morning. She had already noticed a great change in my life and was only too glad to come along to the Church and find the love of Jesus as I had done. We have been attending the Church ever since and found through all the ups and downs of health as we have grown older, God has been most faithful in everything." They both passed away several years ago.

Chapter 12
A Place Of Their Own

Michael began to be exercised about the need for a school. He could afford to send his children to a good private school when the time came for secondary school, but he realised that most parents in the Church could not do such a thing. The local secondary school left much to be desired, teaching the children the mechanics of sex at the age of eleven with no moral content and other things that the parents were not happy with. Different parents would come and tell him about the problems their children were having with the school, and it stirred his heart more and more. The search for a property began which could combine the needs of the Church and school; they inspected many sites for about two years but there always seemed to be something wrong with them in the end. However, it did serve a useful purpose in that they had a much clearer idea of what they wanted.

In April 1980, they came across the property Bell House School, and they knew immediately that God wanted them to have. It was ideal in every way having already been a school, which circumvented all the problems of going for planning permission. Confusion set in when the owner suddenly changed his mind and refused to sell - what was going on? They looked at another property, but they had no heart to be enthusiastic until Michael was talking with a couple of the men in the Church in August and declared that he was sure that God had intended them to have the previous property. On the strength of this, he phoned the owner. Instead of being flabbergasted by this idiot on the other end of the line telling him that he felt sure God wanted them to have his property, the owner calmly told him that he and his wife had decided to sell that morning! He was going to contact the estate agent the next day to set up the sale. Michael told him not to bother and arranged to see him the next day instead, when they discussed terms and other details. He was asking £175,000, but the Church only had £200 in the bank.

They needed several miracles from God to get everything ready in time and the money necessary. The Reids and the Linnecars decided to sell their houses and contribute the proceeds towards buying the property. The buyer who turned up for the Reid's house stipulated the condition that they must be out by September 1st. When Michael rang the Bell House to find out when they could vacate, they suggested September 1st as well, which left them a very short time to complete all the legal niceties. The bank and the solicitors had to act very fast. The agreement that was drawn up for the joint mortgages of Reid and Linnecar made banking history— they had never done such a thing before.

The way in which God directed them to the bank was extraordinary. No bank was interested in providing a mortgage for a Church or a school. Finally, Michael rang the headquarters of Barclays Bank and demanded to speak to someone who had the power to give him a proper answer to his enquiries. He was put through to a senior manager, who instead of turning him off with excuses like all the others had done, listened sympathetically to his story about wanting to open a Christian School. He immediately recommended he ring another manager who would have the power to give him a decision. He tried to ring straight away but was informed that the previous man he had spoken to was on the line.

When he got through to him and explained who he was, he was astonished to hear the voice at the other end of the line saying that he had been instructed to give him whatever he wanted! They and the Linnecars went up to London to the headquarters of the bank, and it was duly arranged in two weeks for them to buy the property. As they were departing, the manager asked Michael if he wanted anything else, to which he replied that he would like to borrow £60,000 to build a building suitable for the Church to meet in. He straight away agreed and told him to let him know when they needed it! The people in the Church gave very sacrificially as well towards the other costs so that in all they had about £210,000.

The property comprised a large late Georgian house, stable block, and swimming pool, with a market garden next door recently added; the land comprised seven and a half acres. All the buildings were in a state of disrepair—the Bell House having been a school with a couple of hundred girls running through it was badly in need of redecoration and remodelling into separate apartments for the Reids and the Linnecars. The stable block roof needed replacing completely, and the market garden was full of derelict greenhouses. One of the first problems they tackled was the stable block roof. It was no mean task as it is a listed building, and they were not allowed to change the old-fashioned peg tiles. They borrowed a book from the library to help them as no one had any experience of that type of roof. It was the first of many building projects, but somehow it was special as everyone was so involved with helping that it knit their hearts together. The cobbled floors and the horse stalls had to be taken out, and offices were built in their place together with a large room that had been a garage which became the first home for the school.

Arrangements had to be made to include another apartment in the Bell House for an elderly lady whose testimony was unique. She was born and brought up in Germany during the period of the First World War when her family knew what it was to suffer starvation. Upon the rise of Hitler, she knew that she could never sign the Nazi pledge, so she escaped to Africa with only the clothes she stood up in and some gold coins hidden in her hat band. She was interned by the British government in Tanzania when war broke out as she was classed as an enemy alien. At the end of the war, she was offered a British passport which she accepted. It turned out to be God's provision for events years ahead. After many years in Tanzania, where she ran a coffee plantation as the only white woman for miles around, she had to return to Germany because of crippling arthritis. In 1979 she came to visit friends in the Church and was intrigued to find out what they had got caught up in.

During one service, she pulled Michael's arm and demanded that he pray for her, which somewhat surprised him as she seemed a very formidable lady. However, the next day she requested to see him. She asked him what he meant by sin, thinking to justify herself that she had never murdered or something serious like that. She remembers him asking her if she believed in God. She replied that of course she did, but inside she knew she was not telling the truth; she had long since rejected the Catholic God of her childhood. God healed her of terrible emphysema, which would leave her gasping for breath, and sometimes she would have coughing spells that would last as long as half an hour. The pain caused by the arthritis also disappeared, so as a result of these two miracles, she decided to move from Germany at the age of 76.

When she moved to England, her friends phoned Michael, very worried about Jaky as she had spent the night wandering up and down unable to sleep and groaning. They begged him to come and see her and find out what was wrong; however, he decided upon further inquiry to leave her in God's hands and refused to come. Another desperate phone call ensued the next day, but he still felt no liberty to go to her until the next morning when they rang to say that she seemed to have come to a place of peace. Her story to him was that she was groaning under such conviction of sin, and all her past life came before her for the first two nights. She kept trying to push it away until the third night when she cried out to God—instantly she had a vision of the cross and knew that Jesus had borne all her sin in his own body on the cross. What joy and peace came to her after this experience to know that her old life was gone forever!

Chapter 13
The Church Of Tomorrow

January 1982, the great day arrived for the school to start with seventeen pupils covering a great age range, one full-time teacher, and plenty of helpers. They started with a programmed learning system as it seemed to be the only way of covering the large age range and lack of funds to pay any more teachers. When the Church building was finished later that year as a sports hall, the school was able to move to larger accommodation at one end of the new hall. As they tested the children's progress, the misgivings they had about the system were confirmed. The children were regressing in their knowledge of maths, and the one-sentence answers in the 'paces' were not teaching them to think logically or to be able to write a reasoned essay. Her Majesty's Inspectors encouraged them to completely throw out the system by telling them that they would only give full recognition upon this condition being fulfilled. When the time came for full recognition, the Inspectors were so pleased with the curriculum that had been written for the school that they took a copy away with them to show to other small schools what could be done. The whole process took less than two years.

All along, Michael insisted that Peniel Academy is not a Christian School in the accepted sense of the term. By this, he means that the school follows a normal curriculum with carefully chosen textbooks in which they do not attempt to 'Christianise' the subject matter. The teachers are all Christians, and so by their life and ethos, they will produce an atmosphere in the school to enhance the children's education to the best of their ability. Mr Linnecar pointed out that children only have one crack at education, so it was not fair to experiment at their expense. The three 'Rs' were very much emphasised, teaching the children to read phonetically. They found such a method even greatly improved the performance of those diagnosed as dyslexic before they came to the school.

About thirty per cent of the Church had degrees or higher qualifications, so there has been a very useful pool of wide-ranging abilities to draw on for teachers. If ever they have lacked, they prayed and asked God, and he has always sent the right person. At the time of going to press, there are fifteen full-time teachers and twenty-two part-timers. Until 1992, the parents only had to pay for the materials that their children used, but now a flat rate system has been introduced to simplify the system which still only covers about one-third of the costs. No child has ever been excluded because of lack of finance, but it does involve sacrifice to send children to a private school.

A few of the staff are paid full salaries if they are the main breadwinners, but the rest give their time voluntarily. Over the years, the school has developed more and more as they have felt able—and sometimes unable—to cope with the changes necessary. To date, the school has nearly a hundred pupils with ages ranging from four through to eighteen. They are not chosen for their academic capabilities, but only with regard to their parents' commitment to the Church. However, it works out that of those who have left the school, over half have gone on to university or some form of higher education.

     I'M ALIVE

The school is not used as an evangelistic arm of the Church nor an indoctrination centre but as a place where children are equipped for life, both temporal and eternal. It is in the Church services that they are brought into a living relationship with Jesus Christ as Redeemer, Healer, and Lord. The parents are encouraged to bring their children into the services at a very early age where they have the privilege of seeing miracles enacted before their eyes and are soundly based in the Word of God. The junior children take notes on the sermon to help their concentration, sometimes delighting in some of the more outrageous statements of their pastor! From the moment they enter the school, they learn memory verses, starting with one verse a month and progressing to whole passages of up to fifteen verses long. They are also required to write out these passages the following month with perfect spelling and punctuation. Michael had to do this with Shakespeare when he was at school—how much better with the Word of God. The children leave school knowing more of the Bible than some of the pastors that they meet, and they know how to apply it.

The size of the school and the breadth of the age range are reminiscent of the old village school atmosphere. It is reflected in several different ways. All the children mix outside lesson times, the older ones taking responsibility for the younger, as if they were part of a large family, thus cutting across peer groups and preparing them for later life. All study is done through individual tuition and small group work. The emphasis throughout the school is on creating a loving caring atmosphere in which discipline is firm and consistent. The expectations of the children's achievement, motivation, and behaviour are high, but allowances are also made for their differing talents and abilities.

Having two very keen sportsmen as the headmaster and deputy has meant that despite the lack of facilities at times, hey have emphasised the importance of the children facing up to the challenges of sport and mixing with the outside world in pursuit of winning. They had to choose an individual sport as the school was too small for team games in the beginning. Their choice alighted on table tennis in a somewhat strange way as the headmistress of the senior school reported in the second issue of 'Trumpet Call' in 1988.

"Do you know the connection between goldfish and table tennis? I am not sure that there is one, except that the man who came to clean the fish tanks at the school also played table tennis—and that is how we were launched onto the world of ping pong. We started six years ago with one table, a few bats that had been retrieved from attics, and a net that obligingly let the ball down onto the opponent's side if you hit the ball against it hard enough! That, and a few aspiring (perspiring) students. Our first taste of success came in 1983 when two of the boys reached the finals of the under-11 boys of Essex schools. One emerged triumphant to go on to the finals of the schools for the whole of England. His success was short-lived, and we realised that if we wanted to improve and help the children reach their full potential, we would need proper coaching on a regular basis." Since that decision, the children have had a variety of coaches, the most recent one having been the number one player in England for a few years. They have gone on not only to play at the national level but at international levels and win, and they play regularly in the national league in which they have two teams—one in division two and one in the premier league.

Sport is not the only area in which they excel, as they have been encouraged in the field of music and have entered the Southend Festival many times coming away with prizes for individual instruments, choir singing, and poetry reading.

A question that is often asked is, how do the children cope when they have to go out into the outside world when they have left school; surely, they have been too sheltered? In a recent edition of 'Trumpet Call,' it was shown how three of the pupils had succeeded in the outside world. All of them were not doing well in the state schools that they attended. One of them was slipping through the net as she got further and further behind in her reading and writing. The school diagnosed her as dyslexic but did not help her to overcome it. She came to Peniel school at the age of thirteen where she was given extra coaching and encouraged to work hard herself to do things well. When she left school, she had gained seven grade 1 CSEs and got a job as a secretary, and the last job she had before having a baby was a responsible job in an employment agency which she helped to manage. She says that she was lazy and had given up trying before she came to the school.

Another girl had problems with truancy from school and getting mixed up in drugs, etc. She had missed so much school that she was way behind in all subjects. She says, *"As a teenager, I became so unruly and rebellious; however, it all changed when I came to Peniel Church and God met me and changed my life. At Peniel Academy, the attitudes and atmosphere helped me to stay straight otherwise I would never have got the qualifications that I did. They gave me a second chance."*

When one of the boys joined the school at fourteen, his reading age was three years below the norm. He was a very capable child but never had any encouragement to live up to his potential. He left school with eight grade 1 CSEs and took up an apprenticeship as a toolmaker with Ford Motor Company. That went so well that they reduced his length of training from five years to four; now he is a group leader in charge of twenty men and rumoured to be the youngest in that position. Contrary to what people think, these young people have become useful members of society out in the world who are contributing a great deal to their employers. There is no way that they are hindered by being 'sheltered' in a Christian School.

Chapter 14
The Church as a Family

As with all growing families as they expand, more space is needed. When they first moved into Peniel, they thought that they would never fill the space in the Bell House. In May 1982, they finished the building in which they hold Church services; when they walked into the empty finished building, they felt that it was like an enormous aircraft hanger. They thought they would never fill it! Now eleven years later, they have had to introduce tiered seating to fit chairs in every available space and are planning to extend to seat about 700. It is interesting to note the pattern of expansion. In the first ten years, the Church grew to over 200, from 1986-1992 it doubled in size with half of that expansion being in the last two years.

The market garden had an old shed, which they transformed into an area for the creche and playschool, plus a science lab in which they have the equipment to teach up to A-level biology and chemistry. Next came the school block, which is a three-storey building containing a large hall for table tennis and a school dining room, plus thirteen classrooms. It is equipped well enough for international matches to be held there, of which there have been many. Teams from all over the world come to practise in the excellent facilities.

There were several lovely instances of God's wonderful provision in connection with this building. First of all, when Michael had the plans drawn up, the local planning office did not agree with what he wanted, so he suggested that they show him what would be acceptable. The county architect himself then proceeded to draw up the plans for nothing, including the main features that Michael wanted. One of the things that was weighing quite heavily on his mind was that he had overseen the previous building project of the Church building, but at the end of it, he was exhausted. This one was several years down the line and the Church had grown, etc., and he knew that he would not be able to give his full attention to the building.

Two of the men in the Church came to him with a proposal - they would give up their jobs for a year to oversee the building of the classroom block. God had answered his concern before he had even mentioned it! These two men did as they had promised, and at the end of the year when it came time to find another job, they both were re-employed by their previous employers with a raise in salary! Neither employer had promised them any prospect of re-employment when they had given up their jobs. While they were working on the building, the Church paid them enough to keep ahead of all necessary payments, but it was not the same as their salaries.

Another problem was how to pay for the building. Michael did not want to go into debt again, so when an estimate came for an outside contractor to build it for £450,000, his heart nearly failed him. That was another reason why the offer from the two men was so timely. With their help in overseeing the building and the voluntary contribution of labour from different members of the Church for the finishing work, it was completed for £280,000. Michael did not have to make an appeal for money; God just provided it through the generosity of people in the Church.

Since that time, God has provided in other ways and sent a couple to the Church who have given their time to overseeing any building project. He was in property development and has done work on old buildings, so he has proved invaluable. His wife takes a great interest in interior design. When he moved from his other Church, he was going to leave the T.V. equipment that he had bought to use in the Church he left, as Michael had no interest in it. However, his previous pastor became so nasty about him leaving the Church that he decided to bring it with him anyway. Archbishop Idahosa was shocked at Michael's attitude towards filming the services. Michael felt that it would somehow intrude on the presence of God in the services and be offensive to Him. With the Archbishop's persuasion, he realised that his attitude needed adjusting.

Over the years, the Church has added to and improved upon the standard of the cameras and equipment, and he has trained a team of helpers so that now their programmes are of broadcast quality, and they have a fully functional editing suite. The videos that they have made in the last two years have gone out all over the world and on television in several countries and have proved a tremendous blessing to many. They are an excellent method of evangelism as people watch the miracles as they happen in the services and see testimonies of them being interviewed by a doctor afterwards.

The problem of lack of space had become very pressing by 1992 with the school bursting at the seams, desperate for two more classrooms at least. Michael could not make up his mind whether to go for new planning permission for another large building

I'm Alive

or keep with that which he had already got for an extension to the Church, a building with a basement comprising three large classrooms. Time slipped by and there was still no answer for the problem. The only short-term solution seemed to be to put up temporary accommodation in the form of portacabins. Once again, that was how the situation looked without God intervening. Life is so exciting when He is in the picture because He never ceases to amaze with His wonderful care and provision.

A neighbour whose property adjoins Peniel at the end of his garden came one Sunday evening in May and knocked on the Reids' door. He told them that he was selling his house but before he put it on the open market, was Michael interested in buying it? He agreed to go and look at it with the Linnecars and Ruth as he had had his eye on this property for a long time, the reason being that it adjoined the Peniel property and had a three-and-a-half-acre field at the bottom of the garden. He had mentioned to God that he was interested in it but then forgot about it. As they looked over it, they were only looking at it to see if it would answer their immediate problem for accommodation for the school. As they considered all the possibilities, it became clear that it would be unsuitable for the school even if they could ever get planning permission, which they very much doubted.

Suddenly, they hit upon the idea of the Church buying the house as a manse for the Reids, the Reids moving out of the Bell House, and the Linnecars moving down to the Reids' part of Bell House. The visitors' flats which were in the school building would be moved over to the Bell House to give the school the room that they needed! It seemed too fantastic to be true as this solution answered so many other problems besides the most pressing one of the school. The Linnecars had been finding their accommodation in the Bell House more and more frustrating with a growing family at the top of the house. This was the perfect answer for their family, although they had never really thought of doing anything about it. As the Church has grown, the Reids were entertaining larger and larger numbers which was causing a problem of logistics in the living space that they had. When they walked into the lounge at the new house, it immediately occurred to them that here was a room which could accommodate the growing numbers, although again they had never considered moving either. Another area of needed expansion was for the Church building so the added land has solved any problem of overdevelopment of the site.

Having told the owner that he would buy his house, the next consideration was how to pay for it. Michael approached the bank, who were willing to lend the money to buy it, but it meant having to sign over the whole of the Peniel property as a guarantee. This made him uneasy, not liking the idea of the bank having control like that. Having seen some of the problems that other churches have got into with large loans that they cannot repay for some reason, or another made him doubly cautious. God, as always, had the solution waiting for him in the form of Archbishop Benson Idahosa, who happened to be visiting at the time. Without consultation, he called all the committed people of the Church together and took a collection (a most unusual occurrence for the Church, so some were shocked). In about twenty minutes, people had promised to give about £230,000, which increased to £286,000 when Michael talked it over with the Church at the next meeting. The price of the property was £275,000, so God provided enough for the legal fees etc. as well! Archbishop Idahosa suggested that the Church call the house 'Testimony House' to reflect the miracle of God's provision, which they have done. Everybody got involved in helping to renovate it, and it is now functioning in a marvellous capacity, giving the Reids a great deal more liberty to entertain as they feel fitting.

 I'M ALIVE

Lots of people in the Church have found that having given sacrificially to Testimony House, God has returned the money to them in wonderful ways, showing them that He is no man's debtor. Not that they gave the money expecting a return on it, but it has increased their faith a great deal. One such was a doctor in the Church whose parents lived in Panama. When the time for the collection came, he thought that he might be able to gather together a few hundred pounds. However, when thousands were being mentioned, he realised the only way he could give that kind of money would be for him to give the money that he had been saving up to go and see his parents. He decided that he would be able to save the money again, that the Church was more important and that if God wanted him to go to America, He could provide a way.

Less than a month later, God did provide a way; his company told him that they wanted him to go to a conference in Florida all expenses paid! The night before he left for the states, his parents rang and offered to pay the extra needed for him to come and visit them in Florida. There were many other examples of how God was so faithful to so many, but it would take up too much space to tell all. It was a way in which some of the more recent members of the Church could feel involved, having heard the stories of how God provided for the Bell House.

The next step forward? The expansion of the Church building for which they already have planning permission so that they will be able to seat 650-700.

Another way in which the family has been extended is that in 1992, a group of people began to meet together in Rotterdam, Holland, inviting Michael to come and speak for two days a month. The Reids have been travelling to Holland for several years; first of all, they took the Church three years running to a conference centre for their convention. The leader of the conference centre invited Michael to speak at conferences for Dutch people that he held after having seen the miracle ministry, and God again attended the preaching with some wonderful signs following.

A most remarkable miracle that reverberated around the Christian circles in Holland was that of a lady who, since thirteen years of age, was riddled with arthritis and had spent the last three years in a wheelchair. She had gone to every conference she could and been prayed for many times, but her condition had only grown worse, so she was very well-known. She came to the conference not expecting anything to happen, refusing to be prayed for because others had hurt her in their attempts to get her healed. In the last service, Ruth asked her if she would like Michael to pray for her; she gave an evasive reply, so Ruth told her that she would not ask him to pray unless she gave a positive response. After more evasion, she finally said she would, so Ruth called Michael to come and pray. He told her that she did not have to believe anything; he believed and so did Jesus, and that was enough of a majority.

After he had prayed, she tugged Ruth's skirt and told her that she had felt heat go through her body from the waist downwards and all the pain had gone, but Ruth did not realise that this meant that she could walk. She wheeled herself out of the room into the ladies' toilet, where she got out of the wheelchair and walked! She got back into the wheelchair and returned to the meeting where she told the leader of the conference centre that she could walk, but she did not want to make a show in front of all the people. He encouraged her to get up, and when the rest of the people realised that she was walking, the whole place went electric; they laughed and cried as they watched her dance and jump for the first time in years.

 I'M ALIVE

Neither her doctor nor physiotherapist could believe their eyes when she walked into the surgery. The doctor said that she had been trained always to look for a scientific explanation for everything, but there was no explanation for this. She does not believe in God, but even she had to admit that it was a miracle. When the physiotherapist examined her, he found that she had been healed of something she did not realise — she had a growth on her spine which had disappeared. Two years later, she visited the Church in England and proudly showed them her prowess on a bicycle.

There were many other miracles of changed lives as well as just physical healings; it was so precious to watch the transformation in the people in the four days of the conferences. By the end, the atmosphere would be like heaven on Earth, and the faces of the people told the whole story; they shone with the light of God, having begun the conference all weary and worn down. Some of the people began to visit the Church in England; they so loved what they saw and experienced there that they began to ask God for something similar in Holland.

Michael had no intention of starting a Church in Holland because he was English and because it had never occurred to him. However, as they have gone one step at a time, he has been most amazed at what has happened. A group of people have gathered together and met in a hired hall above a riding stable, sometimes numbering as many as 120, and out of them, a core group is forming and meeting regularly on their own when he is not there. What is the future of the group, and do they have a pastor? God has the answer to those questions; they just have to follow step by step as He leads.

Chapter 15
What is the difference?

One of the things that God challenged Michael about in the early days of the Church was that, since he could see so much that he did not like in Christendom, he should go ahead and build what he did like. Consequently, many of the things that he has instituted or not instituted as part of Church practice and procedures have been quite radical as far as other churches are concerned. God never left a blueprint in the scriptures for how a Church should be modeled, only some indications of what to avoid. This is partly why there are so many different types of churches in the world today.

Built into everything as a foundational rock is his absolute conviction that it is Jesus who builds the Church, as he declared in Matthew 16 and also from Psalm 127 verse 1: "Except the Lord build the house, they labour in vain that build it." In this way, the Church is not a burden to him, nor does he worry about what is going to happen in the future, because as he says many times if God doesn't do it, it won't get done. Since the time of the first visitation of God in the Church, he has realised that God does so much of a better job of running the meetings etc. He believes that God is the prime mover in everything and all he has to do is to be obedient.

He realises when he prays for the sick and sees many miracles it is God who does it, so he feels no personal responsibility for those who do not get healed. He cares greatly but he does not take the weight upon himself. Many have asked him if he had a vision for what he has built, and his answer surprises them. He has only ever gone one step at a time and done the next thing that God has shown him. God knew how to handle him because he knew that if he had shown him all in the beginning he might have run away. When in a group of ministers for the largest Pentecostal churches in Britain, he was asked what his vision was —was he aiming for a 1,000- or 5,000-seater church, or this or that expansion of his ministry? He replied that his only vision was Jesus. The reason he has called the Church Peniel is that it is the place where Jacob met with God face-to-face, which is what he wants for everyone who enters the doors of the Church.

The visitations of God have been a hallmark of the Church. Prior to this, only the early visitations have been mentioned, but there have been many others. In about 1984, God directed the Church to fast and pray every weekend once a month, starting Saturday at noon and going through till about 10:00 p.m., and again on Sunday starting at 10:00 a.m. and finishing about 6:00 p.m. Even the children joined in at their request, and this went on for several months. Michael preached from the book of Nehemiah, which became so alive with the power of God that it penetrated deep into the hearts of the people. It was like heaven on Earth, just as in the first visitation. God never asked them to do the same thing again.

In 1987, Michael had a dream which took his ministry into a new dimension. Miracles had always happened before, but after this encounter, they increased in volume and intensity. He developed a new understanding of the authority that there is in Christ, and it showed throughout his ministry. He went to sleep one night, but it seemed as though he was straight away involved in a tremendous struggle with evil, which continued all night long. The next day he awoke feeling that hell had invaded him, and it remained with him until he went to bed that night. Again the fight resumed until the evil completely threatened to overwhelm him. He cried out to the Lord, and suddenly heaven opened. He saw Jesus and myriads of angels surrounding Him, and he began to stamp and jump on the forces of evil. The song sung by the angels that rang through heaven and deep in his spirit was "The Lion of the tribe of Judah has prevailed over all his enemies." He awoke with the song ringing in his ears and the whole experience coursing through his being —he knew that he knew that he knew, without a doubt, that Jesus had the victory over ALL his enemies.

He explained what had happened to him in the Church that night, and as he did so, the power of God just fell on the congregation. Some were taken up into heaven in visions, others fell off their seats repenting of their sin. One time Michael ran down the Church shouting "Fire," and when he turned round, everyone was felled in the Spirit like mown corn. Was the fasting and praying connected with the subsequent visitation of God? Many would say that this is a necessity for God to move, but God never told them that there was a correlation; otherwise, they might have supposed that they had found the 'method' of getting God to move.

The question of the 'formula' or 'secret' of revival has been asked many times, and sometimes the enquirers have thought the answers given facetious - like stacking the chairs. At one conference in Holland where Michael was asked to preach on revival, his 'formula' consisted of three steps all the same, which was to get out of the way and LET GOD... He then proceeded to show them what revival was, as God moved in the most wonderful way, as already described in an earlier chapter. At the beginning of 1991, God sent

   I'M ALIVE

in another ministry with a remarkable gift of knowledge and healing, and He used him to encourage Michael and the Church at that time. The meetings would go on until one or two o'clock in the morning as no one wanted to go home because He was moving in such a precious way. Since that time, the same man has come back again, but it has never been the same again. Michael is fond of saying "God does what He wants, when He wants and how He wants." Some of the people who have experienced several of the times of refreshing are quick to recognise 'the whispering in the mulberry trees' as the meetings seem to move up another gear and God is more present to move than normal.

Many ask Michael if he operates in a 'team ministry,' to which he replies in the negative because he does not want people to be confused about the way God has led in providing those who work alongside him. He definitely believes in gifts of men being given to the Church as in Ephesians 4, so as the pastor, the buck stops with him. However, God has given him some wonderful men and women who function in different giftings, without whom the Church would not be able to continue. They are definitely 'hand-picked,' as it were. His closest workers (team, helpers, associates) have been with him from the early days of the Church and have been a tremendous help and encouragement through everything that has happened.

God has added others as the need arose, and each has provided 'that which every joint supplies.' He listens to their advice and opinions, but in the end, he has to do what he thinks God wants. Some are shocked when he says he has no elders, no deacons, and no problems. He takes this from the fact that Paul only told Timothy to institute elders when the ministry left a Church, not while they were still there. Many functions in the Church in their different areas of expertise and do a great job, but if they don't have a title, then there is no problem about 'detitling' them when they cease to do the job.

His emphasis has always been that he wants a family Church where every age group is represented evenly as in a family. Consequently, without trying in any way to select those whom God sends, the whole age range is very well represented. Many remark upon the warmth of the atmosphere as soon as they walk into the Church, and they are very surprised when so many come up to talk to them and show an interest in them. Included in the numbers that God has sent have been about twenty-seven different nationalities. There are no racial groupings as such, and all get along very well together.

What about evangelism? Obviously, as the Church is growing so fast, something must be drawing the people in. Three times a year, 70,000 copies of a newspaper are printed called the 'Trumpet Call.' 50,000 of those are delivered into the homes in the area by the people of the Church. The paper records the wonderful miracles that have been happening in the Church and also makes some social comments on topics that seem relevant to what is happening in the nation. The first newspaper was printed in 1986 of which there were 20,000 copies. It has progressed amazingly as the reporting and design of the paper have improved each time.

One of the editors of the newspaper has always had a secret longing to be a journalist, and he is also very shy. God has provided the perfect vehicle for his expression through his literary skills and sense of humour and helped him overcome his difficulty in expressing his deep desire to share with others what Jesus can do for them. The other editor has more recently joined the Church and is a professional journalist, so has added another dimension to the paper. The paper is also sent all over the world by different

　　　　　　　I'M ALIVE

members of the Church and to the mailing list which is growing all the time.

Many people from the area have been drawn to the Church through reading the paper. Sometimes it has taken the reading of several issues before they have plucked up the courage to come. Many have come for a miracle but have not returned because they have got what they came for, or they live too far away to come regularly. In the last two and a half years, there have been about 4000 visitors, some flying in from Europe and more far-flung corners of the Earth, many of them desperate for a miracle. It is sometimes hard to see people not come back after they have had such a wonderful miracle from God. It was the same in Jesus' day, so a greater ratio of retention cannot be expected. Only one out of the ten lepers came back to give thanks to Jesus.

Dr Judson Cornwall came to the Church as a guest speaker but left more enriched than he came. He kindly gave his testimony to 'Trumpet Call.' *"I have known that I was a diabetic for the past five years. The doctor told me that it was the 'old man's' form of the disease. With a controlled diet and regular exercise, I kept it under control, but there was no cure for it. Since I travel the world at teaching conventions and conferences, maintaining full control of my diet was often impossible. In April 1992, I was the guest speaker at Peniel Pentecostal Church. I asked Dr Michael Reid to pray for me in the healing service that was to follow the message. When he and his associate Peter Linnecar laid hands on me, a pleasant warm sensation began to descend downwards on my spine. With it was a precious sense of the presence of God. This warm feeling continued for about twenty minutes.*

I felt that God had healed me, the noticeable symptoms of diabetes disappeared, and my energy level rose appreciably. When I returned home, I told my wife that I had been healed. She was a little cautious and begged me to keep on my diet and exercise regime until they were certain. It was the sound wisdom of a loving wife. My schedule was so full that I did not have time to go to the doctor, but when we changed medical insurance, it became necessary to have a complete physical examination by a new doctor. I covenanted with my wife that we would not tell him of my history of diabetes.

When the examination was complete, the doctor asked me if there was anything specific that I would like him to examine. I then mentioned to him my family history of diabetes which was the cause of my grandfather's death and a contributory cause of my father's death, and I had reached the same age when it became debilitating to them. The doctor immediately sent me to the laboratory where a blood sample was taken. Three days later, he phoned my wife to report that I was in amazingly good health for a man of my age, and he could find no evidence of diabetes in my blood. In the months that have followed, I have maintained a high energy level with no evidence of diabetes whatever. God made good his covenant promise, I am the Lord that healeth thee." (Exodus 15:26)

Ever since he had a bookshop in Ripon, Michael knew that it was an excellent form of evangelism, and he had it in his mind to repeat the experience. This time the shop was called 'Trumpet Call' so that people could connect it with the newspaper, which has proved to be a winning combination. It is not strictly a bookshop and has developed, over the time that it has been open, into a very successful coffee shop upstairs, with the downstairs being devoted to books, gifts, and secular family videos specially picked for not being too full of violence, sex, etc. The local MP opened the shop congratulating the Church for opening such a service to the community at large. Very often it is either the shop or the newspaper which is people's first contact with the Church. It is staffed by voluntary labour from the Church and demands quite a commitment from those who do staff it, but they find that they

　　　　　I'M ALIVE

get the opportunity every so often to share their faith with others and to be able to help them. There is nothing like the personal recommendation of others to draw someone to Christ, which is something that visitors have remarked upon. Each one they have talked to has their story to tell of how God has intervened in their lives and changed things.

It has already been mentioned in a previous chapter how God provided the equipment for the Church to produce videos of the services. Over time, the cameras have been replaced and more equipment purchased until they have a fully functioning editing suite from which they can produce broadcast quality programmes. These have been another great source of evangelism as people can watch the miracles happening before their eyes. Some of the videos have been shown on television in Europe and Africa, and they have the facilities to subtitle in a foreign language, most of which have been in Dutch so far.

Videos are fast becoming the modern form of communication as fewer people read books. However, alongside the videos, the Church does produce books and has its own publishing company called Sharon Publications (another area in which God has used the previous training that he encouraged Michael into at the time when he resigned from the ministry). Four of the books produced have been written from Michael's sermons, three of them in connection with Judson Cornwall. He has kindly offered his expertise in writing plus his inspiration to compile some very challenging books. There is always some new angle of inspiration, or else challenging the accepted 'fashions' in doctrine that circulate through the churches now and then.

Less than three years ago, Michael felt that the Church should have a choir after having visited a couple of churches in which the choir enhanced the ministry of the Church. As always, God had provided ahead of time someone to take on the job. A wee Scots lassie is choir director and has worked a miracle with the blending of voices of many who have never sung in a choir before and know very little about music. The overall impression is dynamic, so much so that they have twice won the top prize for choirs at the Southend Festival with two different adjudicators. As a group of people together, they project a wonderful sense of life as they sing. It makes all the difference when they are deeply committed to what they are singing instead of it being an intellectual exercise.

Although Michael loves music and knows what value it has in lifting people's spirits, he is quite at home ministering when there is no music or singing. When faced with a situation where there is a small group who may not be able to muster up enough musicians, he is just as happy to launch straight into speaking. He also feels it important to make the point that Jesus did not find it necessary to have a singing group with guitars and other instruments accompanying him. He just got on with the job in hand of preaching, healing the sick, and delivering the captives.

I'M ALIVE

Chapter 16

The Distinctive Ministry of Bishop Michael Reid

By James Peter Jandu

"I am not a miracle worker, I am not a healer, and I haven't got a gift of healing, but I do know someone who has; His name is Jesus, and He lives in me." — Bishop M. Reid, 2010

I watched as he stepped away from the podium with deliberate strides, placing his heel to toe, each step and word resonating with divine authority. The room shook with the force of his voice: *"No miracles, no Jesus!"* Pastors squirmed in their seats, confronted by these audacious words.

Questioned on Premier Radio, he replied: *"...Jesus was a miracle worker wherever He went, He did miracles. If Jesus lives in a ministry, then there are always going to be miracles, miracles of healing, blind eyes opened, deaf ears unstopped, cripples walking; that's normal Christian living.* "The host aptly replied: *"...You're kind of saying that...60-70% of churches who don't see that regularly, that Jesus isn't in them."*[4]

No stranger to controversy, his message sent shockwaves through the Church community, and numerous miraculous stories circulated.

One such miracle occurred upon a vicar's request when he prayed for a twenty-two-year-old girl, who had been in a coma for about two weeks and was staying at the vicar's home.

He went round and found her in a coma. Turning to the vicar's wife, he said, "Let's have a cup of tea."

They sat down and chatted for about an hour and a half until around 11 p.m. "Right, we'll go upstairs now. She'll be normal, and she'll be back with you before 12," Bishop Reid announced.

The vicar looked at him like he was a nutcase. Bishop Reid said, "Let's go into the bedroom."

The vicar and his wife, along with Bishop Reid and his wife, all stood in the bedroom. "Would you like to pray?" Bishop Reid asked the vicar.

The vicar prayed as a vicar would. He knelt at the end of the bed and began to pray using a prayer book, "Lord, let thy servant depart in peace."

Bishop Reid interrupted, "This woman doesn't need the prayer book; she needs Christ. She doesn't need a word from the book; she needs a word from God."

He approached her and said, "Young lady, you can hear me. I know you can hear me because your spirit's alive, though your body looks dead. Now, what I want you to do is to sit up, wake up and be healed."

----

4 Premier Radio, January 29th, 2009

 I'M ALIVE

She sat up and threw up the foulest vomit all over the bed; she was completely healed.

Bishop Reid looked at the time; it was five minutes before midnight. "I told you she'd be delivered before midnight," he said.

Global Ministry

He established one of the most successful ministries that mirrored Biblical times and offered valuable lessons to its followers. It was well-known through its outreach programmes and built assets by showcasing God's goodness. His mentorship by veteran ministers helped shape him, and he extended similar support to others. Prophetic words foretold suffering due to the envy this controversial ministry gathered, yet this couple remained faithful to their calling.

A Close Bond with Archbishop Benson Idahosa

Bishop Reid had a close bond with Archbishop Benson Idahosa, founder of the Church of God Mission International, in Nigeria, which has over one thousand branches in Nigeria and abroad. Their bond was so strong that the Archbishop extended his home to host him.

"I remember a time when I first met Archbishop Benson Idahosa… we made a covenant with each other…Where you go, I go; where you lodge, I'll lodge. Your God will be my God." — February 2008

The Archbishop befriended Peniel Pentecostal Church from May 1986 to February 1998, which marked his last visit. Bishop Reid joined Archbishop Idahosa on missions to over 40 nations, including a successful crusade in Ukraine. One night, at around 3 a.m., Bishop Reid prayed on his hotel balcony in Kyiv: *"Lord, there must be a man in this city who can lead a Church."* Not long after, during one such crusade, the Archbishop and Bishop Reid were approached by Sunday Adelaja, an assistant in television production, who expressed his divine calling to start a Church. A year later, Archbishop Idahosa encouraged Sunday to begin his ministry. This led to the birth of the Embassy of the Blessed Kingdom of God for All Nations in Kyiv, Ukraine, and it became Europe's largest Church with over 25,000 members.

On one such crusade, the Archbishop and Bishop Reid were approached by Sunday Adelaja, an assistant in television production, who expressed his divine calling to start a Church.

After Archbishop Idahosa's death, Bishop Reid revealed his surprising financial state, with only $300 in his account. He had selflessly dedicated all his resources to God's work. His tombstone, which was without his name, bore only the inscription 'Man of Faith.'

"Help, Bishop!"

Bishop Reid made substantial spiritual and financial contributions in Africa, which earned him recognition from Presidents and government officials, often receiving presidential treatment. Christian TV stations, including God TV founders, sought his assistance before launching. Prominent Christian TV ministers asked for his help when in need and received his willing support. The Church also backed initiatives like Bill Wilson's Metro Ministries, one of the largest children ministries in the world

Despite his influence, he always made time for people of all statuses. For instance, I introduced him to Bishop Jonathan Ansar from India, who, after meeting Bishop Reid, abandoned the unbiblical spiritual warfare doctrine and greatly appreciated his transformative insights.

Spiritual insights were often imparted with a touch of humour. During a meeting with Colin Dye, Pastor of Kensington Temple, Colin asked, *"How do you witness miracles in the U.K. like in Africa?"* He humorously replied, *"I don't tell GOD I'm heading home."* A prominent Word of Faith preacher approached him on another occasion: *"Bishop, I've heard about your miracle ministry. Can you pray for God's anointing as I preach tonight?"* His response was firm yet eye-opening: *"No. The problem with you Word of Faith preachers is that you don't believe what you preach. Go, you are already anointed!"* The preacher understood and left joyfully.

He had a profound influence that was attested by thousands of ministers, and his world-class ministry projects have blessed countless individuals.

Absence of Self-Enrichment

Bishop Reid's reputation for generosity teaches a vital lesson; the message, *"Give all you have, and I will provide,"* guided him.

"...the people I help the most are the most treacherous...in the end.... One time, a family in the Church... I'm talking about 34 years ago; a fellow lost his job...I couldn't bear to see them without a job. So, what did I do? I paid their mortgage and food bills, bought clothes for the children, and for four or five months, I paid everything out of my salary...They hate me [now] with just cause, you see. They can't get over the fact that they couldn't show gratitude and appreciation...the ones you helped the most are the most mean-spirited now..."

In its early days, and after relocating to Budworth Hall in Essex in 1979, the Church's finances were largely sustained solely by generous contributions from the Reid family. Later, he owned a business and instead of taking a generous salary, he selflessly donated its annual profits—up to £200,000—to the Church, for nearly seven years; this may have amounted to as much as £1,540,000.

In 1981, they sold their gold, jewellery, as well as their family home in Green Walk, Ongar, Essex and utilised the proceeds to invest in acquiring both, the Bell House and the Market Garden land, which later served as the Church site.

Another time, Dr Ruth Reid received a £30,000 bequest from a will and wholeheartedly donated it to the Church. On a separate occasion, Dr Ruth Reid's sister, Francis Macartney, expressed her intention to leave her house, valued at £185,000, to them in her will. However, Bishop Reid requested her to bequeath the house to the Church instead.

Despite receiving generous honorariums during his extensive speaking engagements, often as high as £10,000 per occasion, he selflessly donated them all to the church he Pastored. This unique practice accumulated hundreds of thousands of pounds over 32 years, while his salary was based on his congregation's average earnings.

Though he interacted regularly with renowned global ministers, he declined hundreds of preaching invitations, including a regular one for a prestigious U.S. ministry's conference that was held in the U.K. His choice was aimed to protect his reputation from questionable [financial] doctrines, emphasising his commitment to his divine calling over ministerial connections and financial gain.

When ministers demanded fixed honorarium to speak at his Church, he responded firmly: *"Don't tell me how much to give. Rest assured, you'll be well taken care of."* Bishop Reid disliked money being the primary focus in ministry.

The Reids never took an official holiday in 32 years of leading the Peniel Pentecostal Church. Their global preaching travels, while extensive, were far from easy. I joined them on a trip to India in 2010 and witnessed their exhaustion. Bishop Reid: *"...wherever we went, from when we landed to when we left, we had meetings planned. It wasn't a holiday; we worked. Even the young people who*

     I'm Alive

came with us were shocked and exhausted within three days, and said, 'We don't know how you carry on.' I did it all the time. I'd meet people in the morning, afternoon, and evening and seeing people between the meetings. So, it was hard work continuously. "Without a doubt, these were not leisure trips but ministry investments.

The Church also had an unusual tradition. After being healed, a man attended the Church for around eight months. One day, he asked the Bishop, *"How can someone donate to the Church?"* Bishop Reid laughed. He asked the question because no offerings had been collected during the services. During my visits to his Church, I never witnessed offering collections. I later discovered a discreet letterbox-style hole in the wall at the entrance, for voluntary contributions.

Bishop Reid, August 2003: *"In 27 years, you can count on two hands the number of times I've preached on tithing...we don't take collections, there's a box at the back, if you want to give, so be it, if you don't, God bless you. I don't need your money...but what I do want to see is God get hold of your heart and your life."* Regarding offerings, Julian Fagan comments, *"No, never, no, maybe one time he would do for a visiting speaker, but genuinely speaking, I think we just took one offering once for new carpet, but probably in the eight years I was there, I can just count on my hands...at my old Church it was money-oriented and it was extravagant and showbiz, everything you see on these Christian channels all the crazy stuff...try to screw people out of money."*[5]

Though he acknowledged and respected ministers, he fearlessly and openly challenged them. Once, he questioned a renowned U.S. pastor, known for his End Time prophecy books: *"Surely you don't believe the rubbish you write. Why do you write these books?"* Allegedly, the preacher responded by making the 'Pay Me' gesture – the motion of rubbing one's thumb over the tip of the index and middle fingers,

---

5 Former member, Interview May 2010

an action that symbolises money. He also fearlessly confronted a famous prosperity preacher who owned a jet plane. He asked: *"Your Church has tens of thousands, and many are poor. Why do you take their money while they are left poor?"* In response, just like the other preacher, this individual also made the 'Pay Me' gesture.

He once recounted a visit to Dubai, where he stayed at the same hotel as a renowned evangelist who occupied a $25,000-per-night room during his city crusade. While touring the opulent hotel, Bishop Reid was offered a $1,200-per-night room at a discounted rate of $600 for a single night; he, however, chose to stay in a $300-per-week hotel instead.

He showed remarkable generosity, directing funds towards God's work, and even hosted sizeable Church events outdoors at his residence; his lifestyle was neither wealthy nor impoverished. Unlike many ministers, he never pursued personal enrichment through his ministry. In an interview in 2010, he stated: *"I never tried to enrich myself, wasn't interested."* He could have become a multi-millionaire but chose honesty and financial integrity instead. Such a trait has the potential to breed adversaries that lurk in the shadows—voracious wolves silently snarling, hungry for power, influence and wealth.

"I never tried to enrich myself, wasn't interested."

Ministry, Community Outreaches and Initiatives
Political Controversy

In 1998, 119 Peniel members joined the local branch of a Tory association within two days, boosting funds by around £5,000. Bishop Reid's companies had donated at least £2,500 to Eric Pickle's fighting fund and the Conservative Party in the three years up to 1999. This stirred controversy but aided in Eric Pickle's election.

Jerry Springer Protests

Bishop Reid hit the headlines once again when he led the protests outside BBC's London offices on Friday, January 7th, 2005, when it aired the controversial musical 'Jerry Springer – The Opera'. Working with an alliance of Christian groups, he described the musical as 'filth'.[6] Protesters gathered outside the offices and expressed discontent by burning their TV licences.

He told Reuters: *"The use of foul language together with mocking Jesus Christ and portraying him wearing a nappy with sequins is highly offensive to Christians, and we felt that it was totally wrong."* He added that the BBC seemed hesitant to broadcast content that offended minority groups, but Christians were fair game.

However, he distanced himself from extremists who were reportedly responsible for making death threats to BBC executives. Following the delivery of a petition to BBC Chairman, Michael Grade, Bishop Reid stated: *"We are Christians. We are not extreme. We do not make threats. Our case for calling on the BBC to postpone the blatantly blasphemous programme is an excellent one, and we don't want it hijacked by extremists. If relentless swearing and showing Jesus as a sexual deviant is allowed, what next?"*

The BBC received over 60,000 complaints regarding the broadcast, including 7,940 to the media regulator Ofcom and an additional 8,860 complaints afterwards. Martin Scorsese's film 'The Last Temptation of Christ' had received 1,554 complaints when it aired in 1995, previously holding the record for the most complained-about programme on British TV.

This protest catapulted Bishop Reid into the spotlight of a secular world.

---

6 The Guardian Sun January 9th 2005

Protesting Against Sexual Orientation Regulations

Founded in 2005, the Christian Congress for Traditional Values played a pivotal role in coordinating demonstrations outside the Parliament, protesting against the implementation of the Sexual Orientation Regulations that addressed discrimination based on sexual orientation, which posed challenges for particular faith groups.

Following a three-hour debate, Lord Morrow's endeavour to repeal the Sexual Orientation Regulations was defeated with a majority of 131 votes. Two to three thousand Christians assembled outside the House of Lords, demonstrating their support for the motion. Approximately 100 gay and lesbian individuals were present to express their dissenting views.

In the same month, a CCTV campaign that featured a mobile poster with the message 'Gay Aim: Abolish the Family' was found to have breached the advertising standards code, as determined by the Advertising Standards Authority.

Rumours hinted at a conspiracy tied to this protest. Bishop Reid suspected a British MP, who was connected to a church member and supportive of the LGBT cause, of plotting his downfall. This scheme was allegedly facilitated through financial transactions, possibly in Ireland.

The Peniel Church

The Peniel Pentecostal Church was launched on November 14th, 1976 at the Arts and Activity Centre in Ongar, Essex, with only three members. As the congregation grew, it later moved to Budworth Hall in Essex in 1979. The Church acquired property in Coxtie Green, where they met in a large black building. Bishop Reid humorously claimed to have the *largest black Church in the U.K...* 'The 900-seat venue reached its maximum capacity on most Sundays.

They strategically placed billboards in key spots around the U.K. to boost outreach, leveraging unsold ad spaces at a discounted rate from an industry insider during slow sales periods. Individuals travelled from close and distant places, encompassing various ages, races and economic backgrounds, to hear the preaching that was bursting with the life of God and profoundly touching lives.

In August 2001, ahead of their 25th anniversary, Bishop Reid commissioned an independent Congregational Attitudes and Beliefs Survey, which was conducted by London Christian Research to assess the health of the Peniel Church. On 'Survey Sunday' in October 2001, members filled out forms, and Bishop Reid had no role in selecting the questions or reviewing the responses. The November 2001 report revealed some intriguing findings.

When asked what they valued the most at the Church, 90% declared that they appreciated the Bible teachings, followed closely by the pastor and the presence of God, both at nearly equal percentages. These ranked lower because the pastor also taught the Bible. Julian Fagan said: *"First time I heard Bishop, that's exactly what I wanted to hear...Bishop just basically gave it to me straight...I thought that's...how the Bible is supposed to be preached, and the resounding phrase 'if you don't like what I'm saying, go jump in the lake' and he wasn't trying to keep anyone or tickle your ears or keep people sweet."*[7]

Additionally, 33% primarily appreciated the family-friendly atmosphere, 30% admired the caring congregation, and 27% valued the school, Peniel Academy.

Regarding their faith, 94% reported a growth in their conviction (44% significantly), 53% maintained the 1996 attendance levels, and 42% attended more due to commitment, teaching and enjoyment.

---

7 Interview May 2010.

Furthermore, 85% read the Bible weekly, 30% daily, and 98% were baptised in water.

44% of attendees were aged between twenty to forty-four years, a rarity among English churches at the time. Unlike others with older demographics, which are often skewed due to active Sunday schools, Peniel mirrored the community's national age distribution.

With 48% male attendees, it matched the general population's 49% rate; most English churches leaned towards 60% female. Here, single men and women were equally represented, unlike most churches, where single women outnumbered single men.

They had high educational attainment and mostly held steady employment, with minimal unemployment. A third of the regular attendees held advanced degrees or qualifications in fields, including law, medicine, dentistry and various other high-ranking positions in business.

The Peniel Church had the highest frequency of attendance and commitment levels nationwide, surpassing even newer churches, with consistent percentages across age and gender groups. A remarkable 75% of the Peniel attendees felt a strong sense of belonging – three times higher than the typical 25% in other churches.

People of all ages joined Peniel, primarily through personal invitations. Additional reasons included miracles, Bishop Reid's sermons at other churches, and TV exposure. Notably, 20% of those in their twenties grew up in Peniel, a rare example of organic Church growth.

The U.K. Christian Research noted that the Peniel Church exhibited statistical evidence of a vibrant and charismatic community, with robust Biblical teaching, extensive Bible reading and a willingness to share faith. The congregation experienced growth in faith, increased Church attendance and instilled a high level of belief compared to

 I'm Alive

most other evangelical churches. They concluded that their success could be a model for other English churches.

Bishop Reid: *"Most churches out there don't want to know, so what can you do? We have pastors meetings...conferences, we reach out to people, but people don't want to know...but we are what we are, and we're here to stay and grow..."*

"...the report did worry about what would happen when I died, well, I hope you bury me...but it's a wonderful report; everything was healthy, they were wondering...am I preparing a successor? Well, I'm not about to die, I don't think, but if I do, well, God will take care of His Church because it's His Church, and that's the way it should be...I think it's nonsense about who's the heir apparent, I don't know anyway."

Around 2010, he and his wife mentioned discussing a successor and expressed confidence that they had received guidance from God regarding this. In the past, attempts were made to replace him by those who harboured grievances about the Church and wanted him gone.

Bishop Reid: *"There's only one per cent of people that don't like what's going on in the Church, I know, I got it from this report...the people of God want what God wants; they aren't after what they want for themselves...selfish, self-centred individuals who love money and love this world's goods and serve mammon and not God and are frauds..."*

Around 2010, he and his wife mentioned discussing a successor and expressed confidence that they had received guidance from God regarding this.

Associate Pastors, Peter Charles Roland Linnecar and Carolyn Mary Claire Linnecar, came from different religious backgrounds— Peter was evangelical and Carolyn had a brethren background. Peter was thick around the middle with a bald head and fingers like sausages. He arrived as a struggling pastor, having spent two years with Jamie Coleman, a London Bible School graduate who ran a Church in Harlow without conversions. Bishop Reid advised Jamie to pursue a different career, ending his ministry aspirations. Eventually, Peter was made a director for Michael Reid Publishing from March 3rd, 2000 until he resigned on August 2nd, 2006.

"...it's one thing I bless God for all the years...Carolyn and Peter joined us...nearly 24 years ago... I'd rather have a person alongside me with the heart of Peter than someone...so smart and clever. Why? Because I value the heart of a man more than their supposed abilities. I'm not saying Peter hasn't got abilities; he has; he chose a wonderful wife, and that was the smartest thing he did. I chose a wonderful wife, and that was the smartest thing she did..." [Audience laughs]

"...in 25 years, I can stand before God and say 'thank God for the people God's given us. Don't think this Church came just because of me; it didn't. God brought the right people along at the right time... I'm grateful for the way Peter and Carolyn have been with us and Meidre has been there... what would one do without Meidre in the back office? ...when Benson [Idahosa] was...with me... I'd ring up Peniel and say can you put me through to the old girl in the back office and Benson used to say...'I know who you're after; it's the old girl in the back office, isn't it?' I said, yeah 'It's Meidre. You can't get anyone more faithful.' Has she ever made mistakes? Yeah, but not as many as me because that's why I'm the pastor. I made more mistakes...you can't find a better bunch of people you really can't..."

Through the Church life's ups and downs, he dusted off the fallen, encouraging them to try over again. In 2009/2010, Peter Linnecar, then the Principal at the Peniel Academy, and his wife Carolyn, faced police questioning with regards to historical child sexual assault accusations, including rape allegations. Around June 24th, they received a letter notifying them that *"The fact no action is being taken does not preclude an aggrieved party pursuing proceedings"* and *"Should additional information become available, the matter will be reviewed, and this decision may be reconsidered."*

                    I'm Alive

The ministry supported them during the allegations. [For confirmation, contact the Child Abuse Investigation Unit in Essex, involving Acting Detective Inspector Steve Nelson (Badge Number: 683), and Ofsted, the school regulatory body, also investigated this incident.]

Some held unfavourable opinions of a key leader. Orville Thomas, a former member. He states: *"[Church leader] once issued a serious threat to me. He made it clear that he would cause me GBH and keep me down in whatever ways possible...I invited a friend to watch The Father musical; when my guest, who worked in a club, saw [...] at the Church, he was surprised and claimed [...] and his son were regulars at the strip club where he worked."*

Over the years, many individuals expressed their gratitude for the ministry.

"Only eternity will show the gratitude...for what you've done for us, for the life...that you've laid down. We want to thank you for what you mean to us." – Carolyn Linnecar, Pastor at the Peniel Church.[8]

"We've gone through a few scrapes, but any time we've needed help, he's always been there." –Doug Austin, member of the Peniel Church.[9]

"There have been tears, there have been challenges, but I wouldn't swap it for anything...I can't describe its effect on our family, especially... the school, it's priceless." – Jon Avery, Member of the Peniel Church.

"...he was a man who had great compassion for people, a love for Jesus Christ, and miracles were happening in his Church. He made a great impression upon me." – Professor Roy Hayden, Dean of Theology at the Peniel College of Higher Education.

"I spent three months looking for churches, but nothing ministered to my heart until I met a man.... He became my father, as he is today." – Colin Cleminson, Assistant Pastor of the Peniel Church.

---

8 Trumpet Call, Issue 39, July 2003

9 Trumpet Call, July 2003

The Peniel Academy

The Reids, along with many Church parents were concerned about their children's education, finding the local Ongar Comprehensive School lacking from a Christian perspective. After a two-year search, they miraculously acquired Bell House at 49 Coxtie Green Road, a functioning school with easy planning approval. The entire Church united to raise funds through various means. In January 1982, the Peniel Academy was founded, starting with 17 children in the stable block and catered to students aged between 2 to 19. The school mainly accepted Church members' children, occasionally making exceptions for missionary families.

Using his teaching expertise, Peter Linnecar played a vital role in founding the school and managing regulatory matters with the Department of Education. While working full-time at FIA, he volunteered for occasional teaching and served as the Vice Principal under Bishop Michael Reid, who was the Principal. Dedicated Church members volunteered full-time to teach and run the school. Dr Ruth Reid: *"...everyone mucked in together to educate each other's children."* Parents were required to provide a year's attendance, financial contribution, and active involvement to enrol their children, ensuring educational stability to avoid school changes due to Church dissatisfaction. As the Church expanded, the Peniel Academy grew, necessitating the acquisition of Brizes Park in 1998, a listed mansion spanning 74 acres.

Dr Ruth Reid: "...everyone mucked in together to educate each other's children."

Children learnt that the Church was an integral part of their lives, and attending Sunday morning services was mandatory. At age six or seven, students of the Peniel Academy were obliged to take sermon notes, which teachers later evaluated at school.

I'm Alive

During his school days, Bishop Reid had memorised extensive Shakespeare passages. His suggestion to replace Shakespeare with passages from the Bible was initially met with doubt by the teachers of the Peniel Academy. Nevertheless, he persisted, creating a tiered system of passages for different ages. Children exceeded expectations, graduating with extensive memorisation of the New Testament and significant passages from the Old Testament. Parents also learnt these passages to instruct their children at home.

When he advocated for Bible memorisation among the children, he didn't realise the significant role that memorisation had historically played in Hebrew education. Ruth explained: *"Later, as I began to research for my thesis, I discovered that it would have been a substantial part of the way Jesus learnt as a child. Hebrew children in Jesus' day would have had to repeat their lessons to the teacher verbatim. Because of this, Jesus could confound and astonish the doctors and teachers in the temple (Luke 2: 46-47). He would have known great tracts of the scriptures, which the Holy Spirit would have been able to bring to His remembrance with understanding."*[10]

The aim was to run the school differently from the norm. While some leaders favoured a profit-driven model, he opposed it—nominal fees helped sustain the day-to-day expenses. Dr Reid stated: *"The school is not run as a business that has to make huge profits. The sacrificial giving of time and money means that the fees charged are a third to half of the normal cost of sending a child to a private school...so that all Church members can afford to send their children to the school."* She reiterated: *"We kept the fees as low as possible...on the basis that the parents would provide help with teaching, cleaning and any help that was needed, that they would contribute."*

Almost all teachers were Church members, leading to remarkable academic success, often ranking among the top five for

---

10 Hey Everyone, Teens Love Miracles, p 74-75

GCSE and A-Levels schools in the U.K. Bishop Reid states: *"...we were number three for exam results in the country. We have come second also...every year the next class tried to excel and beat the previous class. Ninety-five percent of the children went to universities.... We beat private and state schools."* During one year, all eleven-year-olds achieved level 4 and above in all subjects, surpassing the government's targets of 75% in Maths and 80% in English. This feat garnered substantial attention from the government and other independent educational institutions.

A letter dated January 19th, 2000, from Miss W Sanderson of the Independent Schools Registration Team to Bishop Reid stated: *"The results...are exemplary. Nearly every child graduates...to gain entrance to the university of their choice...As a result of the inspection of the Academy by the Department for Education and Employment, Her Majesty's Inspector, Mr Robertson, reported that pupils were highly motivated, keen to learn and delightful. Attainment exceeds what would be expected nationally in relation to the capabilities and ages of the pupils concerned."*

Music and the arts were strongly encouraged and every child acquired proficiency in at least one instrument. The Church band included proficient students from the Academy. Children actively participated in performing arts, staging in-house plays and shows throughout the year. They also entered recitation and drama competitions, achieving notable success. Dr Reid explains: *"This is all part of developing the whole person and gives them confidence to speak in public."*

At the school, Bishop Michael Reid emphasised education, not Christian indoctrination. *"It is not an evangelistic arm of the Church nor an indoctrination centre but a place where children will be equipped for life, both temporal and eternal."* The school did well in many areas. Members of the school appeared on Blue Peter, while the school's junior choir was the runners-up in a national singing competition called 'Minstrels in the Gallery' that was broadcast on Radio Two.

In a 2001 Research Report on the Congregational Attitudes and Beliefs Survey, it was mentioned: *The children and young people who attend Peniel are markedly different from the majority of such in other English churches...*[11]

Bishop Reid: *"Tom Matthew, when he came over and he took our young people's camp, he said he had never been with a group of young people like it, who...wanted to listen and learn...[he] said, 'I was just shocked at the difference'..."*

While achieving exceptional academic results, the school remained authentically comprehensive, often prompting disbelief. Unlike many British private and grammar schools, they didn't follow an intelligence-based selection policy.

Most students excelled, attaining impressive degrees for prosperous careers, and demonstrated God's work and testimony. The Peniel Academy students were highly sought-after and significantly valued by employers and universities. Evangelical Alliance reported: *"Employers and universities alike would ask for more of the young people from the Peniel Academy because they know they will be hardworking, honest, and have integrity... David Blunkett was the Minister for Education in the Blair administration, and he remarked that he would like to bottle Church schools' recipe for success and pass it on to all schools."*

— "Faith Based Schools Put to the Test," Idea: Resourcing Members of the EA to Change Society, March/April 2002, 20.

Vince Avery, a former student of the Peniel Academy, reported to Trumpet Call: *"Looking back, I could not have asked for a better education. All the pupils at Peniel are encouraged to achieve to the best*

---

11 London: Christian Research, Nov 2001, p40

of their ability and to give 100% to whatever they lay their hand to do. This work ethic coupled with Biblical Christian principles gives a solid foundation for when you leave school, go to university and then on to the workplace.[12]

The school's chosen sport was table tennis. Bishop Reid: *"We took table tennis because we had a very big age range from four to eighteen. We also had boys and girls, and I didn't want a contact sport for various reasons. I didn't want injuries, so table tennis was a better option."*

With head coach Nicky Jarvis, a three-time representative of England at the World Table Tennis Championships, they consistently won six out of eight age group trophies for six years in a row and, at one point, triumphed in all eight age groups. In 2006, a team of four girls from the school represented England and played in the World Schools Table Tennis Championship in China. They were placed eighth in the world.

Bishop Reid: *"Peter Cleminson was number one in the juniors, and Abigail was offered to train for the Olympics and high-class players."*

Eric Pickles, MP for Brentwood and Ongar, inaugurated the Peniel Academy's new junior school wing on May 16th, 2003, replacing old porta cabins that previously held pre-school and junior classes. He planted a magnolia galaxy tree and unveiled a commemorative plaque, following the pattern of the first wing that opened in May 2002. No construction loans were required; Church members sacrificed their time a resources to complete the buildings after professionals erected the walls and roof.

Throughout its 33-year existence, the school has likely educated hundreds of children affiliated with the Church.

---

12 Issue 34, 2001, 28

Peniel College of Higher Education (PCHE)

The Bible School first started in 1979-80 in Ongar. It evolved into the Peniel Bible College at Coxtie Green Road, and later renamed the Peniel College of Higher Education (PCHE) in 1997, when it relocated to Brizes Park. PCHE became the largest charismatic Bible College in the U.K., attracting numerous international students. It offered high-quality courses based on Biblical principles, with a focus on healing.

Impressively, in 1997, it established an affiliation with the Oral Roberts University (O.R.U.), the world's largest charismatic university. This institution had 5,300 students during the 2001-2002 academic year, who came together from all states, 55+ countries, and 40 denominations. There were only two affiliations worldwide with Oral Roberts University – one in Sweden and the other was PCHE. During the existence of the PCHE, O.R.U. assigned two deans of theology, Sam Thorpe and Roy Hayden, to deliver lectures. The PCHE offered accredited theology programmes at O.R.U.'s U.K. campus. In 2006, the PCHE affiliated with the University of Wales for Master's and Doctorate degrees.

In 2002, the Council for Charismatic Colleges and Universities awarded PCHE with the Racial Harmony award for its diverse student body and programmes.

Global Gospel Fellowship (GGF)

Global Gospel Fellowship (GGF) was established in August 2000, forming a vast network of hundreds of miracle ministries worldwide. Its inception was encouraged by T.L. Osborn, a highly-travelled 20th-century evangelist. Recognising the need to guide pastors and leaders in sound doctrine amidst widespread errors and 'gimmicks', they named the organisation the Global

Gospel Fellowship. The inaugural annual conference included representatives from all five continents.

Regular conferences drew a global audience from many nations, with numerous international and regional seminars and conferences.

Rev. Feb Idahosa of Nigeria exclaimed: *"...I enjoyed hearing about the basics of Christianity again and about what Christ has done. It's not what we've done but what God has done...Bishop Reid made it very plain and very simple."*

Bishop Margaret Idahosa, also from Nigeria, declared: *"It has opened many men's and women's eyes, especially pastors who have been bought up [dogmatically]."*

Ugandan Bishop Robert Kayanja stated: *"...if it weren't for GGF, ministers like me...would not have had the chance of hearing Dr T L Osborn in person. I think that what Bishop Reid and the Peniel Church are doing here is a real investment into the lives of ministers who would otherwise not have had the chance of hearing Dr T.L. Osborn speak at the age of seventy-nine."*

Finally, Dr T.L. Osborn summed it up succinctly: *"I think the name itself is wonderful. It's global...It's Gospel, that's the good part and its fellowship...It's terrific. If you haven't heard the Peniel Choir, you haven't heard anything. It's wonderful."*

The Peniel Choir

In 1989, the Peniel Choir began with 23 members and quickly grew to 100. This renowned choir strongly supported Bishop Reid, regularly performing with him on TV and at various venues across the U.K. and Europe. It also featured in the 10 a.m. Sunday service, where they captivated the congregation each Sunday.

Phillip Billson, a producer at BBC Religion, says: *"The Peniel Choir have that rare gift of breathing the love of Christ into every note*

 I'm Alive

of their singing. The conviction that Jesus is Lord in each member's life shines through all they do. And what a truly inspirational sound that lifts the Spirit and brings glory to God!"

The scriptural songs brought blessings to thousands worldwide.

Publishing

Trumpet Call – Miracles Healing Faith: In 1986, 20,000 copies of the inaugural Trumpet Call newspaper were published and distributed to all members of the Parliament and the House of Lords.

The newspaper started with a tri-annual print run of 70,000 copies but later increased to 100,000. Of those, 50,000 were distributed to local homes by members of the Church. This publication highlighted stories of transformed lives and miraculous events in the Church, and carried social commentary on relevant national issues. Its evolution was marked by improved reporting and upgraded designs with each issue.

Book Publishing: In 1989, the Church's commitment to spreading the Gospel led to the creation of a publishing company called Sharon Publications, later renamed 'Alive U.K.', which was dedicated to promoting Christian materials and outreach.

Bishop Reid's books have garnered a significant global influence. His inaugural book, *'Whose Faith Is it Anyway?'* was published in 1990. This was followed by other titles in a similar vein: *'Whose War is it Anyway?' 'Whose Mind is it Anyway?'* and *'Whose Love is it Anyway?'* His book *'Strategic Level Spiritual Warfare – A Modern Mythology'* was, in some ways, the crowning piece of his literary work. Referring to the book, *What God Can Do For You!* John Glass, General Superintendent of Elim Pentecostal Churches U.K., commented: *"Cutting through the veneer of religion, legalism and ritual that so often veils the face of what the Church is meant to be; this book reveals the core values of the Gospel – Christ and nothing more, Christ and nothing less, Christ and nothing else."*

Peter Kerridge of Premier Radio, commenting on the publication, It's *So Easy!* said: *"A big man with a big personality doing a big work for a big God...The book will inspire you to reach out to the God who can do much more than you can ask or imagine."*

Howard Conder of Revelation TV, regarding *It's So Easy!*: *"Unputdownable...a masterpiece of simplicity."*

T.L. Osborn about *'Strategic Level Spiritual Warfare – A Modern Mythology'*: *"I commend you on the remarkable job you have accomplished in presenting this sound, helpful, and urgently needed work to the Christian world today...I have no doubt that it will be a stabilising influence among sincere Pentecostals and charismatics."*

Countless emails and letters attest to the life-changing impact that the books have had on many lives. Bishop Reid: *"This is my greatest reward and has encouraged me to write again."*

The TV Ministry

On the morning of Tuesday, June 11, 2002, the Church launched their weekly half-hour TV programme—"What God Can Do For You"—on the Trinity Broadcasting Network. Within a year, it expanded to Revelation TV and Life TV, reaching a global audience of millions. Bishop Reid: *"...we have to use every means to communicate the Gospel... He went where people were, and in this modern age, television provides us with a fantastic opportunity to do the same by taking His word into people's homes."*

The programme was highly engaging and successful, featuring vibrant interview-style episodes with diverse guests. Due to high demand, the Church paid nominal fees for broadcasting this programme twenty-two times weekly across various stations. They invested over £150,000 in media equipment to ensure the production was of high-quality content. Dr Reid: *"The TV and media department...would not run without the help of the young people. They love to be involved in these areas."*

Philip Whealy, Peniel TV's Director of Television, remarked in Trumpet Call July 2003: *"[He] is a remarkable man with remarkable gifts. He has always had a heart to reach people. Working with someone like that would have been difficult to create something without life, vitality, and originality... [On] many occasions... God's miracle power has been captured on camera. We do follow-ups on people healed many years ago and still living lives free of pain."*

Bishop Reid also participated in secular TV debates on the creation and the resurrection and he was occasionally interviewed by secular news channels like Sky News and BBC News.

Miracle Conferences

Over 5,000 global visitors came to the Church each year, for the regular miracle services and to attend the annual Miracle Conferences held during Easter and the August Bank Holiday weekends. Bishop Reid and other international speakers delivered messages and prayed for the sick; they were accompanied by the Peniel Choir's musical ministry.

Music & Miracles

'Music & Miracles' were monthly gatherings at the Peniel Pentecostal Church that featured the choir, with Bishop Reid preaching and praying for the sick. Promoted extensively through billboard ads around prominent locations in the U.K., they became vital community outreaches, attracting even those who wouldn't typically attend Church. The billboard next to Sainsbury's car park in Brentwood proclaimed 'Miracles, Healing, Faith: Come and See' and showing him holding a boy with one hand and a microphone in the other.

The Father: The Greatest Story Ever Told

This remarkable musical, 'The Father – The Greatest Story Ever Told,' featured the renowned Peniel Choir and Orchestra. It was written and produced by Philip Whealey, with Bishop Reid assisting. It is a story of love, deception, betrayal and redemption. The incredible production, staged at the Church in December 2007, played to a packed house, prompting an additional show due to the overwhelming attendance. Countless people in carloads were turned away. The storyline unveiled God's timeless, redemptive plan—each song seamlessly blended the lyrics and music, which was further enhanced by the dramatic presentation, mime and passionate narrative.

Simon Eden, a multi-talented BAFTA award winner, reviewed the production: *"Every year, many churches across the country pull out the tea towels for the Shepherds, and young girls get to hold a plastic baby in their Church nativity plays. Very few amateur thespians even contemplate trying to tell the Biblical story from start to finish, let alone writing an entire West-End/Broadway-style classical soundtrack for it and performing it with a live orchestra. Somehow, the Church ... managed to perform such a feat..."*

Dr T.L. Osborn: *"Dr Ladonna and I dedicated an evening to watching both DVDs of 'The Father.'... You have made a major contribution to society...a superb, highly professional production... very moving, spiritually... a great investment of money. Your Church team performed professionally. Phillip's creative work reveals a great depth of insight. Your mime artist is simply remarkable... With all my heart, congratulations on a splendid production for our hurting world."*

The performance received an influx of positive feedback, with many people praising its exceptional quality.

"Amazing. It was so powerful! So many people were saying they just wanted to see it again and again – it just reminds you of what God has done for all of us. When's the next performance?!"

"Thank you – it was absolutely amazing."

"A big thank you to all who have made the musical and the DVD production possible – we have just watched the DVD, and they are just WONDERFUL! And the bonus disc is as good as the actual performance... This is, without a doubt, the best DVD set anyone could ever buy! We are so excited, blessed and thankful to the ministry for making this all possible!"

"My wife and I just wanted to express our thanks for the musical – it was absolutely amazing."

"...the musical was simply brilliant!"

Before introducing Bishop Reid at the production's conclusion, Andrew Love remarked:

"...The person who's going to come now...into whom God put a treasure...the treasure of faith, years and years ago and everything you see here, the choir, the children, the Church, the sound system—everything was inspired by a man who himself was inspired by God, into whom God breathed His life, and he has been the inspiration behind all of this and the product of his ministry is what you see here."

The ministry thrived with a buzzing, well-attended Church that was at its peak. The December 2007 performance of 'The Father' was exceptional and inspiring, eliciting powerful emotions. Those fortunate enough to witness it were captivated, moved and transformed by the performances. This musical stands out as one of the significant highlights during the 32-year history of the Church, under the leadership of Bishop Reid. A tremendous spirit of cooperation and love was expressed throughout the whole performance. A London theatre was booked in May 2008 for the West-End theatre public; however, it never took place. In 2008, some who had earlier praised Bishop Reid unveiled their true feelings and intentions, but God is never caught off guard.

Prophetic Words Regarding Peniel

Treachery and Rebellion: In a private conversation with me, Bishop Reid recounted an early ministry experience. He told me that while he observed [...] approaching the front door from his window, God revealed that [...] would betray him in the future.

In 2003, he received a divine revelation about an upcoming insurrection. *"I told my son, Matthew, they are plotting to take over and that there would be an insurrection...he said, 'Oh, you're just exaggerating'."*[13]

In 2003, he received a divine revelation about an upcoming insurrection. "I told my son, Matthew, they are plotting to take over and that there would be an insurrection...he said, 'Oh, you're just exaggerating'."

Benson Idahosa Prophecies: In 1996, during the Church's 20th Anniversary celebration, Archbishop Benson Idahosa honoured the founders, Bishop Michael Reid and Dr. Ruth Reid, with a gift for their two decades of dedicated service.

The video recording of this event serves as a time capsule containing several prophecies for Peniel's future. Notably, the Archbishop predicted that precisely 20 years later, by 2016, the attendees of the gathering would be in a different location.

---

13 Interview May 2010

   I'm Alive

"The Lord said to me, teach when you get there on what I intend to do 20 years from now. Whether you believe in prophecy, whether you're a believer or not, whether you are [inaudible] a journalist of the worst order, a cynic, 20 years from now, these very people, these ones here now, will not be in the same location. God is taking us forward. Do you believe me? Do you believe in the Word of God? So the Lord said to me, read these scriptures and tell them what I intend to do. So I picked up my pen and wrote the Scripture that God gave me...This morning, go with me to second Peter...chapter one and written in verses...five to eight, but the text itself starts from verse three..."

Furthermore, he prophesied that the work would only move forward, without diminishing.

Furthermore, he prophesied that the work would only move forward, without diminishing.

A Dark Period: The Lord directly addressed Dr Ruth Reid, enquiring whether He could guide her through another challenging phase that was reminiscent of a previous dark period she had endured. She asked: *"For how long, Lord?"* He did not reply. She responded: *"Yes, Lord."*

Increasing Dissatisfaction Amongst a Minority

"If you are going to walk with Jesus Christ, you are going to be opposed... In our days, to be a true Christian is really to become a scandal."

– George Whitefield.

Amidst Jesus' preaching and healing the sick, a shadow of deceit loomed as the treasurer siphoned away ministry finances, and a nefarious plot took shape amongst the religious elite. Jealousy simmered due to the attention He garnered; His blend of bold and compassionate preaching kindled both admiration and hostility – an outcome genuine ministers face till today.

Similarly, Bishop Reid encountered criticism and attacks both within and outside the Church. In February 2001, the Church was charged with undisclosed libel damages, estimated to be in five figures, along with legal costs. Brentwood councillor, Anthony Galbraith, falsely labelled the Church a 'cult' and a local threat. Galbraith later formally admitted the falseness of his claims. Bishop Reid specified that the compensation received would be donated to charity.

There was opposition from within the Church as well. A former member, Everton Morgan, explains: *"After Church, she [his wife] would stay in the car as she said there were two types of people – those for Bishop and those against him."*[14]

Bishop Reid: *"…in life, you'll always get people who can complain. They'll always have good reasons for their complaint… there's a lot of truth in what they say…there was truth in the fact there were giants… everything they said was true except that the citizens of those cities quaked with fear. They knew they had lost before the battle began…"*

He encountered efforts to discredit him from individuals whose lifestyle he opposed, including one person referred to as a 'nasty piece of work' by an anonymous online commentator. This person made potentially defamatory allegations on the website 'Reachout Trust', which led to the website owner, Doug Harris, deleting the thread on May 1st of that year. He even apologised for the defamatory content. Additionally, a blogger criticised Bishop Reid for pointing out leaders' mistakes, even though he himself ran a blog that extensively critiqued a leader. Some individuals' excessive protests appeared to be driven by personal grievances and financial interests.

Bishop Reid: *"Who gets the blame…who do they accuse – the pastor –fantastic job, huh? It's always the pastor's fault when things go wrong, but while everything's going right, you know, well God's blessing us…"*

---

14 2010 Interview

 I'M ALIVE

"...an old man...had been a bare-knuckle boxer all his life and had suffered from the stroke...He couldn't open one of his eyes...During the sermon, God spoke to me...I touched the side of his head and told him that his eye would open...His eye started to open, and then he turned to look at his wife for the first time...He could see her...At the end of the meeting, my wife spoke to...one of the [Church] singers and remarked on how beautiful it was. [The singer] responded dismissively, saying... 'just another miracle.' I was taken aback by his response...My wife asked me how anyone could respond like that."

Towards the end, Bishop Reid noticed a shift in the Church, towards prioritising wealth, with some members chasing luxurious cars, homes, and frequent vacations and forming cliques and family circles.

Within the Church leadership, specific individuals opposed his mission trips and criticised his successful TV broadcasts. The board disapproved of his approach to the Bible School, as he permitted enrolment for Africans and financially challenged individuals, which clashed with the board's desire to impose high fees. In a 2010 interview, Bishop Reid revealed that the board sought to reallocate the funds and even considered employing a Church leader's spouse, who was already involved in Church activities. He states: *"She's very lazy and did not turn up and would just vanish and never fulfilled her functions, so I didn't want her. When she was involved in play school, there were always difficulties and demanding things, and I found she was a very disruptive element..."* Another leader urged the Reids to cease their global travels, arguing that the funds spent on airfares should be allocated to employing people he favoured.

One singer from the worship team opposed Bishop Reid, often leaving after the performance to avoid his preaching due to a personal disagreement. This singer repeatedly criticised Bishop Reid behind his back, despite the Bishop helping him turn his life around and providing free office space and support to launch his business.

As per Bishop Reid, most of the dissatisfaction involved several interconnected families that were united by marriage, all of whom held significant influence within the Church. In my interview in May 2010 with Dr Ruth Reid, she explains: *"Strange enough, when we heard they were getting married, we just knew inside that it was trouble, but you couldn't do anything; you just felt, Oh, that's not a good idea!"*

Bishop Reid stated that some people tried to influence his son Matthew against him by inviting Matthew over or visiting him. Still, he chose not to intervene, believing that God would handle the situation in His way.

In 2007, social services investigated reports from eight children at the Church school who had made allegations against Bishop Reid. He remained unaware of the specifics. The effort aimed to discredit him, but social services found no evidence and took no action. Failing this plot, the disgruntled individuals pursued another.

The Church became a charitable company when the charity commission mandated community involvement. Bishop Reid delegated this transition to the administration department, unaware that some individuals exploited it to further their hidden agenda. He elaborates: *"...when the limited company was set up, I was meant to be a shareholder, as was Ruth, but Peter Bostock only made Rachel and Sheila Graziona shareholders, which was convenient for Peter Linnecar."*[15]

Just as Judas, the embezzler, sought an opportunity to secretly betray Jesus for monetary gain—the modus operandi of betrayers—similarly, a plot to seize control of the Church seemed to be underway.

---

15 Interview May 2010.

Chapter 17

Church Assets

By James Peter Jandu

[Details about the property assets are included here because many believe they played a role in the events leading to the Reids' removal from office. I've presented the complex facts as accurately as possible, despite lacking access to clarifying sources.]

Naboth possessed a fruitful vineyard. Upon seeing its productivity, King Ahab seized it using eminent domain. Jezebel, Ahab's conniving wife, forged letters in his name and sealed them with his royal stamp. Naboth was unjustly accused by her of blasphemy against God and the King, resulting in his death by stoning. Jezebel's use of deceit and trickery enabled her to orchestrate the transfer of the vineyard to Ahab. Ahab faced the repercussions of God's wrath. (1 Kings 21:1–19).

In the same way, Bishop Reid's fruitful ministry, abundant in assets, became the envy of countless individuals and ministers worldwide. Hence, it is vital to give a concise summary of the assets in order to underscore their significance to this story.

Church Assets and Financial Matters: An Overview
The Church Building

Initially, Bishop Reid registered the first Church building in his name and clearing the £60,000 mortgage by 1994. He became the debt-free sole owner of the structure, before eventually transferring its ownership to the Church, which then appreciated to millions of pounds in value. The Church, resembled a plain barn or village hall, situated amidst a cluster of buildings and was enclosed by a high metal fence with automated gates. In the front yard, a significant historical gift from the Ark Royal, a large gun, pointed outward.

The Bell House

In April 1981, after an extensive two-year search, they found the Bell House on 49 Coxtie Green Road, Pilgrims Hatch, Brentwood, Essex, to be a suitable home for their school and their rapidly growing Church. They needed £175,000, but through miraculous financial provisions and sacrificial giving from the pastor and the congregation, they raised £212,000 in just ten days, enabling them to acquire both, the Bell House and the adjacent market garden. At the time, the Church had a mere £200 left in its bank account.

The Reids sold their family home in Greenwall, Ongar, Essex: *"When we brought the Peniel Church, we sold our home and everything to help buy it. An old lady, Jackie Winans, also sold her property and gave us the £40,000 as a personal gift, which we put into Church property after we had bought it. We agreed she could live in the Bell House for the rest of her life."*[16] Simultaneously, Peter and Carolyn sold their home, making a profit of approximately £10,000, which they contributed to purchasing the Church building.

The Bell House was converted into three separate apartments – one for the Linnecars, another for the Reids and the third for

---

16 Interview May 2010

the elderly lady with sight issues, who'd contributed to the sale of her house. The guarantee of a lifelong home for her was faithfully upheld, as she lived in the Bell House until 1992.

The Linnecars received one-third ownership of the property, although they should have rightfully received only a quarter share. Michael and Peter secured mortgages from Barclays Bank for their portions of the Bell House, each at £25,000, which they eventually paid off in full. Many years later, the ten-bedroom residential accommodation, including a swimming pool, was appraised at £1.2 million, with the Reids holding a two-thirds legal share, valued at £800,000. They had specified in their wills that the Bell House would be passed on to the Church upon the last survivors' death: *"It had always been my intention, and I gave it gladly. To contribute to the survival of the Church was one of my dearest desires."*[17]

Later, the Reids relocated to a property they named Testimony House.

In 2003, Peter Linnecar encountered significant financial difficulties as noted in the Church minutes. The lenders were close to foreclosing, jeopardising the interest in 49 Coxtie Green House, Brentwood – the beloved Church property. The AGM minutes dated April 14th, 2007, state: *"RC mentioned the Bell House and the fact that there may be pressure from the bank for Carolyn and Peter Linnecar to sell this year or face repossession. It was agreed that it would be undesirable to have an individual, especially one unconnected with the Church, residing on the property. It was agreed that members of the rest of the board would approach them with a view to negotiation a possible purchase. MSBR [Michael Reid] expressed reluctance for the Church to take on debt. He also felt too personally attached to be involved in negotiations and asked to be left out of it."*

---

17 Dr Reid, ref 2003 trustee Meeting

In Dr Reid's written description of a trustees' meeting concerning the Bell House, she states: *"So, as usual, we were presented with the financial facts with a gun to our heads. This had been [...] 'modus operando' with us every time he needed us to come up with finance to save the business previously."* Andrew Love suggested selling Testimony House and having the Reids return to the Bell House. Despite attempts to blame half of Peter's debt on Bishop Reid due to their past partnership and his prior role as Chairman (from which he'd resigned two years earlier), they refused this solution to address Peter's debts.

"These accusations put me under pressure even more as I considered it totally unfair to blame my husband for Peter's debts, especially as we had always helped him out with large sums of money for the business… the total was at least £40,000."

Peter suggested securing an additional mortgage on the property to clear his debts.

"This seemed like a very bad idea to me considering our age (MSBR sixty and me fifty-eight) at the time. I began to feel very threatened and asked if I needed separate representation from a lawyer…but they all assured me that it was not necessary. I began to cry because I hated feeling we were being pushed into a corner to accept huge debts."

In good faith, although reluctantly, they agreed to an alternative proposal, wherein they signed over their two-thirds share of the Bell House to Peter to help him secure a mortgage and prevent him from going bankrupt. Although Peter assured them that he could handle the repayments, Dr Reid had her doubts and questioned him. This agreement was reached with several conditions during the 2003 trustee meeting and was accepted by all.

The agreement is confirmed in a letter to Bishop Michael Reid, dated May 13th, 2008, from Peter A. Bostock of Curry & Co: *"…you also asked me on the telephone for details of the transfer of your and*

      I'm Alive

Ruth's interest in the Bell House to the Linnecars. That was completed on December 6th, 2004 and I am, as requested, enclosing a copy of the relevant Deed."

The Reids made specific stipulations such as the property was not to be sold and would eventually be bequeathed to the Church, as they were entrusting £800,000, which was a genuine part of their investment for the future.

Matthew Reid, a former trustee, sent an email on December 6th, 2007 that read: *"We need to sort this out ASAP. They have not actually set the value to zero. They have said that once the subsidence is fixed, the property [Bell House] will be worth £750,000. We need to have an idea of what this will take. ...Peter and Carolyne, in good faith, went ahead with buying a new house on the understanding that we [Peniel Church] would purchase this property...."*

This agreement also came with the understanding that the Reids would retain full and unencumbered rights to Testimony House, safeguarding their continued interest in the property. The Board of Trustees, forming a quorum, duly agreed to this arrangement. The AGM minutes dated April 14th, 2007: *"KL explained the licence drafted by the lawyer which gives MSBR and RR a licence to occupy Testimony House for the rest of their lives....All the directors were in agreement that this was the least the charity could do for Bishop and Mrs Reid and were very happy with the idea. It was agreed that they need some time to check the document."*

Dr. Reid: *"I cried for two days after this encounter and signing over the Bell House. We were giving Peter and Carolyn £800,000, which seemed a huge amount of money they did not deserve, although Carolyn was unaware of £200,000 unsecured loans. ..."*

The agreement guaranteed the Reids lifelong residence in Testimony House, ensuring their security and well-being, or so it seemed.

The Stable Block

The Stable Block served as the Church's main office and Bishop Reid owned two-thirds of it. According to him, it was agreed that Peter Linnecar would transfer the remaining one-third to him—as documented in the records—creating a fair exchange.

Bishop Reid: *"...it was also agreed that the other 3rd of the office block would be signed to me, and that was agreed....Peter Bostock, mine and Peter Linnecar's solicitor, got me to sign the papers but the transfer of the 1/3 office stable block was not transferred. So, he had a duty of care.... he never told me he had not made the 1/3 over to me; I only found out later by letter. Peter and Carolyn went to talk to him and said they would do it, but a bit later, and he has since signed the 1/3 over to the Church. He walked away with the Church having signed the property over so he could get a mortgage. He guaranteed both of us that he would not sell the property and that it would be left in his will for the Church. This is what we had always agreed, but he went afterwards to the trustees without my knowledge and told them he couldn't afford to pay the mortgage. He got the trustees to agree. You'll find in some of the minutes I totally opposed the Church paying his debt, and his debts were there for all to see."*[18]

Peter A. Bostock of Curry & Co. sent a letter to Bishop Michael Reid dated May 13th, 2008:

"You asked me about the ownership of the former Stable Block at 49 Coxtie Green Road, and I confirm that it is still registered as belonging to you, Ruth, Peter and Carolyn. I am enclosing a copy of the Land Registry title plan, which shows the extent of the property..... You and Ruth are entitled to two-thirds of the property, and the Linnecars are entitled to one-third.

There was some discussion about Peter and Carolyn giving you their one-third share in late 2004, but that could not be dealt with at the same time as the transfer of your and Ruth's interests in the Bell

---

18 Interview May 2010

     I'm Alive

House to Peter and Carolyn...and it was agreed that it should be dealt with later. Peter subsequently told me that the ownership should be left as it was for the time being...you also asked me on the telephone for details of the transfer of your and Ruth's interest in the Bell House to the Linnecars. That was completed on December 6th, 2004 and I am, as requested, enclosing a copy of the relevant Deed."

The Stable Block had an estimated value of at least £400,000. The commitment to transfer one-third of the Stable Block to the Reids was never honoured; instead, it was donated to the Church. Ultimately, the Reids were unfairly deprived of over £800,000, which is a substantial sum.

Becoming Shareholders

Part of the agreement also included making the Reids shareholders. An email dated September 6th, 2004, dictated to Rachel Whealy, reads: *"I would like to ask if you would be prepared to be a shareholder of the new company...it is the shareholders who have ultimate control over the appointment and removal of directors."* Completing this unfinished task would grant the Reids the power to dismiss the board. What was the reason for blocking their authority?

According to Bishop Reid, the solicitor representing both parties was a personal friend of Peter Linnecar from their time at Cambridge, creating an ethical conflict, which is typically avoided in legal practice. In 2002, Andrew Love, Carolyn Linnecar's brother with an Anglican charismatic background, worked at a prestigious accounting firm. He and Peter Linnecar stepped down as trustees due to the impending sale of the Bell House to the Church to prevent any conflict of interest, given their involvement in the transaction.

Testimony House

The owner of 52 Coxtie Green Road, two doors from the Church, offered to sell the property. After inspection, Bishop Reid decided to buy it. He explained: *"A week later, Benson Idahosa came and asked how much it was and I told him. He said, 'I'll raise the money for you; you and your wife shouldn't be living on site; you need your own home'."*

In April 1992, during a service at Peniel, Archbishop Benson Idahosa passionately recommended acquiring the house, with front and rear access from the Church, as a residence for the Reids. The response from the congregation was overwhelmingly positive, and they showed their approval by raising £285,000 in a single night! The funds covered the purchase of the house and took care of the associated legal fees and renovations. However, Bishop Reid informed the Church board, *"I don't feel happy putting it in my name; just put it in the Church's name."*[19]

Commencing in 1993, Bishop Michael and Dr Reid resided at their new property aptly named 'Testimony House', which was also known as 'the Parsonage at Peniel Church.'

The Bible College Classroom and Block

Initially, the Reids were the owners of this portion of the property, but they later decided to sell their portion of the property to the Church.

Peter Bostock of Curry & Co, in a letter dated November 23rd, 1994, explains: *"The price of £200,000 compares with a market value of £377,000 in 1992, and the transfer will, therefore, include a substantial element of gift."*

In short, the Reids, who were owed £377,000 for the property, accepted £200,000 to donate the remainder to the Church; however, they received only £90,000.

---

19 Interview May 2010

Brizes Park

In 1998, as the Church grew, the Peniel Academy acquired a larger facility on Ongar Road, near Brentwood, Essex. It lay between Navestock and Kelvedon Hatch villages, with amenities like the Bentley Golf Course and a celebrity hotspot restaurant – Alec's, nearby.

The 74-acre estate boasted a Grade II Georgian-listed mansion with a rich history. It included a vast ring-fenced parkland, with access through a quarter-mile driveway that traversed through pristine landscaped grounds before leading to secure electric gates.

The parkland features diverse groups of mature trees, including Oak, Chestnut, Pine, Cedar and Elm along the north boundary, ideal for woodland walks. The grounds also house a self-contained herd of free-roaming fallow deer, adding to the property's unique charm.

Built around 1498 by Thomas Bryce, a London citizen and mercer, Brizes took its name from him. The earlier house was replaced by the present mansion that was constructed by the Glassock family in 1722 and has undergone several renovations over the centuries. In 1949, the Hon. Simon Rodney, a first cousin, once removed, of Sir Winston Churchill, purchased it. Churchill often visited it for weekend retreats. After Simon Rodney's passing in March 1980, Brizes was put up for sale in the same year, and advertised for sale in 1995 and 1997.

The Church purchased the house and five acres around it for £1.3 million, paying in full and subsequently obtained a loan for the additional land, which they repaid within five years. Generous contributions from Church members and parents enabled the restoration of the deteriorated buildings.

The stable block was transformed into kitchens, a dining/ assembly hall, and three classrooms. Additionally, a purpose-built gymnasium, tennis courts and an enclosed swimming pool complex, along with 14 prefabricated classrooms were added to the site, which included a courtyard walled garden and over 30 classrooms.

The children relocated to the new site, and the Bible School relocated to the location of Coxtie Green Road.

Tulsa Home

A house was purchased in Tulsa for their frequent ministry trips. To finance this, Andrew Love facilitated the sale of a section of Michael Reid's land to the Church for U.S.$350,000. This appeared reasonable, given the growing congregation and manageable finances. The transfer involved an accounting exercise of moving $350,000 from the Church.

In 2010, the Church's properties were worth £12 million. Even though he could have become a millionaire, Bishop Reid's remarkable generosity made a lasting impact on the Church, showing a solid commitment to the mission and well-being of its members.

Chapter 18
The Unexpected Turning Point

Then Sheila said, "Oh Ruth, I've got something to tell you..."

The Church faced a crisis when it came to light that Bishop Reid had an affair with his Personal Assistant, Sheila Graziano, who was also the Church's music director, a married lady and a mother of two.

Sheila Macintyre was a pastor's daughter and a twin. She later professed conversion to Christ at the Kensington Temple. Her career as a nanny eventually led her to the Peniel Pentecostal Church.

She served as Bishop Reid's assistant for eight years, succeeding Meidre Cleminson and also took on the role of leading the Peniel Choir as the choir mistress. Excelling in these roles, she received praise, including Archbishop Benson Idahosa's approval. Her relationship with Bishop Reid evolved during her time as his PA. Some believed she had a fascination with Bishop Reid and frequently praised him when talking to others.

In March 2008, after returning from India on Virgin Airlines, Bishop Reid had an upset stomach from a chicken sandwich. His condition persisted for about two weeks, close to Easter. Despite feeling unwell, on the Thursday before Good Friday, he visited the Church and recorded two successful TV programmes about their experiences in India with co-hosts Dr Matthia and David Attar, who shared enthusiasm and positive on-camera testimonials.

Bishop Reid: *"After I had done them, I felt like coming back to bed. Sheila Graziano met me and said we want to have a meeting in the office. Andrew Love came with George [Graziano] and Sam Thorpe. I didn't know what they wanted to see me for in the office, so I went up there…and they wanted Ruth to come, but Ruth was talking to someone that had come for the television. Andrew Love insisted, and then we sat down. Andrew Love said at the beginning, 'This must not go outside this room; it is confidential and will be kept between all of us.' Then Sheila said, 'Oh Ruth, I've got something to tell you. I've had an adulterous affair with your husband for eight years.' That's how it began."*

This took place with Sheila's husband present. Dr Reid: *Apparently I said, although I don't remember, 'Is that all you have got to say?' To be honest, for me, it was like I wasn't there, God kind of gave me protection. I knew my body was there, but I wasn't there, so I didn't feel anything; it didn't hurt me or upset me, and I think I turned to Bishop and said, 'Is that true?' He said, Yes.'"*

During that meeting, Bishop Reid corrected them, stating that it hadn't been eight years and that she had worked for him for eight years. Andrew Love allegedly accused Dr. Reid of being aware of the situation all along, although she was not. Dr. Reid explained his reason for this accusation: *"Because I was not showing any emotions."* The Church leaders were aware it was not an eight-year affair. A letter hand-delivered to Bishop Reid on October 4th, 2008, signed by Richard Cope, Charlie Pring and Steve Wilkinson, states: *"In relation to Sheila Graziano…we have no direct evidence from Mrs Graziano in front of us about the length of the relationship…"* Dr Reid: *"…but they still spread the rumours that it was eight years."*

I'm Alive

The situation then escalated. Bishop Reid: *"[..] threatened me and said he'd got an iron bar down in his car and that he would get me, and he stood up and I didn't know if he had an iron bar with him, so I stood up because I wasn't going to let someone hit me while I was sitting down. He was behaving peculiarly anyway."*

The next day was Easter, and they expressed their desire for Bishop Reid not to deliver the sermon during the Easter service. He replied: *"I wouldn't have preached anyway, as I don't feel well."* They told him Andrew would preach: *"No, you got it wrong. My wife will take the Easter conference, not you."* Bishop Reid: *"...I realised that [...] and [...] between them had planned this whole thing to take over the Church."*

During the Easter weekend, Dr Reid delivered the sermon, and the congregation responded positively. Bishop Reid intended to step back and let his wife take over. However, contrary to Andrew's assurance of confidentiality, the matter was disclosed to others, including the children at the school. Bishop Reid: *"Andrew's excuse was that he always told his wife everything."*[20] Andrew Love later resigned, citing personal issues.

Peter Linnecar suggested that the Reids travel to Tulsa, U.S.A., accompanied by Ian and Carol Veal. Dr Reid: *"They had a meeting with Bishop because it was rapidly spreading around the Church."* Bishop Reid explained what happened following the Easter meeting: *"I was still ill, and Peter and Carolyn came to see us. So I told them what had gone on because they needed to know. Peter said, 'You should take some time off in Tulsa. Nothing will change in the Church; it will be just as if you have gone on a mission trip. The pair of you can have a couple of weeks in Tulsa to sort things out, and when you come back, nothing will have changed.'"*

---

20 Interview 2010

Shortly after informing the Church, they travelled to Tulsa, U.S.A., for three weeks of reflection. Upon their arrival in Tulsa, they found that news of the affair had already reached the newspapers there. Bishop Reid's residence and recognition in Tulsa raised questions about whether the news had been spread intentionally. It was also leaked to the national media in the U.K., and as early as April 7th, 2008, a Sun newspaper reporter arrived at Testimony House.

In their first meeting in the Bishop's office, Andrew Love had emphasised confidentiality. In the Daily Mail on April 9th, 2008, Linnecar also publicly stated: *"...we would ask that you pray for all concerned and respect privacy at this difficult time."* Eric Pickles, the MP for Brentwood at the time, stated: *"I think this is a private matter, and I am always sympathetic for people. Everyone is human. These things happen in life. I hope these two people can sort things out with their families."* The media's information source was unknown, and rumours suggested [...] had confided in someone in the U.S., complicating matters further.

In their first meeting in the Bishop's office, Andrew Love had emphasised confidentiality. In the Daily Mail on April 9th, 2008, Linnecar also publicly stated: "...we would ask that you pray for all concerned and respect privacy at this difficult time."

In the past, Gary Selfridges handled the majority of the media promotion for the ministry. He was deeply upset by the news of the affair. In an email dated June 27th, 2008, he complained: *"... have had to face the opprobrium and mockery of contacts in television and radio..."* [Due to previously promoting Bishop Reid]. On Friday, August 22nd, 2008, he was quoted on the Total Essex website issuing a caution to Bishop Reid supporters: *"...desist from resurrecting... or supporting any other organisation involving Michael Reid..."*

While in Tulsa, three unexpected visitors arrived, staying for a day and meeting with the Reids for a couple of hours. Bishop Reid: *"...they rang me up early morning, so I went to see them for breakfast and took Ian with me."* He was unaware of their intentions; they had come to announce their plans to take over the Church and suggest his retirement. The Bishop responded firmly: *"...no you are not called,... okay yes, I sinned, but you are not called."* They then raised another accusation, and Bishop Reid responded, *"...that is absurd."* Bishop went on to elaborate: *"Peter, Carolyne, and Meidre came to Tulsa because [...] came up with a story that I had had an affair with her, which I hadn't. I was neither blind nor drunk! First, she said it was seven years, then eleven, then fourteen, and finally...seventeen years...but my wife laughed for twenty minutes! Carolyn came with the opinion that [...] wouldn't have mentioned it, she would've taken it to the grave if it hadn't been for the affair with Sheila, and I found out she had talked to Sheila and concocted the story, and she was the one that stood and said I will leave the Church if Bishop comes back..."*

In a written submission by the Peniel Church at the Employment Tribunal, East, they state: *"...as there has been adultery with SG, that of Miss X (despite the later retraction)"* The statement also discloses: *"Her [Miss X] letter expresses concerns that the [her] statements not become public..."* However, someone publicised Miss X's allegations to smear Bishop Reid's reputation, prompting questions like why Miss X initially opposed making her accusations public. And why did she later retract them? These questions remain unanswered.

Two congregation-wide meetings were conducted – one on April 5th, 2008, before the Reids' trip to Tulsa, and the second was convened by Peter Linnecar. Peter Linnecar and his wife couldn't attend the first meeting because his mother was ill in Ireland. She unfortunately passed away on April 4th. While in Ireland with Belinda, Andrew's wife, they discussed their course of action with their father.

In the initial meeting, Bishop Reid sat among the congregation instead of on the stage, a departure from the norm that likely appeared peculiar to attendees. Julian Fagan provided his account of the meeting: *About 250 plus people were there, and Kevin Lee stood up and said, 'There's going to be an announcement, but we are all family, and some will be uncomfortable.' So then Bishop stood up and said, 'I have sinned, and me and my wife will be taking some time out'.*[21] As Bishop exited, confusion spread. Agitated voices questioned his absence. Matthew rose, revealing the cause – the Bishop's adultery. Emotions surged – tears and anger emerged and factions were formed within the board and the congregation. Gary Selfridges pushed for the board's resignation and Ken Hodge's appointment as the pastor.

Upon returning from Ireland, Peter Linnecar held the second meeting at Brizes Park while the Reids were in Tulsa. During the meeting, he announced his temporary leadership of the Church and invited questions. A pertinent question arose: *"Are you called by God?"* Peter repeated the question to make sure everyone heard it but refrained from providing an answer, which the observers noted. Another person rose and mentioned that similar ministerial shortcomings frequently occurred in Nigeria, suggesting forgiveness and Bishop Reid's return. Enraged voices tried to silence the woman, while others were troubled by the hostile reaction toward her, given her apparent alignment with Biblical principles.

Between March 21st and April 16th, 2008, confidential pastoral discussions occurred between Bishop Reid and Peter and Carolyn Linnecar. Regrettably, these discussions were leaked to the trustees and later became public within the Church, violating confidentiality. The discussions involved sensitive topics such

---

21 Interview 2010

     I'm Alive

as minimising the impact on the Church, finding the best course of action, and addressing concerns about the Reids' pension, retirement, salary and wages. Peter had assured Bishop Reid that he would act as a caretaker without making significant changes in the Church until his return.

Bishop Reid was taken aback when he learnt that Carolyn Linnecar had covertly been documenting their discussions and had produced a biased six-page summary. These secret recordings captured their pastoral talks before any talk of disciplinary measures, presenting a skewed view of the events.

The investigation showed a lack of impartiality in handling both parties involved in the adultery. On May 3rd, 2008, Kevin Lee emailed Bishop Reid in response to his request for Sheila Graziano's statement: *"We do not have such a statement."* Sheila Graziano appeared to receive preferential treatment and she continued attending Church. Spokeswoman Anne Brown declined to disclose whether Sheila Graziano was still the music director: *"We have not named the other party involved and will not be commenting on any person other than Bishop Reid."* Even the London Evening Standard tried to reach out to her: *"There was no answer yesterday at her £300,000, 1930s semi-detached house a mile from the Church."*[22] The Peniel Church acknowledged inconsistencies in the treatments of Bishop Reid and Sheila Graziano, stating in a written submission at the Employment Tribunal: *"The only active challenge is on the basis of consistency of the treatment of [Bishop Reid] when compared with [Sheila Graziano] and [Miss X]."* On March 4th, 2010, a man named Martin raised a thought-provoking question in the Brentwood Gazette: *"Why is only one person taking all the blame..."* Sheila seemed to be sidelined by many, while Bishop Reid had been thrust into the spotlight as the scapegoat.

---

22 April 10, 2008

Pursuing Reconciliation: Striving for Resolution and Harmony

"I understand his wife has forgiven him and
we should all follow her lead ..."
— Church Member,
London Evening Standard, April 10th, 2008

Despite the betrayal, Bishop Reid remained willing to assist the Church: *"...my view of it is this: if people have made a mistake, we should be ready to restore them. I would help anyone. I would help them if they really wanted help."* Linnacer stated: *"We believe...our God is a God of love, forgiveness and restoration...."* Daily Mail, April 9th, 2008.

Support for Bishop's return was evident. Ayo Ademakinwa, a former member for twenty years, stated: *"He [Peter] convinced everyone that he was just temporarily stepping in until Bishop returned and people started asking questions...half of the people were not in support and [the other half] wanted to resolve things...and they asked if there was going to be a time of restoration..."*

The three individuals who visited him in Tulsa, stated: *"We feel the people don't want you back."* Facing the three, Bishop Reid candidly told them: *"...while I was there, people begged me not to step down in the Church, and about eighty percent wanted me back..."* He added: *"...it's just the few that didn't want me back but wanted to take over...the rest were not like that."* In April/May 2008, when Peter Linnecar and Anne Brown appeared Live on Revelation TV, callers strongly objected to the removal of Bishop Reid.

An internal email dated April 16th, 2008, indicates that there were voices within the church advocating for his continuation as the leader. Rachel Whealy: *"From the charity's perspective, Bishop Reid is Michael Reid Ministries, and so as long as this remains, my advice would be that the trustees should do all they can to retain him. Would a six-month paid sabbatical be the answer?"* Rachel was laid off shortly after

    I'm Alive

this statement, and at that time, another former employee verified that documents were being shredded. Orville Thomas: *"I spoke with Matthew Reid [Reid's son] in August 2008. I told him I could not support the Church [actions] because they were not Biblical. He explained that the board decided to dismiss his father, and despite his attempt, he still could not clarify what justification they had for taking such drastic action."*

Many within the church opposed his dismissal but stayed silent out of fear. As of August 6th, 2010, online comments still expressed this sentiment: *"I will await for either the coming back of Bishop Reid or for God to choose a man who fears God, but that is God's will, not the will of man."*

Amidst the efforts to silence and undermine the impact of God's work through him, a remarkable figure emerged as a true friend of the ministry – Apostle Alfred Williams from Christ Faith Tabernacle.

Bishop Reid: *"...what happened was strange. There was an individual who returned to England...an African Nigerian who had been in America and had some business in England... Originally, his daughter got bullied at school; when she was about fourteen... the Anglo European School, she was pushed down the stairs, and he couldn't get protection for her...because the school wasn't prepared to help her, probably due to her being black. He came and asked whether I would help. I said, '... let's first just find out, come on a Friday and test her. If she's normal education-wise and there's no other problem, we could probably help her at fourteen.' So, we took her and tested her, and I took her on Monday, so she was out of the school and not bullied anymore, and he was delighted. He had two other children, and I told him, 'We could take them in September, no problem.' I broke the rules to protect the girl. Now, Peter Russell and Peter Linnecar didn't like it, but to me, you have compassion when a kid is being bullied and terrorised in a school. They needed help, and they were Christians, so as far as I am concerned, I would help them.*

...Ruth and I travelled in August, and when he went to book his other two children in, Peter Russell and Peter Linnecar said to him, 'No, you can't do that. You have to wait another year.' But he said, 'My daughter is already here,' but they still said no to him. He assumed that it was me who had made the decision not to take them, so he took his daughter out and put his kids in a Christian School in America because he was worried about their welfare. I knew nothing about this because when we came back, he was gone and they left the Church and went to America.

When he returned for business, someone told him I was no longer the pastor, and he wanted to see me but lost my telephone number. What happened was he found it again, and that night he had a dream that I was starting a new Church, and there was a platform with nothing on it, and God told him to provide the platform. The next day, he came to see me, and we shared with him what had happened. First, I was shocked that his children weren't in school, and I thought what had happened and how Peter Linnecar had dealt with him was appalling. Then he told me the dream he had had. He said, 'Look, there is one person I know who can help you.' He rang up Apostle Williams while he was with us, and Apostle Williams came the next day. He was appalled by the way I had been treated."

Ruth added: *"God spoke to Apostle Williams when Abraham rang him up, and he said the same thing God said to you [Bishop], which was, 'I have done this to purify this man so that he can be ready for the next move of God.' That's what gave Apostle Williams the confidence."*

In July 2010, Apostle Alfred Williams received a vision from the Lord Jesus. Shortly after, while dining with Bishop Reid in a restaurant, he leaned in and blew on him. Apostle Williams explained that this action was how a spell of witchcraft had ensnared Bishop Reid in the relationship. Bishop Reid was taken aback as he recollected the precise moment when this had

 I'm Alive

happened since the notion of witchcraft's involvement had never crossed his mind before.

During an interview I conducted with Apostle Williams, he elaborated:

"I had heard about him; he's a man I know and approve of his ministry. I believe God is using him, so when I learnt what had happened and how the Church leaders treated him, I felt compelled to come immediately. This is part of what we say about the apostolic office – whenever the duty calls, and it is divinely right, you cannot withdraw from it. You will cancel anything to make sure you attend to the cry of heaven, and that was what I saw. When I asked Bishop what happened, he shared the whole story. Afterwards, we decided to visit the people [board] ourselves, along with some other Bishops."

While staying with the Reids, evangelist Billy Burke and his family were appalled by the events and requested a meeting with the Church board to discuss a restoration; however, the board refused. Similarly, many Bishops, nationwide, were horrified by the incident and its handling. A restoration meeting with the Church was attempted by a delegation of prominent ministers, including Pastor Matthew Ashimolowo (KICC), Bishop John Francis (Ruach Ministries), Bishop Mark Nicholson (EICOG), Pastor Kingsley Appiagyei (TBC), and Pastor Lola Oyebade (HOTRIC). Unfortunately, the Church did not respond to the letter. Apostle Williams and Bishop Marc Nicholson sent a letter requesting a meeting with the board in June, but their request was declined.

Bishop Reid: *"Then finally, by October or November, they couldn't get anywhere with the Church. Kevin Lee and Richard Cope wanted to come and see me, so I rang up Apostle Williams and Bishop Marc Nicholson, and when they arrived at my house that evening to see me, I had the people already there, so they confronted them. Kevin Lee said that when the Apostle talked to him about restoration, he didn't know what the word meant. 'What does restoration look like? What does it mean?' But their attitude was, 'We were appointed as pastor, and we have gone on; the past is over, let's forget what the Bishop did, we got a new Church, a new pastor, and a new life, and we don't want to go back'...and they met twice more with them. Then he met with the whole board three times, and the last time they point-blank refused to do what was Biblical. They had made their decisions, and they weren't going back on it."[23]*

During the first meeting with Apostle Williams, the Church board initially agreed with the ministerial team's proposal to develop a restoration programme led by the Bishops and Apostles. On May 2nd, 2008, a group of globally recognised ministers formulated a restoration plan and forwarded it to the Board of Trustees. A minister's team, led by Apostle Williams, returned to the board and the restoration process plan was accepted. Following the restoration process, an email from Kevin Lee, dated December 7th, 2008, after a trustee meeting, mentions: *"...I tabled the idea of a meeting with yourself and Apostle Alfred Williams to discuss in detail the restoration process that was undertaken for Bishop Reid. The trustees unanimously agreed to meet..."*

Apostle Williams explained: *"We wanted to meet a community that believed in the scriptures and submitted to them. When we met them, we inquired about what had transpired, and they shared the same story, which was accurate. However, they told Bishop he could go to America and step back by himself, which aligns with the scriptures. They assured him they would support him going to America for restoration and return to give him the ministry."*

The Church board initially suggested the Reids go to the U.S. for three weeks to mend their relationship, framing it as a mission trip, and there would be no changes upon their return. Trusting these individuals, they flew to America, unaware of the underlying

---

23 Interview May 2010

agenda. Upon their return, some church members contacted newspapers, leading to the Reids being pressured and harassed at their doorstep by the media. Unexpectedly, the church board conveyed, *"We don't want you."*

During their meetings with Apostle Williams, the Church board took a surprising stance: *"We agree with you that restoration is crucial, but we see this as restoration of relationship with God and fellow believers, not necessarily restoration of position."* The Peniel Church stated: *"This is not because the Church has not forgiven him, but because it does not feel that he is the right person to lead the Church…"* Was that the message God had conveyed to them?

Apostle Williams found their actions astonishing: *"…when a minister is going through a period of restoration…that minister ought to be allowed to attend the Church and sit in the congregation. But when we…presented this to them, they said no, they don't want him even at the Church gates. And then we started having suspicion [about] what's going on here; were these people really after restoring this man or after grabbing something…?"*

The board recommended that he conduct his ministry outside the Church. *"Do you seek evidence of restoration?"* Apostle Williams asked. *"No evidence exists,"* they responded. So, Apostle Williams invited Bishop Reid to join him on a mission to Cameroon, where Bishop Reid preached and witnessed numerous people saved and healed. He said: *"I returned with the video, went to them, and said 'this is evidence.' They said that we know now he is restored, but if he comes back, we will sponsor his ministry…"*[24] The Church board repeatedly responded, *"Apostle, we will permit him to conduct ministry outside the Church, and we'll even offer financial aid, but he can't return here."* However, they never fulfilled this commitment to support his ministry.

---

24 Revelation TV, June 26th, 2010.

This decision infuriated Apostle Williams: *"You know what I said to them? Two things. Firstly, I asked them about their understanding of the scripture, and I will demonstrate to the viewers what the scripture says about this man... as far as they were concerned, they didn't want him anymore.... I asked them, 'Every one of you sitting here, who among you can raise his finger to say he has never committed adultery in his life?' No finger was raised. 'So, all of you are victims of what you are judging. Who are you to point and accuse your finger?'"*

Apostle Williams further elaborated during a live broadcast on Revelation TV: *"...I said, 'I have not'...When I married my wife, I was a virgin. I say this on television; this is worldwide. I said to them, 'If all of you have slept with more than one woman and you women have slept with more than one man who is not your husband, who are you, therefore, to say that because of the sin of this man, you rip him off of every good thing?' We will stand before the judgement seat of Christ one day. And I told them that even I who have not done that sin have no right before the Lord to point an accusing finger."*[25]

I said to them, 'If all of you have slept with more than one woman and you women have slept with more than one man who is not your husband, who are you, therefore, to say that because of the sin of this man, you rip him off of every good thing?

Now, let's go to the scripture and hear what the scripture says. The book of Galatians, Chapter 6, says, 'Brothers, if someone is caught in a sin,' and in this case, he wasn't caught in the act; it happened two years before this occurrence, right? Bishop wasn't caught in the act; he has stopped it.

The Bible says, 'If someone is caught in a sin, you who are spiritual should restore him gently.' And then he went for that. But watch yourself,

---

25 Saturday, June 26th, 2010

or you also may be tempted. He says, 'Carry each other's burdens,' he didn't say assassinate each other; he didn't say destroy each other... in other words, if you fall as a believer, we are all soldiers of the Lord. What I'm supposed to do is, as a soldier, stop and put my life down to get you up. It's like on the battlefield when one is wounded; others don't say, 'Why did you go out of the line?' They take him, they care for him and they risk their lives to restore him.

I'm amazed that these people have decided to do things contrary to scripture because the Bible says here, 'Carry each other's burdens,' this way, you will fulfil the law of Christ. So anybody who doesn't do this must not be a Christian; they must be anti-Christ."

Apostle Williams was baffled by this group of individuals who had been nurtured by Bishop Reid, some of whom he had supported financially. He reminded the Church board that Bishop Reid had funded the assets, including one that was registered under the Church and another under his name, which the Church still utilised. Despite his unwavering support during their moments of fault and restoration, his generosity was used against him. How could they morally or scripturally justify their actions, considering this history? He concluded: *"...the reason there is no interest in restoring is because the ultimate aim is the assets."*

By the weekend commencing April 5th, 2008, every book, video and picture of him had been removed from the Church. Visitors to the bookshop were denied access to his materials. During a live broadcast on Revelation TV on Saturday, June 26th, 2010, Apostle Williams declared: *"...they have now redone their brochures and removed the name of this founder from the history of the Church... Is that Christianity?"* During discussions about restoration, they eliminated the visible indications of his presence, demonstrating their intention to assume control.

An article written by William Crawley on the BBC website, dated Tuesday, April 8th, 2008, reported: *"Pastor Peter Linnecar has already taken over the leadership of the Church.''* Moreover, a 21-page letter, detailing the recent events, was globally distributed via Bishop Reid's ministry database, introducing Peter Linnecar as the Peniel Church's new leader. It was also posted on their new website. As the Reids were planning their return from the United States to discuss matters, the Church was already broadcasting Peter as the new pastor every half-hour on Premier Radio – a prominent U.K. Christian radio station. In April/May 2008, Peter Linnecar and Anne. Brown announced Peter as Pastor of Penial Church on Revelation TV before any formal hearing had taken place.

On March 3rd, 2010, an article in the Essex Chronicle reported: *"The Rev Peter Linnecar, who started the Church with shamed Bishop Reid, is leading the way."* In the same article, Anne Brown acknowledged: *"He has been at the Church **almost** since the beginning…"* Additionally, the Church created a brochure that excluded the founder's name and falsely implied Peter as the founder by asserting a three-decade tenure as the senior pastor. The reality was that Peter became a part of the Church approximately a year after its inception. Bishop Reid: *"…for the first seventeen years of the Church, I had no elders, no deacons and no problems!"*[26] Peter occasionally did preach, in the absence of Bishop Reid, however, in the earlier years, his travel was limited.

Ironically, the Peniel Church website described a sermon preached by Peter in October 2009 as follows: *"Pastor Peter Linnecar begins in the book of Deuteronomy Chapter 17 showing that it is all too easy to run ahead of God in our lives and make things happen when we should wait until God brings them."*

As the new leader, Peter Linnecar received a significantly higher salary than Bishop Reid did during his tenure as pastor.

---

26 Interview May 2010

 I'm Alive

Questioning His Repentance

On April 5th, 2008, Bishop Reid, aged sixty-four, submitted his resignation from the Church Board and relinquished his pastoral duties. He stood before the Church and explicitly announced that he was temporarily stepping down; he did not mention resigning as pastor.

During this challenging time, his wife stood firmly by his side. Anne Brown: *"They are married, and they are together. She says she has forgiven him. She loves him."* Others believed God had used him, but withdrew support post the affair, distancing themselves. As a result, unfounded rumours circulated, falsely insinuating a lack of repentance. In an email dated June 27th, 2008, Gary Selfridges mentions: *"...His continued lack of contrition..."* Yet, Reverend Peter Linnecar, acting pastor at the Church publicly stated: *"Bishop Reid has been a servant of this Church for 32 years. We are deeply sorry that this has happened. He has recognised his sin and taken full responsibility for his actions and resigned..."*[27]

He publicly confessed his sin before the Church on April 5th, 2008. He also made it clear in a written public statement: *"It is with great sorrow and regret that I have resigned from the Church board and have stepped down from official duties."* He went on to state: *"I confess that I have sinned. I recognise that I have failed in my duties and acted in a way that harmed the Church...I take full responsibility for my actions... I apologise to my wife and family and all of you whose trust I have betrayed and ask for your forgiveness and prayers."*

In a letter addressed to the trustees of the Peniel Church, dated May 5th, 2008, Bishop Reid wrote: *"...but I trust you have noted my sincere apology."* Another letter sent in 2008, addressed to Peter Linnecar, Carolyn Linnecar and the Board of Directors, reads:

---

27 (Daily Mail, April 9, 2008)

"Due to the recent events, both in the Church as well as in my personal life, I have been given to much thought, prayer and counsel. The following is a summation of those thoughts that I hope can begin a wonderful healing process for all. I realise more now than ever that my sin has opened the door for the devil to wreak havoc in the Church and my personal life, involving people that I love the most. This hurts me deeply! I know it has hurt a lot of people deeply.

I have spent so much of my time focusing on other people and helping them through their difficult times that I have I have neglected taking care of my own needs. I feel completely forgiven by God and my dear wife, Ruth, who has also forgiven me with a depth of love that has to be from God.

In some strange way, I feel even closer to people who are hurting both in the Church as well as abroad. Preaching this Gospel, I realise more and more it is an undisputed privilege that I have lost sight of, but as I search the scriptures, I also find many who, just like me, lost sight of that privilege and, for some reason, failed God in some way. What I also find interesting in the scripture is that God always stood by His servants who failed and worked feverishly to restore them to the place from which they failed.

It would be wonderful to see the same people who were a part of the devastation could become part of the restoration process. It would show a great truth that there is hope even for leadership after great mistakes have been made.

It is my only heart and desire to approach a Biblical decision, removing our personal feelings and trusting God will work out all the details."

Additionally, Bishop Reid initiated a private meeting request. Peter Linnecar: *"Bishop Reid and Ruth Reid asked us to go and tee up a meeting with George and Sheila."* A sequence of events occurred on Saturday, March 29th, 2008. He apologised to Sheila Graziano's husband, but Sheila did not apologise to Dr Ruth Reid.

     I'M ALIVE

He also publicly apologised in the Brentwood Gazette on July 15th, 2010: *"In an exclusive interview with the Gazette, the founder of the Peniel Church offered a full apology for his adultery with another Church member and said he 'fell into a trap.' I did fall into sin, I did have an affair, that is a fact and I am sorry it happened. I am human; I am not super-human, and I am able to sin…I did commit adultery, I did confess it, I did step down, I do believe in restoration…it shouldn't have happened, but if anyone has never made mistakes in their life, I would like to meet them."*

Regarding the apology before the Church, Bishop Reid clarified, *"At that time, the so-called board had said to me, 'Do not say what it is that you're stepping down for.' They didn't want me to say it because… the other person in the whole affair was…still in the Church. Instead of seeing that it takes two to tango, they made her out as a victim for their ends. I stood down, telling people I needed to sort things out with my wife for a time."* Some were angered by the omission of his actions when he addressed the Church publicly. Following this public confession and while exiting the Church with Ruth, he explained that there was an uproar, with people *"yelling and shouting."* However, the Church later released a transcript that included the words: *"…I confess that I have sinned **by committing adultery**…"* and published it worldwide. Bishop Michael Reid clarified this matter during an interview on Premier Radio on January 29th, 2009: *"Well, I did not make that statement; it was made by others, so I just want to make that clear."* Instructing him not to mention the sin during the public confession had provoked Church anger, which was possibly what was intended in the first place.

[Bishop Reid posted the interview on his website, but Premier Radio requested its removal. At the time, Peter Linnecar broadcasted sermons on Premier Radio.]

In churches, leaders who sin often step down, undergo a repentance and restoration process that is led by fellow Church leaders, and then return to their leadership roles. Apostle Williams said, *"I came in weekly to discuss with Bishop, taking him through scriptures and praying with him during the restoration process, and we did that for months. And when everything was okay, we were satisfied, together with Bishop Nicholson, that he is restored."* Yet in 2010, two years after Reid publicly and privately apologised numerous times, a Revelation TV presenter contacted my home and callously told my wife that, in his view, Bishop Reid had not repented and should apologise. He claimed spirits would transfer through his laying on of hands; however, this didn't happen when he joined Apostle Williams' ministry in Cameroon. During a live TV broadcast, I watched this presenter spread this false doctrine, but the guest intervened: *"Born again individuals can't receive spirit transfers; the One within us is greater."*

Despite his public and private apologies and a thorough restoration process, some disregarded it all and pursued another agenda with disturbing ferocity.

Chapter 19
Tensions Escalate

"...the people who took over, and it was a takeover, haven't behaved in a Christian manner at all and have violated biblical principles... Christians do not threaten to burn people's cars, smash the windows... and attack...with iron bars."

– Bishop M. Reid, TBGS, May 2011

Threatening Behaviour

In the Church's early years, a converted former séance practitioner threatened to ruin Bishop Reid and his ministry. Dr. Ruth Reid received a vision of worms consuming him. Shortly after, the man called to apologise but tragically passed away while on the phone to the Reid's. This incident was a sobering lesson, yet some still harboured animosity towards Bishop Reid, demonstrating a failure to learn from history.

In the Church's early years, a converted former séance practitioner threatened to ruin Bishop Reid and his ministry. Dr. Ruth Reid received a vision of worms consuming him.

Just one week after the office confrontation about the affair, a shocking incident occurred, right before the Reids' departure to Tulsa the following Saturday. Bishop Reid: *"Andrew and Colin came to see me... They came to the lounge here, and they were absolutely vicious. Andrew told me he had hated me for twenty years, which was nice to know..."* During the meeting, Bishop Reid remembered Colin pacing in their living room, expressing bitterness: *"...I have had issues with you for eight years..."* Bishop Reid stated that Colin said he would ruin his name and ensure he never preaches again. Concurrently, on Sunday, April 6th, 2008, Peter Linnecar claimed: *"...Andrew Love and Colin Cleminson were not against M.R. and they were not trying to take over the Church."*[28]

However, the backlash was about to intensify. Two days before leaving Tulsa and returning to the U.K., Bishop Reid was visited by Tom Mathew, the Dean of Graduate Theology at Oral Roberts University. Tom Mathew: *"I'm worried about your safety as Matthew Reid phoned me and said that the people in the Church would attack you with iron bars and burn your car and smash all the windows in your house if you came back."* Immediately, upon his return to the U.K. from Tulsa, U.S.A., he was greeted at the airport by John Adabanjo, a trustee at the Peniel Church and the second-in-command to Richard Branson for Virgin Group in Nigeria. Bishop Reid: *"John Adabanjo took us into the Virgin Lounge and tried to persuade us to fly back to Tulsa and stay there for six months and that he would pay..."* John was deeply concerned for Bishop Reid's safety.

The leaders of the church issued a public instruction through a statement on April 27th, 2008, urging anyone who saw Bishop Reid on the premises to report it so that he could be forcibly removed. Additionally, a letter reiterating the same message, dated October 4th, 2008 and signed by Richard Cope, Charlie Pring and Steve Wilkinson, was hand-delivered to Testimony House.

---

28 Sequence of events

           I'm Alive

Since Bishop Reid owned the Church's main entrance gates, he had the leverage to cause disruption. Instead, he opted not to assert his rights and permitted the Church to use the gates peacefully, promoting a harmonious relationship. In contrast, the Church's actions increased animosity toward the Reids.

A certain church member would frequently walk his dog past Testimony House, shaking his head and occasionally peering inside. In a Witness Statement on July 2nd, 2008, Bishop states, *"I feel he is also checking whose cars are on my property."* Once, Bishop Reid and his U.S. guest, Bishop Kirby Clement, were walking about 300 yards from the Reids' house where Bishop Clement was staying when a grey Mercedes 320 classic C saloon repeatedly drove by. The driver parked, stared for about ten minutes, and left, shaking his head. In 2008, this individual attempted to drive into Bishop Reid's daughter and granddaughter, resulting in a police caution and blue light protection. She was forced to relocate to an undisclosed location.

In a May 19th, 2008 email to Kevin Lee and the trustees, the Reids state: *"The ban on me going onto the Church property and threat of my removal was read out by John Shelton just before we got back from the U.S.A. It opened the door for this violence and hatred to increase for which the board is responsible."* The ban had significant implications for their family life, as they couldn't worship with their children and grandchildren, who still attended the Church. Additionally, they couldn't collect their grandchildren from school, causing significant distress, especially to Dr. Ruth Reid. The family was also discouraged from interacting or sharing meals. In a letter addressed to Dr Ruth Reid, dated November 28th, 2008, the Peniel Church Trustees acknowledged: *"We agree that as time developed, you did suffer more isolation...."*

Hate Mail

*"Dear Mrs Ruth Reid, you should keep away from the Church.
I'm sorry to be so harsh, but you are as bad as him.
Who do you think you are coming into Peniel?"*

– This is from three generations of a Peniel family

On Friday, May 2nd, 2008, Dr Ruth visited the Church with Billy Burke and his wife and sat in the office. However, to her dismay, she received no acknowledgement. The following day, as they returned home on a crisp spring evening, they were met by a pile of hate mail that had been slipped through the mail slot, uninvited and unwelcome. Each letter contained furious words etched with such venomous intensity that it made their stomach churn. The authors' rage leapt from the page, their grievances unleashed in a torrent of bitterness: a cruel reminder of the darkness that could lurk beneath the surface of seemingly ordinary lives.

"Get real [they] don't want you back. [They] have a new pastor now, and he will not share the pulpit with either of you.....You have lived off the backs of saints long enough now [and] it's time for you AND your family to GO." – From an Onlooker

"What on Earth [Ruth] do you think you are doing coming back to the Peniel Church? We know your tactics. You think a Ruth Reid smile, and a bit of back rubbing will get you recruits to your cause. Don't shame yourself again by creeping into the Church and hoping a few kind people will lose sight of what you have been [and] will give you a hug. From a family that worships God and not man and a family that has dedicated its services voluntarily for years to the Peniel Church."

"You're just as greedy as he is [Peter Linnecar]. Go back to Tulsa. But don't darken our Church [Peniel] again, literally. We have let the light in, and we don't want your darkness back again."

          I'm Alive

When they sought help from Kevin Lee, he declined and their attempt to contact Peter Linnecar went unanswered. Later, the Church denied any involvement. A solicitor's letter asserted that the Church had *'not been threatening.'* However, when presented with the evidence, they admitted that only *'one or two Church members'* were responsible for the hate mail. The Trustees acknowledged the threats in a letter to Dr Ruth Reid dated November 28th, 2008. *"We agree that the board had received threats and that this had been passed to Dr Matthews."* Indeed, over a hundred people were involved, and at least two members of the four-member pastoral team displayed intense animosity toward Bishop Reid, with one threatening to tarnish his reputation and prevent him from preaching ever again.

The matter was finally reported to the police, who were appalled by the situation and issued a Crime Reference Number: D321D/15302/08. Fingerprints were collected from the letters as part of the investigation, and the original hate mail was retained as evidence. The police confronted Peter Linnecar and Kevin Lee and explicitly stated that the actions were a criminal offence. Only after this did Peter Linnecar briefly address the congregation on Sunday, May 4th, 2008, instructing them not to send hate mail. That Sunday at 2 p.m., Kevin Lee delivered a brown envelope to the Reids' home, which was addressed to Dr Ruth Reid. Despite Bishop

Reid's attempts at polite conversation, Kevin was apparently rude and left abruptly. The letter contained an apology to Dr Ruth Reid for the hate mail but lacked an apology for Bishop Reid:

Dear Ruth,

I want to take this opportunity to write this short note on behalf of the pastors and trustees [most of whom have now left]. This is in light of the letters you received yesterday evening. We have read copies of the letters, and given the hurtful tone, we completely understand that this will have caused you considerable pain. Therefore, we felt it important to let you know that this is in no way representative of the majority of the Church. Moreover, the pastors and trustees are united in denouncing the actions of the individuals who sent these hurtful letters.

We love you; we are for you and will stand in defence of all innocent parties.

Love from all trustees and pastors.

Kevin Lee

In spite of this, the hate mail continued to trickle in. In an email sent at 6:00 p.m. to the Reids, dated May 19th, 2008, Kevin Lee wrote: *"I was very sorry to hear from PC Andy Ennis that you have again received letters of a distasteful and threatening nature."*

Allegations of Harassment

Upon Dr Reid's request for a police update on their investigations, an astonishing response arrived in a letter dated September 18th, 2008, from Samantha Jarvis, the Neighbouring Policing Team Inspector at the Brentwood Police Station. *"Brentwood Police are currently experiencing an enormous amount of calls [complaints] referencing yourselves and previous Church members."*

When the police reached out to the Church, they coincidentally received an *"enormous amount of calls"* accusing the Reids of sending harassing letters. Bizarrely, coordinated complaints accused Bishop Reid of harassment through his letters, but these letters, available for public scrutiny, contained only kind words. The Brentwood Gazette publicly quoted them on September 24th, 2008:

"The Gazette has been given an exclusive look at letters sent by Michael Reid to his former flock at the Peniel Church. The nine letters… sent out to residents in just one month include details of two settlements offered to him and his wife Ruth, in the months following the revelation of his affair with another Church member…rather than encouraging Church members to follow Mr Reid to another ministry, the letters are his attempt to set the record straight and that he has no intention of trying to return to the Peniel.

In the sixth letter, Mr Reid acknowledges that one of the subjects, which has antagonised Peniel members, is his refusal to accept the Board of Trustees offers and says: 'In no way were we going to do anything to create problems for the Church members. We love you.'

And in the seventh, he adds: 'We would never destroy what God gave us the vision to establish.'

The first of the letters, sent on August 24th and signed by 'Bishop and Ruth Reid,' explains: 'My wife and I are alive! We would both like to apologise for the unexpectedly long time since we have been in touch, and we want you to know that our concern for you is as real as ever.' While the second makes reference to his 'adulterous affair, which I have never denied nor would do so,' while the following three surround Biblical passages concerning sin, forgiveness and personal responsibility, the fifth adding: 'Do not allow others to turn you into something that you are not.'

The eighth letter again repeats the earlier message, stating: 'Be assured we would never do anything to disrupt the survival of God's establishment, which He used me and my wife to nurture, develop and grow for 32 years.'

The ninth letter, simply attaching the second offer made to the couple, was sent on September 14th, just three weeks after the first.

When asked to comment, Mr Reid said: 'I am aware you have my letters, and I am quite happy for you to use them.

The Peniel Church refused to comment."

The nine letters from the Reids lacked any harassing content, leading the Peniel Church to withhold comment.

Inspector Paul Thompson initially led the investigation, but during a visit to the Reids' home, the police officer was rude and insensitive, pushing past Dr Ruth. Bishop Reid asked the officer to leave. The officer callously suggested they sell their property and move out if they were upset, and advised Dr Reid to scream at the garden trees to vent out her anger. He convinced Bishop Reid to sign a caution for sending harassing letters. The Reids reported this, and the officer was reprimanded by his superiors. Regrettably, this incident triggered more threatening behaviour from other police officers, instilling in the elderly couple a genuine fear for their safety.

Bible Studies Obstructed

Amidst the ongoing harassment, they started home Bible meetings, but deliberate efforts were made to hinder them. A letter from the Peniel Church's solicitor to Bishop Reid's legal representative stated: *"In a letter dated September 26th, 2008, Wrightway Solicitors argued that Bishop Reid's assertion of not intending harm to the Church was contradicted by his acceptance of donations through his website. This implied deliberate efforts to redirect Church members from Peniel to his new venture."* They implied that receiving website donations and similar actions were deliberate attempts to redirect Peniel's

 I'M ALIVE

members to his new venture, prompting someone to notify the council. The Brentwood Gazette reported: *"Council planning officers were tipped off by a member of the public that the property was being used as a place of worship – a change of building use, which would require planning permission."* The newspaper continued: *"No action will be taken by council planners over reports that the home of Bishop Michael Reid is being used as a place of worship."* A council spokeswoman said: *"A Bible Study group meets each Sunday at this address. Based on the investigation, it is not currently considered to be a material change of use of the premises at 53 Coxtie Green Road due to the current nature and scale of the meetings. The case will now be closed."*[29]

Witnesses confirmed that Church members, including at least one former trustee, harassed people arriving for a Bible Study outside Testimony House. Members of the Peniel Church used tactics such as hiding in bushes to photograph cars and their owners, and became aggressive when confronted.

In his statement, Rob Cleminson, Meidre Cleminson's son, stated: *"During June 29th, 2008, Kevin Lee and I were on Church security duty, which means we were based in the Peniel Church car park. At about 10.30 am, we walked to Testimony House... and stood outside next to the lamppost... Michael Reid then went on to ask what we were doing, to which Kevin replied that we were enjoying the sunshine on the pavement."*

In an official witness statement dated July 2nd, 2008, Bishop Reid describes a confrontation: *"They were standing on the pavement. I asked Kevin, 'What are you doing here intimidating people coming to my home?' Robbie was four feet away, and Kevin came up to me and stated, 'I've every right to stand here. What are you going to do, hit me?' I said, 'Stop harassing me and my family, clear off.' He came to within*

---

29 Wed, April 08, 2009

a foot of me, menacingly. He said, 'Go on, move me.' I found his attitude menacing and mocking."

Despite heated confrontations, the Peniel Church members persisted in intimidating Reid's supporters.

Threats of Financial Ruin

Around 2008-9, Bishop Reid met Meidre Cleminson, who warned him about the Peniel Church's intention to potentially bankrupting the Reid family by slapping them with legal costs if they pursued justice. Shortly before an Employment Tribunal, Rob Cleminson contacted Bishop Reid, suggesting a settlement discussion and revealed the Church's readiness to bankrupt the Reid family if the legal battle persisted, citing the Church's insurance could cover such costs. He also mentioned the tribunal's likely decision to dismiss Bishop Reid.

The Church reached settlements with several individuals under confidentiality agreements. Bishop Reid was repeatedly offered payments in exchange for signing a non-disclosure agreement to prevent him from speaking against the Church. Threats were made that signing the agreement would be required to receive any financial settlement. An email dated June 9th, 2008, reads: *"You both agree to strict confidentiality obligations and non-derogatory comments provisions about the Peniel Church and its members/employees/pastors trustees/attendees."*

Impact on Family Relations

Following her dismissal, Dr Ruth Reid responded with a letter to the trustees on February 13th, 2009: *"I have virtually lost all my children and grandchildren, and you have dismissed me for not having chosen to lose my husband as well. Don't you feel that rather than punish me through threats, isolation, demotion, humiliation, barring me from worshipping in my Church, and then termination of my position, you should be supporting me?"*

The dismissal strained the Reid family's relationships, leading to minimal communication with their children by August 2010. They were also denied visits to their grandchildren. Dr Reid shared a poignant story: *"...God's good; I was praying in the morning saying, 'I miss my grandchildren so much.' I went to the garage that evening down the road, and who should I see there* [begins to weep] *but Danielle and she flung her arms around me, so God let me see them even if the parents didn't. She was with her other granny, so that was lovely, but that's the last time I saw them."*[30]

Bishop Reid also shared a heart-warming tale highlighting his strong bond with his grandchildren: *"November comes, Christmas is looming. My six-year-old grandson is sitting at breakfast; I notice he has a catalogue with him – this is serious stuff. He opens a catalogue and pushes it across the table, and he says, 'Grandpa, I'd like that for Christmas, can you afford it?' I look, 'Is that all you want?' He said, 'I've put a sticker on the page so you won't lose the place.' He said, 'Grandpa, if you can afford that, could you afford everything else on the page?' Then he said, 'You can keep the catalogue.' That's my grandson. Hey, on Christmas morning, he looked for the box where he knew what was in the catalogue would be. It was the first thing he went for. He got everything that was on the page."*[31]

The Reids also revealed that Peter and Carolyn had arranged an interview between Matthew Reid – their son – and Sheila Graziano, along with another woman who claimed to have had an affair with Bishop Reid. To many, this appeared as an attempt to disrupt the family.

---

30 May 2010 Interview

31 GGF, May 6, 2005

Bishop Reid was stunned by the intensity of the animosity: *"...how they stirred up everyone to hate us, from a happy Church from when we did The Father, the musical, to destroy everything... Did I sin? Yes, and I admitted it in front of the Church, but never in a million years would I have believed the viciousness and vindictiveness that came out of those people. I find it still hard to believe."*[32] Many viewed the Church's actions as unbridled cruelty and hostility.

Facing Pressure to Depart

Bishop Reid: *"I remember years ago, when God impressed me to move from Ongar to Brentwood... standing up in the Bedworth Hall in the upstairs room...the very meeting when I said it. 'Well, I know where I'm going; I'm going to Brentwood. Those that want to come with me come with me, that's it.' I know what God said; that's what we do, and we did."* —2001 sermon.

Now, many years later, a few of the remnants left in the church wanted them to leave Brentwood. The Reids were publicly confronted on multiple occasions:

"...my wife and I went out to a restaurant ...and someone came up who had a grudge [about] thirty years ago...and attacked me in the restaurant when I was sitting eating lunch. And he [had] ended up in prison before because of what he did, not what I did. I just happened to give evidence. So there are people who have grudges."[33]

"...my wife and I have wanted to get on with our lives...and we've been harassed. My mother grew up in Brentwood,...where I've grown up.... Why should I be driven out by foreigners? People who moved from Croydon...Northern Ireland, or...other places. I'm a Brentwood man; I love Brentwood, I love the people in Brentwood. [We] find that the average person is very sympathetic, and Brentwood is a good town...

---

32 Interview May 2010

33 TBGS, 2011

                    I'm Alive

I think the people of Brentwood need to know that my wife and I are very happy....Okay, there's a few people in there that have deviant attitudes, but apart from that, it's great."[34]

Amid this relentless onslaught of harassment, Bishop Reid faced another horrific ordeal – arrest on historical rape allegations.

Historical Rape Allegations

On August 27th, 2009, at 4 a.m., five police officers arrested the then sixty-six-year-old Bishop Reid, at his home. He was accused of historical rape against his daughter, which allegedly occurred over 30 years ago when she was just five years old. At the time of his arrest, his daughter was thirty-seven years old. The suspicious timing of these accusations became evident when they were leaked to the national media through a pre-prepared press release that followed the arrest.

Dr Ruth Reid stated: *"It was all over the newspapers."* On September 10th, 2009, detectives questioned him, as reported by The London Evening Standard, The Metro, The Essex Chronicle, and The Brentwood Gazette. A presumption of guilt in the court of public opinion allowed his opponents to exploit the situation. Emails were dispatched all across Tulsa, U.S.A. and the story spread like wildfire. Terry Law, a friend of the Peniel Church and a former acquaintance of Bishop Reid, was surprised by how fast the news spread throughout Tulsa, Oklahoma, through newspaper reports.

On that terrifying morning, upon opening the door, they promptly arrested him during an incident that lasted for about 20 minutes, witnessed by Aidy Simmons, Peter and Serena Cleminson. When he asked why he was being detained, they explained that they were following instructions from the case officers. He was not allowed to inform the other occupants about the nature of the

---

34 TBGS, 2011.

arrest. Furthermore, no warrant was issued and he was denied the chance to make any calls, leaving his distraught wife without support.

Dr Ruth Reid explains: *"They said he couldn't get changed without one of them present; he wanted to go to the toilet, and they said, 'You can't go without one of us present.' I mean, it was a horrendous experience."* They both described the experience as 'extremely aggressive'. Adrian Simmons (Aidy) recounted his experience of the incident: *"I live with the Reids and was present when the police arrived. The extreme noise woke me up. My initial thought was that it was bailiffs because they were extremely aggressive, loud, rowdy and very rude to Mrs Reid. It was freaky!"* Dr Reid mentioned during her discussions with an Essex Police Officer in July 2010: *"One of the officers that came was very calm and did not mistreat us. He seemed aware that the others were over-aggressive."*

Experience at the Brentwood Police Station

Once at the Brentwood Police Station, he questioned the officers about the 4 a.m. arrest; however, they claimed no knowledge of scheduling such an early arrest. The situation seemed incongruous, leaving him bewildered as the puzzle pieces failed to align. He remained in a cell, awaiting questioning, from 4:30 a.m. until 11:30 a.m.: *"I was given no food, just a cup of tea, and that was it till 11.30 a.m..."*

After 1.5 hours of questioning, he was granted bail until November 28th, but the two accompanying officers denied him permission to provide additional statements during the initial interview. During the interview, DS Jones made derogatory comments about adultery. Another officer mocked his Christian beliefs with a disparaging remark. *"...I finally finished with the police at 2 p.m. and had no money, no mobile phone and I had to walk home having had no lunch."*

 I'm Alive

As he walked, the two police officers who had questioned him drove by in an unmarked vehicle, laughing at him.

"I'll tell you what, I will never support the police in anything. Totally out of order, they could've called me in for an interview if they wanted me for an interview. Then they gave a statement to the newspaper that I was arrested at 4 o'clock in the morning on the allegations of rape."

Surprisingly, the police didn't interview his daughter, the accuser, until six months after the arrest, suggesting a deliberate prolonging of the allegations. Dr Reid states: *"We do know that Sarah did not make the statement till February of this year."* For ten heart-breaking months, from August 2008 to May 2010, a dark cloud of grief descended on them.

In April 2010, Dr Reid was called in for questioning: *"...First, when Michael went to the station to answer bail, they rang me as soon as he was out of the house and said would I mind if they came and interviewed me informally. So they came and interviewed me informally..."*[35] A few months later, she was called in for questioning again because her daughter had accused her of also being involved in the assault. She faced the threat of arrest despite her willingness to cooperate. *"A few months later, they asked me to go to the police station for an interview, and they said if I didn't come willingly, they would arrest me."*

Regarding the incident, Dr Ruth Reid stated: *"...the police officer did tell me why the investigation is going slowly because Sarah had made other allegations and she has to follow those up, so, to be honest, I was quite relieved... I thought they would see that she was making lie after lie, but the other distressing thing was the effect it had on our family. Even Matthew was upset when he heard about the second allegation. He wept in front of the board; it devastated him. He took on the mantle to help them get rid of his father from the Church."*

---

35 May 2010 Interview

Commenting on her statement, the Essex Police said: *"Her statement was deemed not credible."* Additionally, during the initial police interview on August 27th, 2009, Bishop Reid informed the officers that his daughter suffered from Münchausen Syndrome and even suggested a book for them to read, *"Playing Sick? Untangling the Web of Munchausen Syndrome"* by Marc D. Feldman, M.D., to help them understand that her claims were the symptoms of this illness. He also wrote to A/Detective Inspector Nelson of the Child Abuse Investigation Unit, stating that they must be aware of this illness as a Child Abuse Investigation Unit.

Münchausen Syndrome involves feigning diseases or trauma for attention, often resulting in fabricating or exaggerating allegations, including rape, stalking or harassment when seeking sympathy and medical attention. While she had previously accused others of similar crimes, they did not experience the 4 a.m. arrest or the intense national media scrutiny that he did.

Following a lengthy public investigation, the police recommended dropping the case to the Crown Prosecution Service, which they eventually did, citing baseless allegations. On May 7th, 2010, the case was officially closed.

Case Discrepancies

The case was marred with inconsistencies. The arrest should not have been supervised by Acting Detective Inspector 683, Steve Nelson, an officer involved in another incident. He failed to interview both Bishop Reid and the non-police witnesses—despite having their names—about the arresting officers' actions.

On July 1st, he met with Bishop Reid, claiming interest only in questioning the officers from his unit, not those from Brentwood Station. His report mentioned only four arresting officers when actually there were five. Additionally, he mistakenly asserted the absence of a female officer despite witnesses confirming otherwise.

They conveniently omitted the female officer's presence after Bishop Reid expressed concerns about her, and the other officers, insisting that he leave the door of the toilet open while he used it and the bedroom door open while he changed.

The investigation report cited APS Jackson's direction for the 4 a.m. arrest, attributing it to resource constraints. The findings, in conflict with other perspectives, state: *"Only one, maybe two officers entered the property..."* In truth, five officers entered – three into the bedroom and two on the landing – as verified by witnesses.

However, witnesses dispute assertions that Dr Ruth Reid, aged sixty-four, was not threatened with arrest when she mentioned calling her daughter. In reality, she was threatened with arrest if she made the call, with the claim that it constituted obstruction of justice.

The case contained numerous discrepancies, raised suspicions and contained contradictions that harmed Bishop Reid's reputation.

Additional Inconsistencies

Sarah did not report the incident to the police or newspapers. The Church was aware of Sarah's prior accusations against others, and two members – Esther Reid and Rosemary Boot – went to Scotland to "offer support", and later informed the police about the rape allegations on behalf of the accuser. They expressed their doubts to the police about the veracity of the accusations after speaking to her, stressing her history of fabricating stories. Peter Linnecar publicly expressed his disbelief in Bishop Reid's guilt to the congregation. Yet the Church sent emails to all members, anticipating newspaper publication the next day. A spokesperson told the Brentwood Gazette: *"Although these allegations do not relate to the Church in any way, if requested to do so, we will cooperate fully in any ongoing investigation."*[36]

---

36 September 2009

Bishop Reid: *"Yes, the Church had some involvement; I don't know how exactly, but I do know people from the Church went to the police accusing me of rape. It was a totally false allegation. My son knew it was false, yet his…wife went all the way up to see my daughter and then went to the police. I think the Church leadership…told her it was important and should be reported because I used to work at the school. A certain Church member was President of a cycling club, and some police officers belonged to it, and that's how I think the contact was made. It was Harlow police as they deal with serious crimes, but the fact was they hadn't even got a statement from my daughter when they arrested me, so it was on the say-so of people from the Peniel Church, so it was a…conspired allegation which they knew was not true."*[37]

His employment history with the Metropolitan police and his unwavering support for law enforcement made the excessive aggression of the arrest inexcusable. Moreover, releasing the allegation to the national media through a pre-prepared press release was unnecessary and harmful. Considering his prominent role, authorities should have recognised the situation's sensitivity. Sadly, this incident severely damaged his reputation and profoundly impacted his ministry, revealing the depths to which malicious individuals were willing to go. It also divided their family. Dr Reid said, *"Yet they tell people we love Michael and Ruth."*

One can empathise with the constant uncertainty they faced, along with the persistent threats, hate mail and malicious acts they were subjected to. Their hearts must have felt like a cold, metal fist was squeezing it. It's unsurprising then that this elderly couple, with limited family support, suffered declining health.

Resilience in the Face of Health Struggles

Bishop Reid: *"…that day, I'd heard my wife had cancer, and they told me she'd have one month to live… [Fights back tears]."* The news hit

---

37 2010 Interview

　　　　　　　　I'm Alive

Bishop Reid like a sledgehammer to the heart, as waves of sadness washed over him, almost pulling him under. The same evening, April 13th, 2011, while at home watching Manchester United play Chelsea, he sensed something was amiss and said to the person with him: *"Ring for an ambulance. I'm going to have a heart attack."*

"I had no pain. I just sensed it."

The first responder, an ex-police officer, arrived in seven minutes and was praised by Bishop Reid as an *"excellent man."*

"...he brought his ECG thing...and he said, 'Who's having a heart attack?' I said, 'Me.' He said, 'But you look normal?' [he] came over felt my head... [And said] 'Let's take your pulse,' and it was still ticking, and he said, 'Oh well, I'll give you an ECG,' so he opened the case and started to get the things out..." While placing an oxygen mask and checking him, things suddenly changed. *"Within about three seconds, I stopped breathing, and my heart stopped...he unceremoniously, so I'm told, pulled me off the sofa, got me with my feet up on a chair, and began resuscitation."*

The ambulance arrived and revived him. On the way to the ambulance, his heart stopped three times, each time requiring resuscitation. When they reached Queen's Hospital's A&E department, his heart stopped again: *"It went into fibrillation ...And they revived me again."* After roughly 2.5 hours of stabilisation, he was transferred to the chest clinic.

"...if I hadn't...got the person to ring for the ambulance..., I'd be dead now...the staff, the ambulance staff, the man who came first were excellent....the nursing staff and the care at Romford was excellent at Queens...A&E...the chest clinic, they were brilliant on the wards...they look after you. I had a blocked artery, which they cleared and put a stent in..."

The first responder later visited Bishop Reid's home and seemed nervous when his wife answered the door. He feared that Bishop Reid had not survived, explaining, *"...because only 2% of people who go through that... survive."*

"…heaven wasn't ready for me yet. So they sent me back…I died four times and stopped breathing…if I'd gone to heaven, you wouldn't have got me back. You could have given me electric shock treatment…I wouldn't have come back."

"I wanted to beat my wife to heaven…they had to switch to another hospital, and it's a miracle, all the consultants said you shouldn't be alive; no one has their heart stopped four times like that and they survive…"

Rumours claimed he was scheduled for a heart bypass surgery: *"People make up stories. They always have. They have nothing better to do…. I'll get back to exercising…pills and get my strength back and then get on with my life."*

Three years earlier, the Peniel Church had been aware of the couple's illness and requested them to submit medical certificates from April 7th, 2008 to May 30th, 2008. Dr Ruth Reid, in particular, needed a heart monitor due to stress-induced palpitations. In a letter to the trustees dated May 5th, 2008, Bishop Reid explained: *"I am physically and mentally exhausted, and I have been unable to organise a colleague to come with me…I genuinely do not think I can cope mentally or emotionally…"* Ruth stated: *"I was very, very upset, devastated by the rejection."* Rejection and hostility undoubtedly worsened their health issues.

Responding to the hatred, a former member, Julian, stated: *"When I heard about it, it…saddened me. Mamma Ruth represents the softer side…To think that people would send hate mail and put them under so much pressure that Mamma Ruth even had heart trouble is just messed up. Even from a non-religious perspective, it's inexcusable to treat anyone that way. In religious terms, it's devilish and not of God to treat people like that."*[38]

---

38 Interview May 3 2010

 I'm Alive

The Church acknowledged their health challenges. In an email dated April 16th, 2008, which was addressed to Bishop Michael Reid, Kevin Lee states: "*...you are currently signed off sick, and it is important you regain your health. During your time of sickness...*" Despite being aware of their poor health, the perpetrators cruelly continued to torment the couple, intensifying their emotional and physical distress. It appeared as though they wanted to wipe the Reids off the face of the earth.

Chapter 20
Understanding the Employment Tribunal

A Brief Overview

*"…I tell you what, our senior pastors, I wouldn't change
them for anyone. I could trust my life to him…I can travel
around the world…do what God's called me to do, and
I know they'll be faithful…"*

– Bishop M. Reid, 2001.

Bishop Reid was initially led to believe that he would be reinstated as the pastor, but he was subsequently dismissed, along with his wife. The argument that the man might have made a mistake, but his wife did not, fell on deaf ears. He'd entrusted these individuals with the role of trustees, only to have them betray his trust. An Employment Tribunal was held to address his unfair dismissal.

For 32 years, there had been no existing employment contract between the Peniel Church and Bishop Reid. He declined to sign an employment contract due to disagreements with its terms. The Church did not make revisions or provide an alternative, opting to impose a contract of their choice and expecting his unconditional acceptance unilaterally. His refusal led to unfair accusations of being uncooperative.

During the Employment Tribunal, a crucial piece of evidence surfaced – an email from Ms Whealey to Kevin Lee, Chairman of the Respondent's Board of Trustees, dated April 29th, 2008: *"I told her that he (the Claimant) doesn't have a written contract, as he is well aware, but we have given a copy of the Staff Handbook."*

On April 24th, 2008, he received a written notification of his suspension and an invitation to a disciplinary hearing. However, no such letters were sent to Mrs. Graziano. It was asserted that she had resigned, making disciplinary actions unnecessary. However, Mrs. Graziano had not yet submitted her resignation letter, which she did later, on April 27th, 2008. Failing to suspend Mrs. Graziano amounts to unequal treatment of both parties.

A Few advocated for His Departure

On Friday, March 28th, 2008, a significant meeting occurred at Philip and Rachel Whealy's residence, which included Peter and Carolyn Linnecar, Andrew Love and Colin Cleminson. During this gathering, [...] and [...] vehemently pushed to prevent Bishop Reid from ever returning to the Church. Andrew reportedly went as far as saying he would prefer 'dead evangelicalism' over having Bishop Reid as the Pastor of the Church.

Many of the Church, especially early on, voiced their support for him to remain the pastor. On April 15th, 2008, some staunch opponents, including a dedicated adversary on the Reachout Trust forum, left comments affirming this: *"...there will be a number of members who will support any attempt Reid makes to regain his position..."* Many were misled regarding this by competing factions who sought to oust him in a strategy to gain control.

In the Employment Tribunal, the claimant's closing submission stated: *"It was stated in the statement that 'Meidre tried to point out that the adultery had given people the opportunity to vent their own personal offences about the way in which MSBR dealt with them over the years.' This confirmed what had been suspected all along, that the dismissal of the claimant was purely opportunistic and that the real reason or the Principal reason for the dismissal was not because of the misconduct of adultery."*

The Church submitted redacted documents but was compelled by the judge to reveal the concealed content. Among these documents was one that contained the minutes from a board meeting, discussing a plan to force him to retire at the age of sixty-five. This was recorded in the tribunal's minutes, signalling their intent to gain control of the Church. The secrecy of this plot raises questions about why they did not discuss this openly with Bishop Reid.

Modified Statement of Faith

The Peniel Church submitted a manipulated Statement of Faith as evidence, which included a previously undisclosed clause about marriage that had not been present in any earlier versions. According to their written submission to the Employment Tribunal in East London [51.1]: *"Adultery was in clear contradiction of the Statement of Faith that was a condition of employment (230,245)."*

The Statement of Faith in the Staff Handbook presented at the Employment Tribunal included this clause on page 5, 1.3: *"In the sanctity of marriage between a man and a woman and that this is the only context in which a sexual relationship is appropriate."*

Judge Haynes, a non-Christian, expressed surprise at finding a marriage-related clause in a Church's Statement of Faith. Bishop Reid was equally astonished, as he had never been informed of these alterations.

I'm Alive

Bishop Reid clarified he had never seen this version of the Statement of Faith in the handbook. Meidre Cleminson claimed Bishop Reid attended a meeting where the statement was presented, alleging he had tossed the book across the table upon reading it. However, he denied this, stating he had never attended such a meeting. His absence was confirmed by the meeting minutes that were presented as evidence during the tribunal, exposing Meidre's false claim.

In July 2010, Jennie Whealy revealed to Bishop Reid and I that [...] was responsible for adding the new clause. Jennie had been on the team that assembled the Staff Handbook and was responsible for typing it.

John Onifade led the defence for Bishop Reid. During the proceedings, he presented evidence to substantiate the claim that the Statement of Faith had been tampered with and was, in fact, a forgery. He states: *"...the next day, we brought that evidence to show that the clause was added to the tribunal and showed it to the judge, and the other side said, 'We do not dispute it; we don't say anything about it.'... 'Do you agree that this was not there originally?' and they said, 'Yes.' We presented the evidence to the judge, and the judge said there was no need for him to have it as the respondents did not dispute it to say that the document was doctored. We left the hearing that day and celebrated this because when you present a fraudulent document to a tribunal, it ends the case. I explained that there was a case like this in Scotland, and when it became apparent that the evidence was doctored fraudulently to dismiss a person, it was the tribunal that called the police! The person was arrested and jailed. They were an employer. You would expect the same thing to happen in this case."*

However, the judge ignored the relevance of this evidence and chose not to consider it, even though the evidence remained unchallenged. Additionally, it was noted that other employees had previously engaged in adultery, and despite this, their employment was never terminated.

The case outcome hinged on this clause, and he was found guilty of breaching it, leading to his loss in the tribunal.

Unfair Tribunal

The fact that other employees had committed adultery without their employment being terminated raised doubts about the fairness of Bishop Reid's treatment in comparison to them. John Shelton, a director, trustee and Chairman of the investigation board for the Peniel Church, testified as a witness during the tribunal. During cross-examination, when asked why Mrs. Graziano was not suspended similarly, he could only offer evasive responses: *"...a lot was happening at the same time"* and *"many people were hurting."*

Surprisingly, during cross-examination, John Shelton sided with Bishop Reid's representative and admitted that had he known all the facts presented at the tribunal, he would not have supported the dismissal. He voiced his belief in Bishop Reid's unfair treatment, showed visible distress during the questioning, and later decided to leave the Church.

A Brentwood Gazette reporter sat with the Peniel Church at the Employment Tribunal but did not approach Bishop Reid for a statement. The newspaper later published a report claiming that he had refused to comment.

On March 31st, 2010, John Onifade lodged an official appeal in favour of Bishop Reid and personally submitted the papers to ensure the process's integrity. The clerk-in-charge stamped all documents and issued a receipt. By April 2010, John had not received an acknowledgement letter. Upon inquiry, he was told one document was missing, and he promptly faxed the 17-page document once more. They claimed to have sent a letter dated April 1st, requesting the missing document, but John had not received it and requested a copy of it. Surprisingly, as of August 10th, 2010, he had still not received a copy of the alleged letter.

While overlooking a single sheet might be understandable, it's highly improbable that both John and the clerk missed a 17-page primary document of the appeal. This raises suspicions of foul play in the document's disappearance.

Subsequently, John received a letter stating that since the 'missing' document was faxed on April 26th, it would be considered at the new appeal submission date. However, they then claimed that this new date meant the appeal had been lodged late and, as a result, it could not be considered.

Suspiciously, they asserted that John had written a request for an extension of the appeal date. However, John vehemently denied this, insisting on a copy of the alleged letter. To date, no such letter has been provided.

The initial judgement from the Employment Tribunal was initially expected on February 2nd, but it was not received until February 19th. This delay raises questions about its cause. One might speculate that the hold-up was intentional, to ensure that the appeal was deemed late and subsequently rejected.

In addition, John received information that his telephone had been tapped. Additionally, his car tyres were maliciously slashed. Notably, John Onifade had never lost an Employment Tribunal case before. The circumstances strongly imply the presence of foul play influencing the outcome, though specific supporting details cannot be shared here. The readers can draw their own conclusions.

Not only was he dismissed, but Bishop's wife also faced the same fate, even though she shouldn't have been held accountable for her husband's actions. Additionally, her solicitor's failure to submit her appeal on time resulted in her case not being heard.

Dr Ruth Reid responded by letter to the Peniel Church Trustees on February 13th, 2009: *"...you have dismissed me for not having chosen to lose my husband as well..."*

Pension

Bishop Reid entrusted Church responsibilities—including pensions—to individuals he considered trustworthy, which enabled him to travel. However, it resulted in regrettable consequences in his later years.

Peter Linnecar was responsible for setting up the pension fund for the staff, including his own. However, he failed to set up adequate payments towards the Reids' Church pension.

Peter Linnecar personally informed Bishop Reid of his £45,000 pension, which was then relayed to the congregation. On March 21st, 2008, Carolyn Linnecar stated in a conversation: *"Peter said he would check but thought the funds would produce approximately £45K pa."*

After 32 years of unwavering dedication, the Reids each received a meagre pension from the Church, amounting to only £2,400 annually. In sharp contrast, Peter Linnecar received a weekly salary from the Church of £1,923.07, and his wife's additional compensation only exacerbated this inequality. Fortunately, Bishop Reid had a monthly pension of around £1,600 from a fund established during his business career.

Rumours circulated that they had excessively profited from the ministry through their salaries. Bishop Reid: *"One of the lies they spread was that the family was taking £500,000 a year from the Church."*[39] The figure was suspicious as the Church accounts for the years ending on August 31st, 2008, and 2007 showed staff costs of £588,508, whereas, for the year ending on August 31st, 2006, staff costs

---

39 Interview May 2010.

 I'm Alive

were reported at just £163,037. They reached a total of £500,000 by aggregating the travel expenses from their multiple mission trips, which often included other members too; nevertheless, all these expenses were incorrectly considered as part of the Reids' income, creating the impression that he took £500,000 as personal income.

"The only way I could prove it to some people was to show them my PAYEE slips, which proved it was just lies."[40] The payee slips indicated a modest salary of £52,000, reflecting his belief that a minister's income should align with the congregation's average earnings.

It's entirely unfounded to claim that the Reids financially exploited the Church. They dedicated themselves wholeheartedly during their service, making significant sacrifices and firmly trusting that the Church would support their retirement. This commitment was formally documented and evidenced by discussions with solicitors. They never anticipated receiving such an inadequate pension, amounting to just £2,400 each, which equates to a mere £46.15 per week.

Their financial situation was dire – no substantial income, small government, business, and Church pensions and limited savings. The economic situation they were left in was an unjustifiably malevolent act.

Lost Earnings and Investments

As the Church expanded, Bishop Reid couldn't devote time to his thriving business, which generated an annual net profit of around £185,000. Peter took over the company, and in 1986, Bishop Reid granted him a 50% share in McCarty & Dowie, valued at £2.5 million, based on potential buyer offers.

Bishop Reid conveyed to me: *"If I asked how things were going, he would say fine, when in actual fact... he was running up big debts, but*

---

40 Interview May 2010.

I never knew... He would never give me information about what was coming in and what was going out. I kept asking, and he wouldn't give it in the end.... I dread to think how we've been conned and how much we personally have lost."[41]

Church funds were used to supplement the wages of his business employees, including paying their spouses for no work. This deception was exposed when Rachel raised concerns about the school finances, prompting an investigation that revealed embezzlement of the Church funds. Bishop Reid summoned those involved and reprimanded them, stating: *"Using Church funds in this manner is unacceptable!"*

Peter was swiftly barred from accessing Church funds for five years and prevented from preaching during this period. Congregation members may have been perplexed by Peter's abrupt cessation of preaching, unaware of the embezzlement and its repercussions. On June 21st, 2010, an individual named Dan posted a comment on the Brentwood Gazette website: *"The Church...30 years ago started...very healthily. Things only soured in the last ten years... Peter Linnecar was set aside, unknown to many in the congregation, when this...happened – it was just noticed that he wasn't involved in anything anymore. So, though having been core to many things at the start of the Church and the school, he... wasn't involved in the last decade."*

Peter continued to manage the business, but it eventually faced bankruptcy. Peter and Carolyn lived in the Bell House and created business offices there. [...] used the Church funds for utility bills via unauthorised banker's drafts. On another occasion, the Church credit card was used to fund a family trip to Venezuela. Once Bishop Reid uncovered this dishonesty, it took nine months to retrieve the money. Out of kindness, he chose not to expose [...]

---

41 Interview May 2010

or involve the police, sparing him from potential imprisonment. Instead, he distanced himself from Peter, halted his preaching and had minimal communication with him for about five years.

Dr. Reid: *"However, the one thing that comforted me was the reassurance that we had a secure place to live for the rest of our lives in Testimony House. Haha!!!!"*

Chapter 21
Eviction from Testimony House

"The Board was in full agreement that security of tenancy must be provided to Bishop and Mrs Reid...Hope it is clear enough."

– Meidre Cleminson, 2007

Despite the financial challenges faced by the couple, the Peniel Church's decision to potentially evict them from Testimony House was one of the most painful experiences for the couple.

Bishop Reid: *"...the house was bought for us to live in the rest of our lives, the Archbishop...wanted it in my name, but I put it in the Church's name as I wasn't looking to enrich myself, and I never did. Maybe unwisely now, it seems, but that's the way it was."*[42]

Ayo Ademakinwa attended the service: *"In 1992, Archbishop Benson Idahosa came to the Church and said that the congregation needs to be grateful for this great work done by Bishop and Dr Ruth Reid by contributing enough money to buy their own home. That night, enough money was raised to buy Testimony House ...When the money was raised, it was given to the Bishop and Ruth to buy their home,*

---

42 Interview May 2010

but they refused to be selfish and requested the money to be put in the Church's purse. When the house was purchased, they were promised that they could live in it forever, even outside ministerial engagements. I know because I was there. I also gave a substantial amount of money towards the house that night."

As mentioned earlier, Bishop Reid originally owned 49 Coxtie Green Road; however, he later gifted it to the ministry. The Reids also signed over their two-thirds ownership of the Bell House to Peter in an agreement that secured them lifelong accommodation rights. Bishop Reid: *"...they persuaded me, and the trustees guaranteed that Ruth and I could live here [Testimony House] for the rest of our life, and if something happened to me, she could stay on, and if it was necessary for her to move they would buy an equivalent property somewhere else so she was provided for, so on that basis I signed that document to help Peter Linnecar out of debt."*[43]

Dr Reid states: *"...The worst thing of all was that we were no longer able to give the Bell House to the Church on our deaths, and I had little trust that Peter would keep his promise to give it, which, of course, proved to be true..."*[44]

Lifetime Occupancy Licence

Documented evidence revealed discussions between solicitors and Church trustees regarding granting the Reids a lifelong occupancy licence for Testimony House, in line with the ministry's charitable objectives, even if they no longer served as ministers.

A December 8th, 2006, letter from Stone King solicitors to Jennie Whealy addressed the topic "Parsonage Lifetime Interest for the Bishop and his Wife.": *"...I have discussed with Robert the practical constitutional routes that might enable the trustees to give greater*

---

43 Interview May 2010

44 Interview May 2010

comfort to the Bishop and his wife...the trustees are able to lawfully give a good deal of comfort to the Bishop and his wife as the 'sweep up' clauses within the objects allow the trustees to go beyond this period of active ministry."

Minutes of an AGM meeting held on Saturday, April 14th, 2007, state: *"Kevin Lee explained the Licence drafted by the lawyer, which gives Bishop Reid and Mrs Reid a licence to occupy Testimony House for the rest of their lives. All the directors agreed that this was the least the Charity could do for the Bishop and Mrs Reid and were happy with the idea. Jennie Whealy to forward the Licence to David Attar, John Adebanjo, Richard Cope, John Shelton and Meidre Cleminson for them to check. It was agreed that Kevin Lee could sign on behalf of the trustees..."*

Referring to the notes from a directors' meeting dated February 7th, 2007, an email from Meidre stated: *"Licence to Occupy: Bishop Reid, Mrs Reid and Rachel Whealy left the room to allow the Board to discuss the above issues. The Board was in full agreement that security of tenancy must be provided to Bishop and Mrs Reid. Advice has been sought, and a report from Stone King is available."* In the email's closing remarks, she mentions: *"Herewith ends the notes!! Hope it is clear enough."*

In September 2006, a proposed licence agreement introduced unusual and unfamiliar clauses that were not found in any prior verbal agreements. Due to the strange wording, the Reids chose not to sign it. No revised licence was subsequently offered.

The Reids had resided in Testimony House since 1992. On April 23rd, 2010, the Church requested a copy of the house occupancy licence agreement, alleging that the Reids had not provided supporting evidence for their claim, as asserted by the Peniel Church solicitors. The Reids contended that the existence of the documentation implied premeditation, thereby rendering

I'M ALIVE

both verbal and written agreements that were legally binding in terms of fairness. Peniel solicitors: *"Except for a purported claim in Testimony House, none of these issues have any relevance to the possession proceedings that we are instructed to pursue."*

In another letter dated December 8th, 2006, the Reids asserted, *"The Licence will be enforceable as a contract against the Charity whether the individual Trustees change or not."* However, in a letter dated April 23rd, 2010, the Peniel Church claimed a legal obligation to ensure the house was vacated because a continued rent-free occupation by the former charity employees contradicted the Church's charitable objectives. Contrary to this assertion, they were not legally obligated to evict them; in fact, they had the legal authority to act per their current governing documents as they deemed appropriate – the same governing documents that were in effect when the Reids first took residence.

These documents explicitly state:

4. (1) (ii) to support any Minister or Ministers and full and part-time Christian workers in any churches established and maintained by the Charity or in ANY SIMILAR CHURCH and any other Christian missionaries, evangelists or youth workers.

4. (1) (v) to establish and maintain accommodation for persons in necessitous circumstances.

1. (1) (xxii) to do all such other lawful things as are necessary for the achievements of the objects.

No evidence was offered to prove that rent-free occupancy by the Reids opposes the Church's charitable goals.

The Peniel Church and the former Michael Reid Ministries shared closely aligned objectives with his current ministry, 'What God Can Do Ministries,' allowing them to accommodate him as a founder in Testimony House, within their respective purposes. Moreover, if offering them security for their future during their time at Peniel was considered reasonable, why would it not be deemed appropriate after they had left the Church?

Confronted with these facts, the Church reevaluated its course of action, as reported in the Brentwood Gazette on March 3rd, 2010: *"At last week's Employment Tribunal, it was revealed Michael Reid and his wife, the Rev Ruth Reid, are still living on Church property and that an eviction could ensue. However, Anne [Brown] explained that the Church trustees are still discussing what action to take."*

Bishop Reid owned their main office building and refrained from seeking eviction or rent payments. In contrast, the Peniel Church issued eviction threats and presented offers for the Stable Block, which the couple deemed to be unfair. He turned down their £130,000 offer for a property that was actually worth £400,000, which resulted in false accusations of refusing their sincere efforts.

Despite signing an agreement to vacate the property in 2012, Bishop Reid was unwilling to vacate the property since 2009.[45] He claimed that the Church used *'undue influence'* to force him into signing the consent order to leave the property. Facing looming threats of eviction and legal costs, he felt compelled to do so. This took place while he was recovering from a heart attack and mourning the death of his wife, whom he had been married to for over 30 years.

In June 2010, the Peniel Church filed legal papers to summon the Reids to a court hearing before a judge on August 10th. By July 2010, they had enclosed most of the property around Testimony House with a fence and secured the gate to the Church grounds from their home by screwing it shut. The High Court dismissed his case, and the Church was granted an order to evict him.

---

45 Metro, Tue June 11 2013

 I'm Alive

Initially, my primary concern while assisting Bishop Reid was ensuring the security of his residence. Eventually, when he was sixty-nine years old, the Church provided him with a home valued at £465,000, allowing him to live there rent-free for life. However, he described the property as a 'hovel'.

Incorporating the Sale of Stable Block into the Settlement

The Reids sought a fair settlement, while the Peniel Church aimed to decrease payments, while still acknowledging their debt to the Reids. In a letter to Dr Ruth Reid, they said: *"To mitigate against the potential injustice to you, we would like to make an offer to you."*

After meeting the Reids, Kevin Lee promptly emailed on June 3rd, 2008, expressing a strong desire to reach an agreement with Cartwright Solicitors quickly: *"...We hoped you would be presenting on behalf of Michael and Ruth a proposal to find an amicable and speedy resolution to the current situation. Regretfully, you did not...we are prepared to give you until 6 p.m. tomorrow, June 4th, 2008, to do so."*

In an April 23rd, 2010 letter, the Church accused the Reids of refusing all offers. Settlement amounts were predetermined with little negotiation, and the couple faced pressure, threats and continuous eviction warnings to ensure their compliance. The Peniel Church offered a £500,000 settlement that imposed restrictions on the Reids – no comments about the Church, no new Church within a 20-mile radius, and no entry to Peniel premises without written trustee permission.

The settlement involved selling the main office block, valued at about £250,000, valuing Bishop Reid's two-thirds ownership at £170,000. As a result, the final settlement offer was £330,000, falling significantly short of what the Reids deserved for their years of service. He owned two-thirds of the Stable Block; the remaining third, owned by Peter, was supposed to be transferred to Bishop

Reid, but the solicitor never completed this transfer. Bishop Reid: *"So I'm left with the situation of 2/3, but now they are trying to force me to sell it down-priced to them. It's the only property I own in this country."*[46]

Peter eventually transferred one-third to the Church without informing Bishop Reid. He approached the trustees, who approved the transfer because he couldn't cover the mortgage payments.

In a letter dated April 23rd, 2010, the solicitor stated that a Church-nominated RICS surveyor would assess the Stable Block's commercial value. Curiously, they insisted on selecting the property appraiser themselves, leaving doubts about why they didn't permit Bishop Reid to obtain an independent valuation.

In a surprising twist, the Peniel Church's solicitor asserted in an April 23rd, 2010 letter that their client could legally offer only £40,000 as a settlement, a significant reduction from the original offer of £500,000. However, no concrete evidence supported this assertion, suggesting it relied on personal advice rather than legal obligations.

Some Christians suggested he should relinquish everything without pursuing legal action. Despite having legal rights to the property, Bishop Reid remained reasonable and didn't obstruct their use of his property. Additionally, he had the right to the royalties received from the sales of his DVDs, books and tapes, potentially totalling a substantial six-figure sum, but the Church refused to acknowledge this obligation. Eviction notices were served to reclaim the property he resided in, accompanied by a £40,000 settlement offer for his lifelong service.

In the face of the Reids' unfortunate financial predicament, the others prospered off his years of labour.

------

46 Interview May 2010

    I'm Alive

Chapter 22
God's Emissary

"Before I formed you in the womb, I knew you; Before you were born,
I sanctified you; I ordained you a prophet to the nations."

– Jeremiah 1:5

The Call

In Bishop Reid's living room hung a picture of Winston Churchill. Despite his flaws, Churchill displayed the ideal qualities to lead Britain to victory in World War II. His stubbornness and ego were countered by his boldness, bravery and unwavering determination to defy the odds and confront Nazi Germany. His rise to power in 1940 significantly impacted world history. Likewise, Bishop Reid's contribution to Christianity was marked by a divine call from a potter, with profound wisdom and purpose. His apostolic and prophetic mantle served as a global voice to the nations, mirroring God's voice, which can be both gentle and thunderous, evoking both pleasure and anger.

The Scripture unequivocally states that God selects and appoints whom He will. Divine selection perplexes the human mind since it clashes with our desire for control. Therefore, individuals not born from above may become upset when God uses those they deem ineligible: *"...the son born according to the flesh persecuted the son born by the power of the Spirit. It is the same now."*[47] Undeniably, God, in His divine foreknowledge, intentionally chose Bishop Reid for His purpose.

The Message

"It is a poor sermon that gives no offence; that neither makes the hearer displeased with himself nor with the preacher." – George Whitefield.

Many people attest to his steadfast Biblical preaching. Nevertheless, Bishop Reid's unwavering preaching stirred up hostility among a minority. Such was his dedication to his message and reputation that he remained resolute in his sermons, refusing to compromise by speaking at lucrative pulpits stained by greed.

He resisted constant pressure to lower his standards concerning the Bible, the Church, the Bible School and the Peniel Academy. He stressed the importance of instilling morality in the children regarding the Church school. He prohibited romantic relationships for those under sixteen, to prevent complications and allowed only friendships. Despite parental disagreements and some children's resistance to sports, he promoted physical activity and a healthy diet. Additionally, his unwavering commitment to financial integrity unsettled some leaders who disagreed with his decision to allocate funds to support financially challenged overseas students seeking to attend the Bible Schools.

Bishop Reid: *"They didn't like my stand on many issues because I was outspoken. However, they liked the success. All the time, they were militating for freedoms that I didn't believe in..."*

---

47 Galatians 4:29

"When they got married, one of the rules I had was no alcohol on the Church premises. But Colin wanted to violate the rules, and they also wanted a jazz band. So he put a marquee down in his garden, and I went there and was appalled. It was the worst wedding I'd been to. Some of the girls had backless dresses on, and they looked like whores. They were dancing, they were drinking, wine was flowing and the whole thing was unbelievable. And that was for their wedding. I said something on Sunday; I said I was appalled by it. I walked out; I couldn't stay. I had the food at the reception and then just walked out. They were dancing till one o'clock in the morning. Those types of things are not Christian."

Following his removal, many observed a decline in standards: *"...and the moment they got power, they made the school a democracy. They voted on the rules, so everything I put in place to make the school successful and disciplined, they got rid of because Peter is not a disciplined person, and Carolyn. I was appalled."*

After Bishop temporarily stepped down, Everton was astonished by the emerging revelations: *"It was as if they were glad that he wasn't there anymore. They were saying, 'We can preach with freedom now....' They wanted freedom to do as they wanted."* Julian corroborated this: *"Some people were relieved and felt free, saying things like, 'Thank God Bishop is gone,' while others [had] felt oppressed and controlled."*

Everton: *"One of the staff who worked at the college, her name was Faith; I asked her what Bishop had done that made her turn against him. She said, 'You don't know, Everton. If you knew, I've known Bishop longer than you, and I've been here a very long time. Anyway, we all got freedom now.' I asked, 'Freedom from what?' She didn't explain but just said, 'We're free now. He's not here anymore.' But she wouldn't say what Bishop had done. I found out the hard way by being noisy."*

People often express resentment towards God by targeting His messengers, a pattern observed throughout the Bible and history.

Questioning His Role as a Bishop

Doubts arose about his bishopric, with some labelling him a 'self-styled' Bishop. Indications suggested that the Peniel Church may have officially adopted a stance of not recognising his bishopric, addressing him instead by his first name. In the Essex Chronicle in March 2010, Anne Brown stated: *"Some people certainly left with Michael..."* By April 2008, observers noticed that the title 'Bishop' was not being used when mentioning him. An Elim Minister confirmed this: *"...[in April 2008] one of the staff [Shane Whittaker] from the...Church rang me and asked if I had heard the news about 'Michael' and the title 'Bishop' wasn't used..."* Julian Fagan: *"...they refer to Bishop as Michael almost on purpose...the thought I have is when did he stop being a Bishop to you, when did you deem it right to take away the title Bishop because as far as I am aware that's something God almighty did and he was ordained by Bishops, he didn't want to be but he was..."*[48]

Tom Chacko, a Revelation TV presenter at the time, told me that according to I Timothy 3, Bishop Reid no longer met the qualifications of a Bishop and should therefore not preach again. I explained that I Timothy 3 serves as a guideline and that if we err, we have an advocate in the Father, who forgives and restores. He subsequently asked for our email exchange to be treated as *'private,'* to which I responded: *"Anything I have said or written to you can be made public as I have nothing to hide."* I asked whether he had engaged in adultery. He responded, *"No, never."* I asked if he had ever lusted in his heart, a concept defined by Jesus as adultery. He consistently refused to answer, avoiding the question until he abruptly ended the conversation.

---

48 May 2010

   I'm Alive

In my conversations with Howard Conder, the owner of Revelation TV, he consistently displayed kindness and compassion when discussing the situation. However, he declined to have Bishop Reid on the station.

The I.C.C.C. consecrated Bishop Reid as a Bishop. Established in 1982, the I.C.C.C. is a unifying alliance of national and international ministries, comprising thousands of ministries and hundreds of Bishops, across six continents. Bishop Reid served as the national presbyter for the I.C.C.C. and was a member of the College of Bishops for several years.

As per the I.C.C.C.'s official website, their episcopate was acknowledged by Pope Paul VI in 1978. *"...the pope saw it as a gesture of genuine desire to identify with the historic Church, and he defended the actions of the three Pentecostals and called for McAlister and DuPlessis to be brought before him for commissioning as Bishops of special recognition and rights, thereby establishing them both as direct descendants of apostolic succession."* Robert McAlister consecrated Archbishop Benson Idahosa, who in turn consecrated Bishop Michael Reid in Benin City, Nigeria, in 1997. This confirms that for many, he is a genuine part of the apostolic succession.

His consecration was confirmed by Bishop Margaret Benson Idahosa, Presiding Bishop/President, Idahosa World Outreach, on Thursday, October 22nd, 2009. *"I herewith confirm that the above named, [Rev. M.S.B. Reid ThD. DD] was consecrated as a Bishop by my husband and co-labourer in the Lord's vineyard; His Grace, Most Rev. Prof. Benson Idahosa (of blessed memory), the founding Archbishop of Church of God Mission International Incorporated, Benin City, Edo State, Nigeria, in the year 1997 His mandate as conferred by the Church to function in that capacity remains."*

His global spiritual oversight of thousands of pastors qualified him as an active Bishop. The gifts and callings of God are without repentance; God's calling is irrevocable.

Resistance to his Post-Peniel Ministry

God entrusted him with a new mission – to establish and nurture the 'What God Can Do Ministries.' However, it did not come without determined opposition.

Though the Church, verbally and in written communication, both publicly and privately, professed their affection for him and expressed their willingness to support his transition into ministry, a dedicated clan remained steadfast in their efforts to obstruct him in every way possible.

While the Reids were in the U.S., the Peniel Church leaders, on April 27th, 2008, made an announcement that they would return to the U.K. the next day. However, during their time in Tulsa and upon their return, the Reids' friends were either told that they had chosen to stay in the U.S.A. permanently or that the Church didn't know their whereabouts.

Supporters were eager to reach out to the couple. But their phone number was redirected to the Church, preventing direct contact. A man planning to visit the Reids had only the Church number to rely on. In response, he was told: "*We don't know where he is. We don't know what his telephone number is.*" The church knew they were just two doors away, where they had been for decades.

In another case, his profound impact on pastors in Abuja, Nigeria, fuelled their desire for his return to Nigeria and sparked significant plans. Despite a pastor's two-year effort, including numerous calls to the Peniel Church, he couldn't reach Bishop Reid. He eventually travelled to the U.K. by faith, but sadly, he still couldn't establish contact, even after visiting the Peniel Church. In another case, it took an Indian man nine months to find them.

I invited individuals to meet Bishop Reid twice at his home, but they mistakenly went to the church, two doors away. When they asked for directions, they faced hostility and were told that his location was unknown.

Apart from trying to stop his home services, the Peniel Church also took legal action against him for using photos of himself, claiming that those images, taken by Ben Cooke and Anthony Weil, were used without consent. A letter dated September 16th, 2008, stated that he should not use church-owned photos and legal proceedings began by October 15th, 2008.

In 2008, Bishop Reid requested access to his extensive ministry database of supporters. Meidre Cleminson's April 27th, 2008 email mentioned the board's intention to assess compliance with the Data Protection Act before responding. No subsequent response was received. Later, a comprehensive 21-page letter was sent to all database members discouraged any collaboration with him. Donald Panth, Bishop Reid's representative in India, received a letter suggesting payment and income in exchange for collaboration with the Peniel Church. The letter even proposed funding a joint Bible College. Bishop Reid personally reviewed the letter during his trip to India. However, Donald Panth declined the offer, appropriately.

The Church denied him access to the private phone numbers of his global ministry friends and took various actions to sever contact, including spreading rumors that he was no longer in the ministry. Furthermore, they issued press releases that undermined his credibility. Bishop Reid: *"They just twisted everything, but they made sure no one would come and see me and find out the truth..."*

In 2008, he requested his sermon recordings, considering them his intellectual property and not needed by the Peniel Church. However, they declined, citing audience members' concerns about appearing on the recordings with him. However, legally, unrestricted areas within the church grounds are considered public spaces and the individuals present are assumed to provide implied consent if they appear in the background.

His books were listed online for sale for a penny, most likely to impede sales through his website. Moreover, the church withheld the original digital files of the books, preventing him from reprinting them. What became of Bishop Reid's books? In a December 7th, 2008 email, Kevin Lee explains: *"I was asked to investigate why material associated with Bishop Reid was being disposed of."* Unconfirmed rumours circulated that a few individuals had gathered his products and burned them in a skip, reminiscent of burning books associated with the devil in Acts 19.

They insisted that he refrain from starting a church within a 20-mile radius and accused him of attracting members through website donations, among other deliberate actions. These actions were aimed at hindering his income and the progress of his ministry, contradicting their claim that they would support him.

"People were told I'd moved to Houston, which I never did. And I was uncontactable, which I'm not. They were told I retired, which I haven't."[49] *"But in the end, I think God's hand has been in everything. We're happy, and the people are finding us again. They're finding I'm alive and well. I'm ministering as I always do, and now they're finding the website."*[50]

On November 14th, 2008, the Reids uploaded their inaugural video. He continued travelling globally, conducting crusades and ministering at various churches, witnessing the same miracles as before. *"I'm involved with many churches around the country. I've travelled…and had tremendous campaigns in Cameroon. We're being hosted by the President in Sierra Leone. I go to Ghana, to Nigeria. I'm*

---

49 TBGS, 2011

50 2010 Interview

　　　　　I'M ALIVE

going to Uganda...Kenya...Congo...The thing is that Presidents and Prime Ministers in those countries will accept us."[51]

Despite stiff opposition, their steadfast dedication to preaching, teaching and healing continued to make a lasting impact worldwide.

Later Life: Illness and Death

Bishop Reid: "...she's been gone two years, but I still find a sit down computer, and sometimes I almost want to have a chat with her."[52] Dr. Reid had a captivating smile. Bishop Reid: *"...she had a beautiful smile...and when I was preaching she'd always smile at me, it gave me great encouragement....you preachers, when you're up preaching and your wife's frowning, then you know you're in trouble."*[53]

"People used to go to my wife and say, 'I'm amazed, you come with your husband every year, and you take notes of what he's preaching, and you're always smiling and you seem so absorbed in what he's saying.' She'd say, 'I love him, whatever he says I love him and I just appreciate the gift God's given him.' and I appreciated the gift she was to me."

But she also concealed sadness behind her genuine, radiant smile. During the time I spent with them, I witnessed the toll the hate and intimidation took on Dr Reid. The severe strain adversely impacted her health and overall well-being.

In December 2011, Dr Ruth Reid passed away from pancreatic cancer. Bishop Reid: *"My darling wife, Dr Ruth Reid, was promoted to Glory on Monday, December 5th. She was a beloved wife, mother, and grandmother and I thank God for her life and ministry, which touched thousands of people around the globe."*

---

51 TBGS, 2011

52 Sept 23rd 2013

53 Sermon, 23rd Sept 2013

"...one of the hardest things in my life was to watch my wife suffer, and I was there when she went home to glory. I'd take the pain for her. I'd have taken everything for her, but I couldn't. She went home..."[54]

Her granddaughter wrote: *"My darling Grandma, I love you with all my heart. I'm so happy that you are with Jesus now and happier than anyone else in this world. I will always treasure your memory and the way you were always part of my life. I love you so much. Xxxxxx."*

Bishop Reid, 2012: *"Before she went to glory, she finished her book and it will be published very shortly. It explains what happened in our lives, the trials we went through, the difficulties we went through, and how people... were very treacherous... But God sees everything, and the truth will always come out because it's going to be shouted from the rooftops. And those that think they won [are] deceived [and] will be shown up for what they are."*

"Faith is one of the things that doesn't die with the person, it's eternal... by faith, Abel still speaks."

A Service of Remembrance was held in honour of her life on Thursday, December 15th, starting at 6:30 p.m. at Christ Faith Tabernacle in London. Ruth's casket was on display for viewing from Thursday, December 15th, to Saturday, December 17th, at the Basildon Chapel of Rest, under the management of Cooperative Funeralcare. The funeral service took place on Monday, December 19th, at 10:00 a.m. at St Martin's Church in Basildon. The burial service was held at 2:00 p.m. at the Woodman Road Cemetery in Brentwood.

A Tribute to the Memory of Dr Ruth Reid – 1945-2011

By Bishop Michael Reid

My wife, who's gone home to be with the Lord two years ago, passed on to glory and beat me to it. I want to share part of her life.

---

54 Sept 23rd 2013

    I'm Alive

My wife isn't dead. She's alive because [when you're] absent from the body, you're present with the Lord.

I want to share a living testimony, not something of the past because we have eternal life and that life is eternal, and when we step out of this body, we step into glory.

So many people feel, *"Oh, it's over,"* no, it's just a separation for a moment. My wife and I lived a strange life. [...] She became my wife, and we were so, so in love. We were committed to one another. ...One thing she'd always say was she'd never marry a vicar or someone in the ministry, and when she met me, I was a businessman. When we got married, I conformed to a will, but she already knew that I had a call from God on my life...but she married a businessman, and the reason for that was she'd watched her parents suffer in the ministry. They had a big vicarage at an Anglican Church; it was cold and not the best place to live. There was poverty, and so she didn't want to grow up like that. Not that I believe ministers should be poor, but so often, they are treated very badly by churches.

When we got married, we began to have a vision... to... raise a true church. God spoke to me and my wife and said, *"You know what you don't want, now build what you do want."* God put in our hearts to do something totally different outside of religion, into Christ and Christianity. We might get criticised for it because we were firm in our resolution to live the Biblical way, to do it the way God said, and to give up the vain philosophy that was powerless. We wanted a God who was a miracle-working God, a God of power.

My wife had met the Lord in a... separate experience, and she'd had a real encounter with God... We... had one desire: to glorify Jesus Christ, to let the world know there's a saviour.

We set out on our path, and we were fortunate we met men of God who... challenged our hearts. One of them was Archbishop Benson Idahosa – a man of love, grace, faith and a man of fun – he always had a smile. One thing everyone says about my wife is she always had a smile and she was always welcoming to everyone. She knew her God, and she wasn't ashamed of the Gospel of Jesus Christ. Wherever we went in the world, whether we were meeting Prime Ministers or Presidents, she always had a glowing smile.

She went up to Liverpool, and I was living in Liverpool at the time, and we met there. I went with a friend to listen to a man of God from Romania, Richard Wurmbrand... many people were there, and my [future] wife was there... She looked across the balcony and saw someone on the opposite balcony and God spoke to her and said, *"That's the man you're going to marry."* She thought, *"This is crazy. I don't know who that is."* Afterwards, when we were leaving the hall, we met through a mutual friend, and that was our first meeting. She never told me what God had said to her, but by the second meeting, I knew she was the one for me. God, in miraculous ways, brought us together and our life together was one of God's miracles.

"No miracles, no Jesus" was our saying, and we wanted to build something for God where people could come and find the living God. We had tremendous experiences... and the thing about the relationship is that it doesn't end; it never ends when we're one in God. Even though we might be separated for a moment, we're conscious of the living reality of that person.

In 2017, Bishop Reid remarried in China and returned to England on December 17th with a supportive partner. As he approached the end of his life, his health worsened, but something remarkable happened.

"During the final years of his life, a remarkable transformation took place. His health declined to the point where he seldom spoke unless

     I'm Alive

directly addressed, and even then, he responded briefly. However, when questioned about scripture, he would passionately teach as if in perfect health, a testament to his life's calling and the presence of the Word of God within him."– Rev Dr Samuel Sao, Senior Minister at the Christ City Church.

He succumbed to his heart disease after battling it for five years. On Friday, January 13th, 2023, he peacefully departed at home in the presence of family, friends and loved ones. His funeral service took place on February 3rd, 2023, at 11:30 a.m.

[The Revd Trevor Dearing died on February 24th, 2023, aged eighty-nine. He was the man who'd encouraged Bishop Reid to start preaching again and start a church.]

Whatever God starts, He finishes.

Chapter 23
Meeting Bishop Reid: My Account

"*You're not a Pastor; you're a disaster! You're a witch!*"These were his words to me during our initial meeting.

My encounter with Bishop Michael Reid embodies all the elements of a divine appointment, most notably the impartation by laying on of hands that he and Dr Reid later affirmed privately to my wife and me. Before I go into the details, I will explain the journey that led to those profound encounters.

"You're not a Pastor; you're a disaster! You're a witch!"
These were his words to me during our initial meeting.

I don't recall how I first learned about him, but my earliest memory is when a friend mentioned their discussions with him on doctrinal matters. After researching his ministry, I decided to visit, which only led to more visits in the late 1990s and early 2000s. Back then, I had no idea about the divine plan that would unfold.

Early Meeting and Attending Events

I never met him personally during those initial visits, but I greatly enjoyed his teachings and those of visiting ministers like T.L. Osborn.

I vividly recall his humorous talk about weight loss struggles, joking about working with a personal trainer instead of going to a gym: *"Frequenting a public gym might just put your marriage at risk!"*

At one event, T.L. Osborn recounted an incident when he inadvertently deleted a book he was writing. In a remarkably generous act, he invited anyone interested to receive the new unedited and revised file. I was fortunate to obtain a copy, complete with his handwritten corrections and notes.

Astonishingly, I received confirmation of my revelatory insights through Bishop Reid and T.L. Osborn's sermons; they taught things I hadn't heard from anyone else. This further piqued my interest.

Consequently, I often invited ministers to meet with him, and several took up the invitation. I purposefully avoided being in the room, aiming to let the others have the same encounter I had through his ministry. I recall dropping off Bishop Jonathan Ansar for his stay and studies, and the warmth of the people there left a lasting impression on me.

Two memorable moments from the early days stick in my memory. The first took place during a lunch break at a Global Gospel Fellowship event. I was seated at a table in the large marquee, not far from Bishop Reid and T.L. Osborn. As Bishop Reid stood up and walked past my table, he suddenly came to a halt. His gaze was intense and prolonged. I pondered the significance of this moment, accustomed to prophets singling me out from a crowd and delivering prophecies. Eventually, he casually uttered: *"You'll learn,"* before continuing. Those seemingly casual words would later hold great importance. Many years later, I discovered his perceptiveness; every word he spoke was intentional.

In another situation, I was in the church's front car park with a minister friend. I distinctly remember when Bishop Reid approached us to talk to the minister. He took the book I was holding, "You Have Not Many Fathers" by Mark Hanby, and began flipping through its pages. He returned it a few seconds later and remarked: *"That's incorrect. 'Rhema' and 'logos' are used interchangeably in scripture."* This contradicted the traditional teaching among charismatics. His understanding of the scripture was unmatched by anyone I'd ever heard.

I never imagined that those visits to hear him would one day lead to an encounter and conversation that would profoundly impact my life. The divine sequence began in 2008 when as I approached the pulpit in the church I pastored, God spoke to me: *"Dismantle this work; I have something else for you to do."* Simultaneously, my ministry in India unexpectedly evaporated, and within months, under unusual circumstances, I crossed paths with Bishop Reid.

---

as I approached the pulpit in the church I pastored, God spoke to me: "Dismantle this work; I have something else for you to do." Simultaneously, my ministry in India unexpectedly evaporated, and within months, under unusual circumstances, I crossed paths with Bishop Reid.

From a Facebook Chat to the Initial Meeting: A Journey of Impartation

I was aware of the events at Peniel, but they didn't concern me, and I didn't give them much thought until the evening of Tuesday, 22nd September 2009. As I relaxed on the sofa that evening, my wife's persistent encouragement to join Facebook drifted through the air. I remained unyielding in my disinterest. *"I'll create an account for you,"* she persisted with a smile as she disappeared into our newly finished conservatory-turned-office, re-emerging moments later. *"Come and have a look,"* she invited, her voice brimming with eagerness. I peeled myself off the sofa. *"I'll take a look to keep her content,"* I mused silently.

          I'm Alive

I searched for a specific profile, clicked on the chat function, and curiously typed: "*Hello.*" Unexpectedly, I received an instant reply: "*Hello.*" I assumed his office assistant was replying: "*Is this Bishop Michael Reid?*" I was shocked when the reply confirmed: "*Yes, this is Michael Reid.*" I almost tumbled off my chair: "*Michael Reid, or a secretary?*" I grinned ear to ear as he accepted my request to visit him.

Soon after that, possibly the following evening, I walked across the expanse of his living room; the inviting plush carpet gently sighed under the weight of each step, no doubt, having been a silent observer, collecting tales of preaching exploits from renowned preachers. If I remember correctly, an original signed document from a renowned preacher, possibly Spurgeon, was framed and displayed on the wall.

I felt incredibly at ease; he did not exude an aura of self-importance, unlike other ministers. As we settled in for a conversation, he did not hold back. *"You're not a pastor; you're a disaster! You're a witch!"* His words smashed into me, yet I didn't dispute them. Instead, I experienced an unusual mix of joy and amusement, and an unexplainable understanding washed over me. It marked my first encounter with a minister of this kind – one who spoke the truth without an apology or smarmy politeness. By the end of our meeting, I understood why he had a painting of Winston Churchill, the famous wartime Prime Minister often called the 'British Bulldog', displayed in his living room. However, before our initial meeting ended, something genuinely remarkable took place.

As I stood to leave, he called me over and placed his hands on me. I stood, attentive to the most child-like prayer I had ever heard, void of any theatrics. Unexpectedly, a peculiar sensation washed over me, and all of a sudden, I was startled to see physical scales dropping from my eyes. They resembled long, golden-cream-coloured paper or leaves, each floating down to the floor in a spiral from my eyes. Then bang! Instantaneously, I grasped the undeniable truth of God's sovereignty with divine certainty; no words can adequately describe it. And then again, bang! In another flash of revelation, the certainty of the unshakeable security of my salvation flooded my consciousness. At the same time, an extraordinary sequence unfolded and I witnessed the entirety of the Bible—from Genesis to Revelation—I cannot articulate this experience in any other way.

Unexpectedly, a peculiar sensation washed over me, and all of a sudden, I was startled to see physical scales dropping from my eyes.

In an instant, my theories had vanished, without my permission, request, or debate and were replaced by an unwavering divine certainty that remains until today. Initially, I kept the experience to myself, unsure why I had been graced with that experience. At that time, I was not aware that Bishop Reid, unlike most Christians, embraced God's sovereignty and the security of salvation and possessed an unmatched grasp of the scripture. God's plan was unfolding gradually.

The Unfolding Plan: Dreams, Visions and Revelations

Before meeting Bishop Reid, as I walked past the TV, on my way out of the living room, I suddenly felt prompted to glance back at the screen. A minister was preaching in a tightly packed church: *"Why was God drawing my attention to this man?"* That man was Apostle Alfred Williams.

As I continued attending events at the home of Bishop Reid, things continued to unfold. A verse that had always held a mysterious significance for me since my early days in Christ took

I'M ALIVE

on new meaning when I met Bishop Reid: Psalms 103:7, "He made His ways known to Moses and His acts to the children of Israel." Bishop Reid often stressed the importance of understanding God's ways. I would reflect: *"This emphasis is unique; God inscribed that verse in my mind for such a time as this."*

I noted my mysterious ability to comprehend every word he spoke. This ability finally made sense when God gave me two significant dreams. In the first dream, I found myself seated on Bishop Reid's cream-coloured sofa. Abruptly, I felt a presence behind me, and when I turned, I was surprised to see Archbishop Benson Idahosa sitting on the back of the sofa. Locking eyes with me, he uttered unexpected words that caught me off guard: *"You have been brought here to correct your understanding of the Scripture. You have an apostolic ministry."* Months later, in the second dream, I sat opposite Apostle Alfred Williams in Reid's spacious conservatory. Apostle Williams spoke with conviction, declaring: *"You are an apostle in training."* Until that first dream, I had never entertained such a notion; however, in a flash, everything in my ministerial past made perfect sense.

During my time with them, I refrained from sharing my experiences or presenting myself as a minister despite my long-standing, unmistakable divine calling. By that point, I had been preaching for two decades, covering everything from street corners to numerous pulpits, and eventually, I hosted successful annual leaders and workers' conferences in India.

Months later, I shared the initial dream with the Reids, sparking Bishop Reid's keen interest in Archbishop Idahosa's words. I also recounted the marquee incident. Once, in his living room, I shared my experience of being baptised in the Holy Spirit with someone and saw Bishop Reid glance upward subtly, listening intently. He could discern my calling without any need for me to declare it.

This became evident one day as my wife and I found ourselves seated in the car with them, en route to a destination that escapes my memory.

God Spoke to Them About Me

My wife and I were seated in the back seat, with Bishop Reid at the wheel, while Dr Reid occupied the front passenger seat of their Range Rover. Dr Reid's voice broke the silence: *"Since the beginning of our ministry, we've been looking out for someone upon whom his mantle would fall,"* she began. *"Throughout these years, God never directed anyone our way. We talked about it last night. We both believe it's you. "*Those were not the words I had expected, yet every fibre in my being recognised its truth. I scarcely acknowledged the weighty words she had just spoken, perhaps because I had never hunted acknowledgement, titles or positions.

"Since the beginning of our ministry, we've been looking out for someone upon whom his mantle would fall," she began. "Throughout these years, God never directed anyone our way. We talked about it last night. We both believe it's you."

The topic wasn't revisited again until an invitation to a restaurant, which I believe was their intention. *"What do you want to do in life? What stirs your passion?"* they asked me. One answer burned within me: *"To preach the Gospel!"* I knew their expectations, but inexplicably, I blurted out: *"I want to create documentaries."* It was true – I wanted to create Gospel-oriented documentaries, a goal I later achieved, including one that featured Pastor Sunday Adelaja, the leader of Europe's largest church. However, it wasn't the answer they had anticipated.

I often wonder why I concealed my strong passion for preaching. Years later, I heard Bishop Reid state: *"There are always people who want ministry, seek ministry. I always look for the person who's trying to get out of it because he's the called one."*[55]

I never dared to teach or preach in his presence. On one occasion, he was late for a service and I started speaking. However, as soon as he arrived and took his position, I handed over the service to him, even though he signalled for me to continue. This unwillingness to preach in front of my mentors has been my general approach even when I was the main speaker; I don't chase pulpits.

Sharing these experiences openly at the time would have been as unwise as Joseph revealing his dreams to his brothers. Some people in Reid's circle seemed to believe that they held a special status with him and expected his exclusive attention. However, I wasn't there to compete with anyone.

This all happened when I was around 37 years old. Years later, the Lord revealed to me that once I turned fifty, there would be a significant shift in my calling—and indeed, there was.

Seeking Assistance, Yet Offering Support

I met with Bishop Reid to seek his support, but the tables turned and I ended up providing support to him. As a result, he remained entirely unaware that 2009 marked the start of the darkest period in my life, which began after God gave me a Word of Knowledge dream and enabled me to emerge victorious in all things.

During my visits, I observed several conversations about the events at Peniel; however, I would politely exit the room as if I were a guest. Nonetheless, the fragments I did overhear unveiled a clear truth – genuine support was lacking. Once I became aware of his predicament, I was deeply compelled to offer assistance. Upon committing to his ministry, I shut down my website and ceased all

---

55 GGF, May 2005

ministry-related activities, incurring financial loss. My focus was to safeguard his residence.

I organised a petition as one of my initiatives, hoping it would generate publicity. Despite opposition, a determined group of us, which included Bishop and Dr Ruth Reid, Apostle Williams, my wife and several others, successfully delivered the petition to 10 Downing Street, the Prime Minister's office. A local press article that followed invited childish hostility. As I walked near the Peniel Church, a passing car splashed water on me, and moments later, I saw the same car in the Church's car park.

We assisted with Michael Reid Media Productions, a platform for online content streaming. I accompanied him and fellow team members to acquire the necessary equipment, and even hosted broadcasts occasionally. My family and I made regular trips from Bedford to Brentwood. Over time, these visits turned into extended stays, sometimes lasting for months.

Although we owned a house in Bedford, the difficult circumstances I was facing led to the eventual loss of the property. Meeting him during this tumultuous time became my lifeline. It's truly miraculous that just as circumstances became difficult for him, my life too simultaneously turned chaotic. We supported each other, and God's intervention through this remarkable man rescued me during a critical period. I kept the loss of my house private and gladly assisted him, cherishing the profound impact of his ministry over material goods.

Our sons, Joshua and Michael, often joined Dr Reid for walks with the dogs, Sienna and Badger. I treasure many moments including when we went out together, only to discover when we returned that we'd accidentally left eight-year-old Michael home alone for hours. Unaware of our absence, he snuck into the kitchen

 I'M ALIVE

for biscuits. We returned to find him on the couch, happily watching TV in the living room, unaware that he had been left all alone.

Equally amusing was the evening when Bishop Reid discreetly asked my wife for toast after dinner. While taking it to the living room, she unexpectedly ran into Ruth. Bishop secretly signalled for her to leave and conceal the toast. While I was writing this book, she brought it to my room and later returned to make more toast for him, despite Ruth's efforts in managing his strict diet.

Questionable Individuals

People flocked around Bishop Reid, but I sensed hidden agendas, insincerity, gossip and discord-sowers among them. Some claimed gatekeeper status due to their longer ministry tenure or extensive sermon consumption. Others, including church leaders with the facade of importance, tried to create a rift between me and Bishop Reid. At the same time, others were motivated by financial gain. I confronted a few who grated me the wrong way.

A charlatan 'Bishop' from my hometown was one such character. He often wore short trousers and falsely claimed to own a TV channel; he had a family life from hell. He once posted a photo online of a converted house garage to create the illusion of having a church building – a ten-seater space. Apparently, he called me a "hypocrite" in his French accent. I could have publicly exposed him for profiting from illegal immigration scams that involved fake passports. I could have also revealed that when I attended his church, only one other person was present, despite his claim that it was *"one of the fastest-growing churches in town."*

The most concerning individual was Sithole, who falsely claimed to be "U.K.'s youngest black billionaire" and promised to purchase properties and cars for the ministry. Once, he met us at Pizza Hut – he came using public transport, which was odd given his supposed wealth.

He extended an offer to purchase a car for us, but I feigned disinterest. Initially baffled by Reid's lack of awareness of the shenanigans, I had a revealing moment, when, during a restaurant visit, Bishop Reid mumbled: *"Something is strange about him."*

At times, I subtly alluded to Reid about others, but looking back, I regret not being more direct. I was puzzled about why he couldn't perceive their deceptive behaviour, or if he did, why he didn't distance himself. Perhaps he possessed a wisdom that I lacked. Eventually, I realised that when Bishop Reid sensed deception, he engaged further to discern motives. He was no fool: *"I watch corrupt people; they'll sit amongst you. I know who they are. I'm not a fool..."*[56] Similar to Jesus with Judas—being aware of his actions yet retaining him—it depicted the coexistence of wheat and tares.

Then came the final straw. Contrary to my usual habit, I voiced concern about a man whose presence bothered me. Having collaborated with ministers from his nation for over a decade, I knew their tactics to extract funds. This upset me, so I decided to keep to myself. After significant persuasion, I eventually spoke with the Reids in their bedroom. I was unequivocally told I had no right to question their choice of friends. Considering the potential discomfort of staying in their home, we went back to Bedford with the clear intention of returning.

Unfortunately, while we were away, we received news that made us feel unwelcome. The disappointment was compounded by negative remarks fueled by gossip. In the end, I left and never returned for an extended period. While I was away, I was unaware of Apostle Williams and Bishop Reid's plan to meet me, or of Dr Reid's trip to Bedford. I did receive a text from Apostle Williams inviting us to his service.

----

56 July 22nd, 2001

                              I'm Alive

Contrary to any claims, I did not reject any meeting requests. My departure held no malice, unlike the backstabbing knife used by betrayers and twisted without tears. Abandoning them, when they were surrounded by circling sharks, left me feeling awful, yet God had a plan.

Following My Departure

According to our original plan, we sold our belongings and relocated to India with an open-ended plan. I closely followed his progress as best as I could and kept in touch.

An email dated Saturday, July 30th, 2011, provided me with health updates:

"I'm spending more time now looking after Bishop & Mrs Reid (sort of like a career). It's rewarding being able to give something back to these pioneers of the gospel. Most of my time now is being their hands and feet, so I don't spend as much time in the office, just an hour here and there. Mrs Reid is stable, she has good days and bad days – Bishop's heart is doing great, but his body needs some resting for a few more weeks."

During this period, I frequently shared Bishop Reid's ministry with others. I encountered a preacher who had attended an event in Dubai and remembered Bishop Reid's bold statement, *"Life can be a bitch sometimes."* Yes, that was the Bishop Reid I was familiar with!

We had extensive travel plans for the end of February 2012, including speaking engagements planned in multiple U.S. states, as well as events in Dubai and Spain. However, everything changed when we received devastating news.

After a year in India, we learnt of Dr Reid's passing. We decided to sell our belongings and return to the U.K. on December 26th, 2011. We spent Christmas on the beach, surrounded by coconut trees and the next day, we flew back to England. My main concern was ensuring Bishop Reid's well-being.

Before fully recommitting to assisting with the ministry again, I wanted to gauge if I would receive a warm welcome. I planned to offer him my speaking engagements in the U.S., all expenses covered. My wife and I were fully prepared to support him, having discussed it before our arrival. In hindsight, I should have visited him once before relocating to England, but I was convinced I needed to assist Reid since his wife was absent. Our affection for him was genuine.

Shortly after arriving, Bishop Reid ushered me into his office; the privacy felt reassuring. In our one-on-one interactions, he would often speak openly. Those familiar with us were mostly warm, though a few displayed caution, which I anticipated. However, unfriendly comments from unfamiliar faces hinted at pre-arrival discussions about us, which left us feeling unwelcome. More importantly, I was satisfied he had sufficient support, which relieved me, so we returned home.

Final Letter

On January 9th, 2012, I typed a letter to him, expressing that our relationship had become *"awkward."* I told him that in March 2011, just before we left his home, I had two clear dreams where the Lord revealed that we would meet again, but without Dr. Reid present— and this is exactly what occurred when we reunited.

I conveyed that we were *"eternally grateful to God"* for his ministry's profound impact on us, noting that I had experienced a *"devastating year before arriving."* Upon hearing about his challenges, I hesitated to burden him with my *"personal struggles."* Further, I clarified that our involvement had postponed significant plans, such as moving to India: *"God knows the details of the numerous other sacrifices."* I outlined how foreign ministries would overcharge Western counterparts for events, travel and other costs to defraud them; now I chuckle as I recall writing, *"There were others who were*

 I'M ALIVE

advising you, who we felt had no spiritual experience with God beyond eating a chocolate chip cookie from Mars." On a more serious note, I expressed that our departure must have caused him pain as well, though that was never our intent and that despite our strong desire to be with him, we reluctantly chose not to return.

I expressed our pleasant surprise at the care he was receiving but warned him that individuals around him might impede his progress: *"Fighting for rank and status is a childish game we shun."* I clarified that we did not sense an atmosphere of acceptance from others, and our intention was always to avoid becoming an obstacle in his endeavours. However, I emphasised our commitment to listen to his sermons remotely and potentially attend GGF events. Finally, I concluded by stating: *"My availability to assist you is an open-ended offer,"* and that *"this letter may be shared openly."* The letter ended with the words, *"Your son in the Gospel."*

Sadly, people leaving ministries often face harsh treatment. During my ten years as a pastor, I supported congregation members in finding a new church when they wished to leave ours. Similarly, Bishop Reid extended kindness to me, and any discord I experienced with him solely stemmed from my ego.

U.S.A. Trip

In February 2012, my family and I spent three months in the U.S., ministering in churches, and it was during that time that we met Bishop Carlton Pearson. Oral Roberts had two notable spiritual protégés, Bishop Pearson and Bishop Reid. Carlton Pearson's ministry played a pivotal role in launching well-known preachers like Bishop TD Jakes and Joyce Meyer. Like Bishop Reid, Carlton experienced a significant loss of ministerial status. Our meeting resulted in years of close collaboration. A Netflix movie called "Come Sunday," featuring A-list actors, was eventually produced based on the life of Carlton Pearson.

Bishop Reid's Personality: The Man I Experienced

Sometimes, a few bad experiences can make us unfairly judge someone. I believe he fits into one of four personality types I know well, each with different roles. Not understanding a person's type can lead us to dislike them for no reason or try to change them when we shouldn't. We need to understand people based on their personality type. Things become clearer when we stop expecting them to change and instead learn to navigate diverse personalities. His personality type includes traits such as being a natural-born leader: uncommon, decisive, assertive, tough-skinned, effective, and sometimes bordering on dominance, which not everyone prefers. His ministry mandate required precisely such a leader.

His personality type – natural-born leaders, uncommon, decisive, assertive, tough-skinned, effective and occasionally on the verge of dominance, which is not favoured by all. His ministry mandate required precisely such a leader.

Misunderstandings often arise from misinformation, including personal experiences. Meeting people in person can challenge negative depictions, and our reactions may reveal our level of maturity as well as our internal state.

In him, I saw a man who possessed both confrontation and kindness, embodying strength and fragility. His tough exterior stemmed from a distinctive biochemistry and hidden insecurities. Peter Embling, a former Peniel Church member, accurately described him: *"...full of compassion and love and concern. You might have a tiger in your tank, but you are a shepherd in your heart."*

Rev. Dr Samuel Sao, the senior minister at Christ City Church, offers crucial insights: *"As a student at the Peniel Bible College, I admired Bishop Reid, but I struggled to grasp why he spoke so sternly, particularly to ministers. One day, during a customary unannounced class visit, he was questioned about his direct communication style. His response, explaining that he spoke that way to discern those genuinely called by God, left me satisfied with the explanation."*

His fatherly presence and tough love could overwhelm delicate individuals; however, at his core, genuine concern prevailed: *"...even when I was in plain clothes, the villains would say, 'Hi Tiger' as I walked down the street. They all knew me...."* His humour broke through his tough exterior. At a GGF meeting, I initiated a question with the words: *"I once read a book..."* Reid playfully hinted that I didn't read much. While I chuckled, some found this humour offensive, as it could bruise egos. For me, his abrasive words served as refining sandpaper.

Perhaps God allowed his unconventional nature to help reveal and smooth out our rough edges. I'm reminded of Isaiah being sent [partially] naked to convey God's message, and the rugged John the Baptist yelling, *"Repent!"* John was beheaded at the request of Herodias' angry daughter. According to the Talmud, Isaiah endured martyrdom by being sawn in two, on the orders of Manasseh. Those sent by God are frequently assassinated in the court of public opinion, if not murdered, simply for attempting to fulfil the call of God in their life. Bishop Reid'd love compelled him to speak the unvarnished truth despite knowing it might invite backlash. His apparent severity stemmed from a profound commitment to the Scripture. Although he did occasionally falter in expression; after all, he was only human.

Unlike most, Bishop Reid did not intimidate me. Being known by God, I stand unshaken. Rarely did I directly question him, and when I did, my objections were often driven by ego and bitterness. This was evident on one occasion when I contested his view on helping the impoverished; looking back, I realised he was right, as usual.

Expecting perfection is a mistake typically made by babes in Christ or the unregenerate, resulting in disappointment. Julian and Everton affirmed this during my interviews with them. Julian: *"...some people put Bishop on a pedestal and almost treated him like he was God. It's essential to have a personal relationship with God, and Bishop never preached, 'Worship me, worship me'."*

Everton: *"People treated him as if he was more than just a man of God. I think, personally, they put him on a pedestal. Man makes mistakes, and they had him up there like he was God..."* Following the affair becoming public, Everton stated: *"I sensed the hatred come out of them straightaway, saying things like, 'How can he do this? Who does he think he is?' But I said, 'Hold on, he's a man and no man is perfect'."*

His presence held power that compelled individuals to seek his approval. People yearned to earn his favour, to be in his proximity, to soak in his abundant blessings, and to be chosen by the chosen one. Men, women and children would work hard to gain his approval. In my opinion, this approach stemmed from their misguided insecurities.

Based on my observations, his presence made everyone feel alive and his relatable speech commanded attention. He spoke authentically, devoid of pretence, embodying the hearer's essence while maintaining deep scriptural understanding. And oh! how some loved him while others despised him!

He was indeed an extraordinary, imperfect man with an impressive memory. He could effortlessly locate references from his bookshelf; his ability to recall historical details was remarkable. We once drove past a pub: *"Dick Whittington used to frequent that place."* After a pause, he remarked, *"Not that anyone's interested to know."* I detected his sense of unappreciated knowledge. If we listened carefully, we'd notice he was just like us – human.

 I'M ALIVE

He openly acknowledged being a work in progress, with his theology evolving. He humbly admitted his limitations and credited God, frequently quoting 2 Corinthians 4:7, to emphasise this point: *"But we have this treasure in earthen vessels, that the excellency of the power may be of God, and not of us."* Like us all, he was a student of love, but not the counterfeit version.

I also saw a man who deeply loved his wife: *"...my wife was one of those people who was never, ever rough with me. She loved me, and it didn't matter what I did or said, she loved me. And I'll tell you something, I loved her. It didn't matter what she did or said. Love covers a multitude of sins... A husband is totally to give his life for his wife. Now, when you talk to husbands, they expect the wife to give her life for them. No, no, no, no..."* [57] This is what I expect from a good man.

Final Thoughts

When among ministers, I distinguish between the called and the self-appointed. We had a profound mutual understanding that went beyond appearances; we spoke the same language and were eternally connected – irrespective of time and distance. In regard to Dr. Ruth Reid, I still remember how her eyes sparkled with excitement as she talked about the goodness of God.

Despite not seeing Bishop Reid for a while, my loyalty remained steadfast. Given my connection, John Sweeney, the former BBC Panorama reporter, met with me to inquire about a recording of a meeting between Bishop Reid and MP Eric Pickles, since I was present. Eric later served in David Cameron's Cabinet as Secretary of State for Communities and Local Government. Even if I had such information, I would never betray Bishop Reids trust; his well-being mattered the most.

---

57 September 23rd, 2013

I was pleased when the church acquired a £465,000 residence for him, granting him a lifelong, rent-free arrangement that began when he was sixty-nine. I couldn't help but chuckle when I heard he called the property a 'hovel'.

Towards the end, the faces of Bishop and Dr Reid were a roadmap of wrinkles that told the story of a long, well-lived life. I felt a strong urge to tell that story and carry forward the teachings I had gleaned from him. After over a decade, I yearned to reunite with him, discuss the impartation from his laying on of hands, and convey: *"Woe be unto me if I do not preach the Gospel,"* and receive his final blessing by laying on of hands. In February 2023, I turned fifty and by mid-2023, the urge to connect with him intensified again. I searched online and was stunned to learn of his passing. Though my heart sank like a stone in water, the timing illuminated the meaning of the final words I heard in a dream the night before: *"Never forget what you've been taught."* It felt like the invisible mantle I had carried on my shoulders since being with the Reids had suddenly become irresistibly, yet pleasantly, weighty.

I felt a profound sadness at not being invited to his funeral. I would have travelled any distance to be there.

Surprisingly, I felt an even stronger connection with him after his passing. The Lord frequently brings him into my dreams, where God imparts revelation from the Scriptures. To this day, profound love for a remarkable couple overwhelms me; I miss their presence, yet I sense it beside me. I have a sneaky suspicion that God orchestrates events, personas and timing to accomplish His will. Although it may appear chaotic and agonising from our perspective, as we drink from His cup, His purpose unfolds.

While for many, their departing from this earthly life signified the end, for me, it marked the beginning.

 I'm Alive

Chapter 24
The Peniel Church After Reid

"The programmes used to be so full of life. Today, when the Peniel Church programme is on, we pray it ends quickly!"

– Anthony Kadama.

In everyone's thoughts, an unspoken question loomed – would God restore the ministry assets as He had for Demos Shakarian through a prophetess's vision that pinpointed the paperwork necessary to reinstate him as FGBMF's leader? Many also pondered whether the Peniel Church would soar above Reid's success or collapse into a tiny pile of rubble.

Bishop Reid: *"There were consequences of what they did. Now, it's not a death threat as some people would like to claim."* During a meeting with Church leaders, convened by Apostle Williams, he was disappointed to discover their lack of interest in adhering to the scriptures. He told them: *"If you guys are not happy with him, you get out of the place and go and start your own somewhere. A man laid down his life, acquired assets and then, because of the loophole in the law, you people decide that 'let us destroy him.' I said to them that 'you*

Bishop Reid, 2012: *"...the things that count are...eternal...A building will be gone soon; it'll be burned with unquenchable fire. So people who...think they've got it, hey, it's going to be like dust running through their fingers. You can't hold what was never yours. You can be a thief, but you won't keep it...thieves will break through, steal and destroy. But the things of faith...life...they are eternal..."*

Rev. Canon George Kovoor, Chaplain to the Queen, stated that his cousin, Joseph Mathia, invited him to assist the church in an advisory role due to the chaotic leadership and church management. The website update on May 21st, 2010, showed that the leadership team consisted of *Peter Linnecar, Colin Cleminson, Andrew Love, Joseph Mathai and Peter Ruck.* The ministry team consisted of *Peter Linnecar, Colin Cleminson, Meidre Cleminson, Carolyn Linnecar, Andrew Love, Joseph Mathai and Peter Ruck.* The trustees were *Richard Cope, John Adebanjo, Peter Cheesman, Meidre Cleminson, David Cox, Chris Lincoln, Julia McGahon, Terry Pearce, Charlie Pring, Frank Saunders, Daniel Van Enckevort and Daniel Yardy.*

Initially, the Peniel Pentecostal Church dropped 'Pentecostal' from its name, becoming the 'Peniel Church'. Later, it evolved into the Trinity Church, indicating more than just a name change. In a letter dated April 10th, 2008, Peter Linnecar stated: *"...the Gospel has not changed..."* asserting a continuity in belief. However, in 2010, a church member informed me that the church had transitioned into a *'Free Church'.* In March 2010, Anne Brown stated in the Essex Chronicle: *"... its priorities and practices have changed."* Reports revealed differing views within the Church. Some considered healing obsolete, while others downplayed the importance of miracles. One member doubted the authenticity of the past healings. Bishop Reid pointed out that she once had a missing wrist bone and, through prayer, a creative miracle occurred. She brushed aside this miracle: *"That was different, can't include that one!"*

Peter Linnecar initially adopted Bishop Reid's healing approach but stopped because there were no healings taking place. In contrast, Bishop Reid had numerous verified miracles in his ministry, and he'd often announce them after confirmation by two doctors, before and after the event. On the day Bishop Reid left, it became evident to everyone that something divine had departed with him; it left a faint scent of a dying ember that lingered in the air. A vast majority also chose to leave, their consciences echoing the words *"No miracle, no Jesus."*

Everton Morgan: *"I...confronted Peter Linnecar. I told him that while I was sleeping, God gave me a word for him. God said to me to tell him that what's happening in the church is that the people have made a circle around the Reid family, and they are sucking the life out of the Reid family, draining their life force and I saw the church collapsing. I gave him a Scripture, Hebrews 13 and he wrote it all down and thanked me for the kind words. The following Sunday, he blanked me..."*

Peter seemed troubled by his inability to match Bishop Reid's effectiveness, with an apparent underlying reason. A former Peniel member: *"The first time I spoke to Bishop...I felt Bishop was very down to Earth, but it was more about what he was saying that made a bigger impression...His preaching felt like a breath of fresh air.... Peter Linnecar didn't seem interested when Bishop was preaching."*

Bishop Reid told me that Peter would often make statements during his preaching and then glance upward to gauge if others had perceived the profound message he believed he had just conveyed. Few found his preaching attractive. Everton: *"When church was over, I went over to Peter...I said, 'If you preach rubbish, Peter...you won't see me in this church no more'...he then said, 'Everton, I want you to do with me what you used to do with Bishop.' ...there was once this man with a back problem and Bishop asked him to bend down. I shouted, 'Bishop, put ten pounds there, he'll soon bend down,' and everyone burst out laughing. I always tried to sit at the front, and Bishop would see me and crack jokes about men being 'so big, but not big and round as this one over here.' We'd always had our little banter; the church would just explode. Before I came there, no one used to laugh, but when I came there, I'd say 'Praise God, Alleluia.'"* On one occasion, Everton yelled: *"Don't worry, Bishop, all these people are just snobs!"*

"I asked Bishop how he feels about what I'm doing, and he said, 'Brother, keep doing that, I enjoy that and you're giving the church life.' So I continued. That's why Peter told me to do the same thing I used to do with Bishop. But after going to the church and listening to Peter, I just couldn't; his preaching was so dry that I just sat there and thought, 'No, I can't say anything, the life wasn't there, the fun wasn't there.' I believe the Word of God is something you enjoy. He tried to crack some jokes, but they just didn't come off. After a while, I dreaded going to church. I didn't want to go there as it was really, really boring...The feel of it was dead, and whoever was preaching was preaching crap." He added: *"After everything was blown out, many people left. People I know said, 'Peter was dead and boring.'"*

Julian Fagan: *"For me and my wife, we found the Sunday morning preaching, which was done by Peter Linnecar, to be lacking and not as edifying or challenging as Bishop's preaching."*[58] He further stated: *"Some people we spoke to recently mentioned that they were going to other churches because they didn't feel like they were being spiritually fed. We thought my wife and I were the only ones feeling that way. We didn't make a big deal about it and quietly left, but later, we found out that others also had similar feelings about Peter Linnecar's preaching."* Regarding the continued presence of God in the Church: *"No, it might be a nice social*

----

58 Interview 2010

club, but I don't see the presence of God there in the way that matters. When you go to church and hear the Bible being preached, you should feel convicted and challenged. That's not what I'm seeing there."

Gary, a former member states: *"...the church was filled with bickering and division following the incident...the atmosphere was dead, especially during communion, with Peter leading the service...for me, it was just dead and lifeless."*[59]

When I visited the Church in 2010, the guest speaker, Rev. Canon George Kovoor, Chaplain to the Queen, humorously referred to the leadership as *"A bunch of puddings!"* Bishop Reid remarked, *"So now, they are destroying everything I built over 32 years."*[60]

Decline in Membership

Despite weathering the initial storm, the Peniel Church encountered fresh trouble in 2009. An email dated Sunday, December 7th, 2008, from Kevin Lee stated: *"Peter Linnecar was acting as 'caretaker' during the early process..."* His appointment became permanent, sparking disagreement among a significant portion of the congregation, yet Peniel reported it was thriving under the new leadership.

In an email dated June 27th, 2008, Gary Selfridges writes: *"I know of no one in my church [Peniel] who would trust his [Reids] preaching ever again."* He continues: *"Perhaps you will visit us at Peniel, which is enjoying a free, open and welcoming atmosphere these days."* A year after the mentioned email, Gary left the Peniel Church. On Tuesday, December 1st, 2009, he posted online: *"...my family left Peniel Church some months ago and are delighting in the normality of an evangelical Presbyterian church..."* While it's positive that individuals found fitting places of worship, few, if any, compared to the ministry of Bishop Reid.

------

59 2010 Interview

60 2010 Interview

Ayo Ademakinwa: *"My only encounter with Peter Linnecar after all these years was when he first came to my house after the events, so we thought let's just sort it out; we will support him. I then went to America...Marilyn Hickey saw me and asked, 'What's troubling you?' I told her about the Peniel Church, and she said, 'You need to go back as there is only one leader in the church.' So I decided to leave the Peniel Church...and go with Bishop Reid. I...went to California...to hear Charles Stanley...He asked, 'What's wrong?' I told him, and he said, 'God prepares his damaged tools, and you can't leave the church.' He said a few other things that helped me. Back in the U.K., I went to see Peter Linnecar and confronted him with questions...he couldn't...answer them! I was shocked! So I went to see Bishop Reid, and I got answers! The difference was that [he] gave evidence for all his answers, whereas Peter made accusations and answered deceptively. After that, I was in total support of the Bishop."*

In April 2008, Bishop Reid was removed; within two years, the church haemorrhaged. Apostle Williams declared: *"The judgement has begun over the people; they have now lost almost all the church members, and they are going to go down and down until they come to zero."*

Even up until July 2010, a current church member shared that roughly 80% of the congregation desired Bishop Reid's return. Despite many hoping for his return, it became clear that he wouldn't, and over 600 members gradually left the church, indicating a preference for their previous leader. Bishop Reid: *"...the people have just left in disgust."*

Even up until July 2010, a current church member shared that roughly 80% of the congregation desired Bishop Reid's return. Despite many hoping for his return, it became clear that he wouldn't, and over 600 members gradually left the church,

---

     I'M ALIVE

By 2010, about 200 members remained, with a significant concentration from a few families. Many in the leadership, ministry and trustee team were relatives. Linnecar was desperate to retain members. Anne Brown, in March 2010, wrote in the Essex Chronicle: *"Pastor Linnecar has been going out and visiting people in their homes. It is more about...inviting people into the church."*

Bishop Reid: *"Some of the people I know are there are saying it's so dead. So, I mean, they've got what they want, or rather, they've got what they didn't want. They thought they could just run it, but without God, you can't run a church."*

To raise one's voice in song within the church is of no purpose if God is absent. Only a called minister can breathe fire to release the captives from icy cages.

During their 25th anniversary in 2001, Bishop Reid stated: *"...what builds a church is...the vision of the pastor, whatever way you slice the pie, that's the way it is. If someone doesn't build the work, it's because the person in the pulpit's got a problem...a church has never been a democracy; it's a theocracy..."*

During my visit to the Church in 2010, there were hardly any attendees, and the service felt uninspiring. The only positive aspect was the sound acoustics that Bishop Reid had installed by hiring a professional from the U.S. Apart from that, the atmosphere resembled a dull social club; the glory had departed from the Church.

Closure of the Formerly World-Famous Bible College

In 2009, the Bible College closed down. Bishop Reid: *"...Peter's motive for closing it was to remove people from the location."*[61] Dr Ruth Reid: *"First, they closed the undergraduate part and kept the master's class going until a few months later..."*

---

61 Interview May 2010

Most of the African students supported Bishop Reid, viewing the board's actions as unjust. Dr Ruth Reid: *"We had ninety-eight master's students, and most of them were on our side, and they were experienced pastors and ministries. They were appalled by the way we had been treated. They knew the scriptures about restoration and agreed with Bishop Reid, so Peniel could not bear the criticism, so they just wanted to rid the Bible School."*

The treatment of the students was shocking. Dr Reid: *"...they abandoned them and said they could study in Mattersley Hall...they closed down the library...and wouldn't even let them study in the library. They said they could go and study elsewhere, but a student who has no money normally and to have to travel twenty miles to the library to study would cost a huge amount."* She further mentioned: *"The treatment was appalling; they had come from overseas, mostly Africa and were stranded. They never tried to accommodate, apologise or help the students with the mess they had landed them in."*

Ayo: *"They were disgusted and shattered as most didn't know where to go and had no money. I was going to try and talk to some of the people that ran the Bible School and try and plead with them to let them finish their units for master's to finish their course, but nobody wanted to listen."* Students lodged complaints with the college but frequently received unsatisfactory responses. Bishop Reid: *"They didn't send the details of what they got for their results and didn't mark the papers. Sam Thorpe, the dean, was very negligent... They had no care for the people, but that is typical of those who had taken over; they don't care."*[62]

The Bible School sent their master's students to Mattersley Hall to finish their studies, where they once again experienced mistreatment. Dr Reid: *"Mattersley Hall lecturers abused them...*

---

62 Interview May 2010

They downgraded the marks that Peniel had given them, and the fact was the whole attitude was 'they were Africans,' and they didn't like African students and said it plain to them: 'Oh, you write like an African'....' 'This is African English. That's why we have marked it down.' Well, if they're Africans, what do you expect?"[63]

The institution that was once significant had lost its status, representing the destruction of years of diligent effort.

The Peniel Academy's Decline

Formerly known as the Peniel Academy and later as Trinity School, this once-prominent U.K. educational institution, based at Brizes Park, faced significant challenges. Numerous parent withdrawals led to financial and staffing losses, causing a drastic decline in student enrolment, to under 100 pupils, down from its peak. By 2010, the school's ranking had plummeted to the hundreds. Despite nurturing world-class table tennis players, the dismissal of coach Nicky Jarvis added to its troubles. In 2018, after a decline, the Church school ultimately closed down.

The Trinity Church's financial accounts up to August 2020, acknowledged a current deficit: *"This position will be brought into surplus over the next financial years with the completion of the sale of Brizes Park after the year-end."*

The site was sold for an undisclosed amount and transformed into 39 luxury homes through a £27 million redevelopment, becoming one of Essex's most exclusive and sought-after places to live.

The End of a Celebrated TV Ministry

The TV ministry was another giant that fell. Bishop Reid's TV ministry, *'What God Can Do For You,'* was among the most successful

---

63 Interview May 2010

Christian TV programmes, airing 20 times a week for a number of years. On August 3rd, 2008, it was rebranded as 'Face-to-Face' and broadcast just once a week due to diminished demand. Christian media consultant, Anthony Kadama, remarked: *"The programmes used to be so full of life. Today, when the Peniel Church programme is on, we pray it ends quickly!"*[64] As of May 21st, 2010, the Peniel Church website claimed: *"We receive many messages of support, for prayer..."* The information I received indicated that they received very few calls during the show, leading to its eventual discontinuation due to a lack of interest.

Financial Decline

The church's financial health declined markedly. Financial records until August 2008 indicate earnings of nearly £3 million, mainly during Reid's time as pastor. However, income decreased substantially with reduced membership and the closure of the Bible College and School. As early as August 2009, the year-end financial records revealed a decrease of over one million pounds. The August 31st 2009 accounts were submitted to the Charity Commission on May 24th, 2010, over nine months late and just weeks before the ten-month deadline, in spite of having accountants from prestigious London firms on the leadership team.

Even though it was a minor operation, they employed 32 individuals in June 2010, exceeding the staff count during Bishop Reid's leadership. Surprisingly, Peter Linnecar's annual salary was 30% higher than Bishop Reids, reaching an astonishing £75,000, despite not being the founder and overseeing a significantly smaller operation. For many, this confirmed the suspicion that financial gain played a role in removing the founding pastor.

---

64 May 2010

 I'm Alive

Testimony House was sold for £657,500 on March 21st, 2014, and on August 12th, 2022, it was sold again for £1,370,000.

In November 2015, Peter Linnecar felt unable to effectively lead the church in its changing direction, prompting him to resign as the lead pastor. However, he and his wife intended to keep attending. On August 29th, 2019, the church made a significant announcement appointing Reverend Wesley Vaughan as the new Senior Pastor of Trinity Church, now affiliated with Elim U.K. Wesley, and his family assumed their responsibilities in September 2019. His induction service took place on Sunday, September 15th, at 10.30 a.m. Reverend Vaughan has expressed his desire to distance himself entirely from the past.

Chapter 25
Forgiveness: The Story of Joseph

"...it was not you who sent me here, but God..., you meant evil against me, but God meant it for good...to bring about this present result..."

– Joseph.

The Scriptures are our touchstone for forgiveness and restoration, not opinions based on hurt feelings.

Bishop Reid: *"I forgive them. It's not me that needs to forgive. I think that man's fault is before God. When David sinned, he said, 'Against thee...only have I sinned.' Sin is against God. They have got to try and get right with God, not with me."*

When Preachers Fall

As the evangelist entered the toilet/restroom, a fellow Christian, taken aback, remarked, *"Oh, I'm surprised to see you in here."* The preacher chuckled inwardly. He mused: *"What do you think we preachers hold it in?"*

I encountered something similar. Mid-bite into my sandwich, a young woman remarked: *"James, seeing you eat is strange. I thought you had no time or interest for such things."*

I'm baffled as to why many are surprised when leaders experience moments of humanity; why the expectation for leaders to be flawless? Indeed, preachers battle hunger, grapple with temptation and even question their call in moments of doubt. They, too, wrestle with the *"Lust of the flesh, lust of the eyes and pride of life."* Many well-known preachers have died, quit, or succumbed to scandal, and become victims of backbreaking labour, gruelling schedules and the emotional grind that defined their way of life. Depression, struggles and moments of weakness can lead anyone to engage in out-of-character behaviour.

Crowds crave a mighty man of God who can lead them with great strength. Esteeming humans over God is the error of a novice that leads to frustration and anger when people inevitably fall short. We punish the fallen for our naivety, misunderstanding and disobedience.

During a GGF event on May 4th, 2005, Bishop Reid humbly acknowledged: *"I look back now, and I thank God for everything I went through, taught me a lot. I'm a pastor because I made more mistakes than anyone else, more quickly than anyone else, and God looked at me and said, 'There's a man with experience...'"* Despite his sincerity, his efforts did not meet the expectations of those who sought perfection. Like predators, they patiently waited for an opportunity to pounce and then took pleasure in the misfortune of others.

Last Sermon at Peniel

Sorrow engulfed Dr Reid like an unexpected avalanche, yet the day after learning about the affair, she bravely delivered her Easter sermon that was centred on the story of Joseph: *"So much was going on, and I was a little nervous..."*

"I spoke about Joseph, how his brothers wanted to kill him through envy and jealousy." Unbeknownst to her at the time was that

the sermon would be her final one at the church, and it bore a prophetic message that would become relevant to the events that would unfold.

In the Biblical story of Joseph, he was despised by his envious brothers. The situation escalates when consumed by anger and jealousy, they seize an opportunity to sell him to the passing Arab traders. Eventually, Joseph was purchased by Potiphar, a high-ranking official of Pharaoh in Egypt. He rose to the position of steward under Potiphar. When Joseph spurned Potiphar's wife's advances, she falsely accused him, leading to his imprisonment. However, his skill in interpreting Pharaoh's dream eventually led to his appointment as Egypt's governor. Recognising the impending famine, he astutely managed the country's resources. During the famine, Joseph's brothers came to Egypt, pleading for supplies. After confirming their reformation, Joseph joyfully revealed his identity. He then welcomed his father and brothers to relocate to Egypt.

Dr Reid: *"...and the one thing that I said was that there's a very dysfunctional family in this church. What they want, or rather don't want, is, 'We do not want this man to rule over us.' That's what Joseph's brothers said. But in the end, after Joseph was in Egypt, he worked there, sent by God to rescue his family, he said to them, 'You intended it for evil, but God meant it for good.' And, honestly, God has meant this whole thing for good."*

'You intended it for evil, but God meant it for good.' And, honestly, God has meant this whole thing for good."

"It took them 22 years to come to a place where they reconciled with him. And I said, 'I hope it doesn't take you that long as you're all behaving like a dysfunctional family.'" Dr Reid noted that most of the congregation responded positively, although a few individuals felt

  I'M ALIVE

convicted: *"They hated that sermon, and every time they talk about it, they talk about that one sermon."*

After the death of Jacob, Joseph's brothers feared reprisals due to their treatment of Joseph years before. Joseph wept as his brothers, still unaware of his forgiveness and God's intervention, cowered before their powerful sibling. So he tells them: *"Do not be afraid, for am I in God's place? As for you, you meant evil against me, but God meant it for good in…to bring about this present result, to preserve many people alive. So therefore, do not be afraid; I will provide for you and your little ones."*So, he comforted them and spoke kindly to them.[65]

Joseph knew of his brothers' motivations when they sold him into slavery. But, in the very same event, he saw the overriding hand of God, guiding, directing and ultimately meaning to bring about good in the same action.

In verse 7 of Genesis 45, Joseph told his hateful, jealous brothers: *"God sent me before you to preserve for you a remnant in the Earth and to keep you alive by a great deliverance."*Notice what he said in verse 8: *"Now, therefore, it was not you who sent me here, but God."*[66]

The story of Joseph portrays jealousy, betrayal, and, ultimately, forgiveness. Forgiveness is a product of the fruit of the Spirit. Deep-seated resentment is impossible to dislodge except by the grace of God.

Forgiveness

"I used to attend your church approximately 17 years ago for about 3 years. When I heard that you had left Peniel, I was quite shocked. Have they not heard of forgiveness?!!! I don't think the church would be the

---

65 (Genesis 50:19-21)

66 (NASB)

same without you. I'm glad you have started a new church again. God bless you and your wife." – Lee Richardson, March 11th, 2012

In the tales of downfall, two sides emerge – one seeking vengeance and the second offering compassion and restoration. These archetypes are evident in stories like 'The Prodigal Son' and 'The Woman Caught in Adultery'. The response of the Father and Jesus sets a clear example for us to follow. In the story of Jesus, religious figures called for His crucifixion, highlighting how an unforgiving heart is filled with hatred, which is in stark contrast to a godly response.

Forgiveness entails pardoning an offender. The Greek term for *'forgiveness'* conveys the idea of *'letting go,'* similar to not requiring debt repayment. The Bible teaches that "*love... is not easily angered and keeps no record of wrongs.*" (1 Corinthians 13:5) God's Word is unmistakably clear: "*Take heed to yourselves. If your brother sins against you, rebuke him and if he repents, forgive him. And if he sins against you seven times in a day, and seven times in a day returns to you, saying, 'I repent,' you shall forgive him.*"[67]

Apostle Williams: "*Let's look at the story of the prodigal son, he said I will go back to my father's house, but what has happened is some ministers have been found in adultery or some specific sin, and people have ganged up on him, removed their name from history, taken over their church, go all over the media and publish all their Pandora's box as if they have never committed such sin.*"[68]

The Apostle John succinctly captured it in the scriptures: "*In this, the children of God are manifest, and the children of the devil: whosoever doeth not righteousness is not of God, neither he that loveth not his brother. For this is the message that ye heard from the beginning, that we should love one another. Not as Cain, who was of that wicked*

---

67 (Luke 17:3)

68 Revelation TV, June 26th, 2010.

*one and slew his brother. And wherefore slew he him? Because his own works were evil and his brother's righteous. Marvel not, my brethren, if the world hates you. We know that we have passed from death unto life because we love the brethren. He that loveth not his brother abideth in death. Whosoever hateth his brother is a murderer: and ye know that no murderer hath eternal life abiding in him. Hereby perceive we the love of God, because he laid down his life for us: and we ought to lay down our lives for the brethren. But whoso hath this world's good, and seeth his brother have need, and shutteth up his bowels of compassion from him, how dwelleth the love of God in him?"*69

In the end, our lives are guided by the words spoken to us by God. Only those who belong to Him hear and obey His voice.

Restoration

When a pastor faces a moral failure, it leads to substantial collateral damage. The pastor's family is shattered and the entire church takes a punch in the gut. Emotions surge, and people hastily take sides, with one group pushing for the pastor's resignation, while another advocates forgiveness and restoration.

Given the evident clarity in the Scripture, why do some churches impose severe consequences for moral lapses among leaders? David was pardoned for sexual transgression, and Moses was forgiven despite striking the rock. The adulterous woman received instant forgiveness. The prodigal son's position was quickly restored, symbolised by a ring and a robe, and the only ones upset were the jealous elder brother and the fatted calf! Many Christians criticise anyone who forgives and restores.

I hear fervent protests declaring: *"A Bishop must be without blame!"* Yet isn't the essence of forgiveness the absence of further blame? Treating someone as if their forgiven sin still defines

---

69 I John 3:10-17

them contradicts the Scripture. In Biblical terms, blamelessness pertains to your present life, not your past actions. It contradicts Christianity's core, which asserts that sin negates future blamelessness: *"...not counting people's sins against them. And he has committed to us the message of reconciliation."*[70] Is repentance at the time of new birth more significant than repentance at any other point? If we genuinely embrace the Gospel, then even the most notorious sinner can receive total forgiveness. I'm uncertain of where the notion arises that one cannot cleanse oneself from the mark of past sins and remain blameless in Christ.

Bishop Reid: *"God's gifts and calling are without repentance. The world has a better view of forgiveness and restoration than the Church of Jesus Christ; unfortunately, there's a much more judgemental attitude. King David would not have... remained King of Israel if he belonged to some other denominational church; he would've been thrown out. He not only committed adultery, but he actually arranged a murder, and then he married the woman he committed adultery with. So, I think there has to be a Biblical attitude to forgiveness, and there should be restoration, and restoration means restoration. Why did King David not renounce his throne when he committed adultery and then arranged murder? Why wasn't he stripped of it? Why did the lion of the tribe of Judah come from that line if you believe there is no forgiveness or restoration?"*[71]

Regrettably, not everyone can grasp such authentic love. Unforgiving reactions lay bare, whether one is born from above or just a Christian in name only. The worldly mind pursues earthly perfection, whereas a mind that is aligned with Christ forgives and restores in the manner of God.

---

70 2 Cor 5:19

71 Premier Radio, January 29th, 2009

 I'm Alive

Bishop Reid: *"...thank God there are ministries in this country who have a heart of love and care. Bishop Marc Nicholson...Apostle Alfred Williams...Pastor Ashmilowo of KICC, Pastor Kingsley Appiagyei, President of the Baptist Union of Senior Pastors of Trinity Baptist Church, Lord Griffiths of Wesley Chapel, and others have got together and very graciously helped me and supported me spiritually and some of them financially. If a man in a ministry falls, we come under tremendous pressures at times, and the enemy of our souls wants to destroy."*[72] A pastor candidly stated: *"As far as I am concerned, Bishop asked for forgiveness and they didn't give it, so there is a debt to be paid by them..."*

If pastors feel trapped, how can they openly share their struggles, when people are quick in condemning them for imperfections? Once repentance is confirmed, no Biblical evidence suggests that such individuals cannot return to their ministry work.

Emotional scars map the personal battles waged. Every soldier deserves to come home. The focus on character flaws emerges when empathy scarcity reigns. The truth is that our flaws unveil our emotional wiring and needs. Individuals lacking emotional intelligence focus on flaws, disregarding both the associated pain and the necessity for enhanced relational skills to deal with flawed individuals with grace.

A Message From Dr Ruth Reid: All Plan Of God

Our 40th wedding anniversary falls on 10/10/10! So much water has passed under the bridge since then. I still feel the same about my husband as I did when writing all those years ago! My love for him has never changed. God directed me to marry him and married I will stay until death do us part. God has not changed his mind about my husband, and neither will I. His gifts and callings are without repentance.

---

72 Premier Radio, January 29th, 2009

I honour and respect the gift of God in him, knowing full well that the treasure is in a very earthen vessel.

I have been so privileged to see God move in such amazing ways over the years. As I have stood on so many platforms on a balmy warm evening in Africa, I see so many hundreds rush forward for salvation and then the extraordinary miracles that God does amongst the crowds with no one except the Spirit of God touching them. I think with tears rolling down my cheeks every time, "For this reason, I was born."

It seems that many would like to deprive me of this privilege, and more especially, that man they love to hate, my husband. I do not understand their motives or their intentions, except that I know that they are driven by a power that is stronger than them, called envy and jealousy. Have they managed to harm us? Yes, they have hurt us in so many ways, and their excuse is that we have hurt them, which we did. We have fought so hard for their sakes, as well as our own, to bring about forgiveness and reconciliation. As yet, they are convinced that their way of total rejection and humiliation by ruining my husband's reputation is the only way forward. All the while pretending to love us and saying they are so grateful for all we did for them. Have they done us irreparable damage – NO! As Joseph told his brothers when he saw them so many years later in Egypt – what you intended for evil, God has turned for good, to save many people.

The last chapter is not written...

Conclusion

The enthralling story you've just read was influenced by an 1855 prophecy that forged a connection between Demos Shakarian and Bishop Reid. Despite narrowly escaping death multiple times, he established a historic ministry, a fact acknowledged by both supporters and critics.

Bishop Reid and Dr. Reid believed that God would step in to ensure their ministry's ongoing global impact. Sadly, in the moments before his passing, he likely faced uncertainty about whether his story would be told, perhaps coming to terms with the possibility that it might never happen. Near the end, he died four times, but God revived him, allowing him to declare, *"I'm Alive!"* This book ensures that his story remains alive.

Called by God

In summarising this story, we grapple with the tension between God's sovereignty and human responsibility. God is meticulous in His plans, bestowing us with gifts and callings that surpass our present character while knowing our future failures. He summons individuals, unassisted, choosing Paul over others in the Sanhedrin and Elijah from among the school of prophets. He often selects those we would not endorse. Any discontentment with His choice is a grievance against God.

Bishop Reid had a gift for discerning people, wisely withholding immediate disclosure. His candidness led to betrayal, reminiscent of Joseph's story. Ministry can be a demanding path to burnout drawing harsh critics who are blind to both your humanity and their flaws. In the Scripture, God-called men endured blame, persecution and death. Jesus also faced hatred; He was labeled a glutton, a drunkard, and insane, and was even accused of being possessed. If this were true, why would anyone listen to Him?[73] Sadly, the unchosen often resent the chosen, thinking they know better than God, consciously or not. The blood of the religious boils with envy and hatred. He gave glory to God; they sought glory. This raises the question: What kind of person clashes with God's choice?

The Ministry of Bishop Michael Reid

Rooted in the Word of God, his call till the end remained to preach, teach and heal. It was amazing to witness someone with deep knowledge simplify the Gospel to a level even a five-year-old could grasp. We seldom find such daring preaching buttressed by such careful and consistent loyalty to the Scripture. Taught by God and influenced by seasoned ministers—Archbishop Benson Idahosa being perhaps the most influential—resulted in profound convictions that oxygenated Bishop Reid's ministry to burn with white-hot intensity.

Remaining loyal to the Scripture risks upsetting people. He, as Jesus did, faced accusations of stern preaching, causing family divisions and was labelled a heretic, to which I echo his famous

---

73 John 10:20

words of humour: *"Go jump in the lake!"* Nonetheless, people were drawn to his compassionate demeanour and sound preaching.

He broke time-honoured traditions and built a church that was founded on divine principles with God as the true architect. He recognised that a divine call is the binding force, without which the church would falter. He avoided using gimmicks to create a seeker-friendly church; instead, preaching the unadulterated gospel. A fellow preacher once remarked to him: *"You seem to preach to drive people away."* On another occasion, a woman enquired: *"How can I join the church?"* He answered: *"Keep coming."* Her head tilted: *"So, how do I leave the church?"* To which he responded: *"Stop coming."* Thousands willingly attended, but a few were angered and sought revenge due to his strict Biblical standards.

After 34 years, at the church's pinnacle, the December 2007 musical, "The Father – The Greatest Story Ever Told," was a notable highlight, depicting a tale of love, deception, betrayal and redemption – a prophetic message that unfolded in the subsequent months.

He travelled globally due to his sought-after ministry, delegating church responsibilities. Not serving as a trustee, he remained unaware of operational details, which created an opportunity to sabotage his ministry, ultimately leading to his dismissal.

The Humanity of Preachers

He was as human as anyone of us. As such, leaders may err due to stress, insufficient support or their inherent human nature. After Bishop Idahosa's death in 1998, he grappled with a loss of crucial support: *"My dear friend Archbishop Idahosa and I travelled together to every continent…When we weren't travelling, he would ring me up every week and we would talk on the phone. When he went home to glory, I found it was like my right arm was cut off. We were such good friends..."*

Additionally, during the early 2000s, the ministry saw rapid growth, opening the door to stress and vulnerability due to the workload. Ministerial work is a solitary journey, hidden from the average churchgoer who only sees a person behind the pulpit and not his history of private battles.

Of course, being human, he, too, displayed bad judgement at times, since a calling does not grant immunity from failure. The apostle Paul stated: *"...we have this treasure in earthen containers so that the extraordinary greatness of the power will be of God and not from ourselves."* God used this earthly vessel into his senior years. As men age, declining male hormones can lead to behavioural shifts and an increase in the temptation to seek external validation.

His humanity, lack of support, workload and age, all contributed to his failures. I question the integrity of those who weaponise a minister's humanity by demanding perfection, knowing perfection is impossible.

The Fall

In the 70s, a profound sense of love and unity prevailed in the church. The church flourished under his leadership, with a promising outlook, which was highlighted by the highly acclaimed Christmas 2007 performance of "The Father." The entire performance was infused with a remarkable Spirit of cooperation and love. However, as 2008 rolled in, a significant shift occurred, and things took a sour turn within the church when the years of simmering bitterness erupted like an angry volcano. The aim was to force him into retirement, which was exposed when a judge ordered the disclosure of redacted content, revealing a conspiracy by a group of individuals to seize control of the church. He was unfairly dismissed, robbed of his ministry assets, and eventually evicted from Testimony House – despite his thriving ministry and ending the affair before it was revealed. If there's undeniable proof that God was working through the individual, how should one respond, whether it ended two years or thirty years ago?

Confession and Forgiveness

He privately apologised to those concerned, as well as publicly to the entire church, and subsequently underwent a restoration process led by experienced ministers. For those who clung to bitterness, these actions were unsatisfactory.

Like Joseph and Jesus, Bishop Reid was removed, resulting in temporary benefits for the beneficiaries, which later backfired. Joseph said: *"...do not be afraid; I will provide for you;"* Jesus said: *"Forgive them, for they know not what they do;"* and Bishop Reid said: *"I forgive them."* Regrettably, not everyone practised his response.

The Response

Two Sides Emerge

Among both admirers and critics—with many supporters and a few opponents—some forgave while others cried: *"Crucify him!"* People drew a line and took sides, reflecting Biblical distinctions between sheep and goats, wheat and tares and those born from above versus human will. Forgiveness and true restoration are alien to those who have perfected the art of appearing to be Christian. They cannot fathom placing a ring and robe on the prodigal; instead, they react angrily like the prodigal son's brother, yet the father refused to demote his son, like those who came to Bishop Reid's aid. Of course, people tend to be extremes in their perception of him: some deify, while others focus relentlessly on negativity, rarely recognising positives.

Examining reactions distinguishes those embodying the Spirit of Christ from those representing the murderous spirit of Cain. God does not discredit the one He calls; an anti-Christ spirit fuels that desire. Hence, each person in this story must assess their reaction – vengeance or restoration, help or reject. Against our better judgement, we side with the rebels.

Unforgiveness and Lack of Support

When I came to his aid, I was puzzled by the lack of support he received from other Christian leaders. One minister offered £500 a month for six months to support Bishop Reid. Despite their prominence, international ministers often valued their ministry's reputation over their commitment to God. Equally disheartening was the absence of hundreds of church attendees from his previous church. While some people reached out and were misled about his whereabouts, most chose to bury their love for him. In the silence, everyone's absence echoed louder than any words could.

Individuals pledged confidentiality but later, by sleight of hand, employed the secular media to amplify their dissenting voices, diverting attention while they assumed control. Imagine enduring the smear of your reputation or that of an elderly couple, or your parents, in global media. Picture enduring betrayal, vicious public assault, hate mail, false accusations of a heinous crime, abandonment by ministry friends, and losing everything you've built—all while striving to fulfill God's call in old age. Consider the people capable of such cruelty. Such treatment of these spiritual parents is unjustifiable hostility.

We all face temptations. Even after winning numerous battles, a single loss can lead the Christian 'God-loving' community to murder us despite repentance. Instead of offering support, lies are viciously spread unchecked; character assassination becomes the agenda as attempts to belittle the perpetrator gain momentum; razor-sharp daggers materialise and stab the heart to ensure death is inevitable. In this story, the Christian community's knee-jerk reaction was brutal, revealing a ceiling for the capacity to forgive, resulting in vindictive and petty acts of revenge. Even the kindest can become a demonic destroyer, later regretting their actions, like Judas asking: *"What have I done?"* Many such responses in this story could fill a heart-wrenching book.

According to Peter Kirk's online comment on March 20th, 2010: *"The most informative site about the situation is the Reachout Trust forum..."* The site owner, Doug Harris, surprised me when I emailed him in 2010 to ask if Bishop Reid could share his perspective on Revelation TV: *"Sorry, we cannot help. He should use the same media his accusers used to expose him!"* Other Christian TV stations rejected hosting this 'Bishop' as a guest.

Receiving negative feedback from a big audience is common; large companies deal with thousands of lawsuits every year because of their size. Complaints are inherent in human interactions. However, many who critically lecture on being a minister and managing a church lack first-hand experience. Bishop Reid: *"... critics have never done anything...it's amazing how many critics never do anything."* Like a computer infected with a harmful virus, they are swift to attack and reluctant to forgive, underestimating the extent of God's forgiving and restorative nature. Keyboard warriors relentlessly discrediting someone often suggests mental health issues that stem from gnawing grudges, which manifest in abnormal and unhealthy behaviour. Envy and jealousy lead the unaccomplished to attack the accomplished. The ego is cunning, often masquerading as good intentions, condemning others due to self-condemnation.

Truly, a marriage between unforgiveness and bitterness births treachery when animosity crowds the mind, causing good people to commit evil acts. Certainly, God permits the wicked inclinations and intentions of fallen individuals to fulfil His purposes, as mirrored in Calvary. No human being had the power to raise a hand against the Saviour unless God so determined.

During difficulties, we make emotionally fuelled mistakes, leading to innocent suffering. While most agree the hostility was unjust, self-righteous anger blinded some to this truth. Is this the way we are meant to support one another? May we gain wisdom from the colossal errors of judgement history has demonstrated in how we deal with chosen vessels. Fools rush in where angels fear to tread; those steps haunt us until repentance is sought. We can do better.

Aligning Our Judgements with God's Word: What's Our Response?

When a notable person falls, our response lays bare the condition of our heart. Should we follow secular media's sensationalism, scandal, exaggeration, and distortion or adhere to the Word of God? Should we back the lynch mob by spreading gossip, embellishing stories, and amplifying negative incidents to portray the accused in the worst manner, or even worse, side with the fallen yet remain silent in defence and support?

When we point one finger at others, three point back at us. Paul lists sinful behaviours to the Corinthians and declares: *"...this describes what some of you were."* Our lives contain unpleasant elements, yet we often focus on others' faults, projecting self-hatred and sticking pins into them. We become pharisaic and sanctimonious when we forget our origins and God's grace. The contrasting behaviour of Bishop Reid's supporters and opponents vividly illustrates the fruit of Christ and anti-Christ. I wrinkle my nose and squint my eyes at the irony of demanding Biblical standards while failing to forgive as the Scripture prescribes; this is a monumental display of hypocrisy.

We must not wag fingers at others but point to the Scripture, where gifts and callings are irrevocable, signifying that God can choose and use imperfect individuals. Stumbling doesn't inherently make you evil; it underscores your humanity. Regardless of the case, our response should be seasoned with grace. We fail to recognise that the root of sin is, in fact, the absence of grace. *"Where sin abounds, grace abounds much more,"* declares Paul the apostle.

How did Jesus handle those who sinned? The religious elite brought an adulterous woman to Jesus. His initial response is telling: *"The one without sin, let him cast the first stone."* He exposes their heart in this solemn assembly as He gracefully takes charge of the proceedings; no extended counselling or prayers of deliverance; just pure, undiluted grace from the master's lips: *"Then neither do I condemn you, go now go and sin no more."* Few in today's churches respond as Jesus did; instead, they resort to stoning with words and actions, taking pleasure in others' misfortunes.

Restoration

A comment from an Elim Pastor sheds light: *"I think it's...wrong. A man and his wife have given 32 years to found and build a ministry...If you had taken Bishop and Ruth out, the church would be gone as he was the man called with the vision, and he built the ministry."*

He goes on to say: *"...he should step aside from public ministry... during which time there should've been a group of senior ministers... people with a stretched-out hand for support and to help him build his life again...it could've been handled differently...there should've been a church court formed,...and not letting it get outside of the church walls."*

From most perspectives, church leaders had three options: either grant him his ministry assets and stand by him, or alternatively, grant him his ministry assets and move to another church, or thirdly, betray trust by seizing his work and discrediting him. If disheartened with the ministry, why not join another or start their own, letting the founder continue his work? There was no legitimate justification for seizing what he had built through God's calling in his life. Instead of choosing an honourable route, what motivated the exploitation of a legal loophole? The Bible: *"The love of money is the root of all evil."* The irresistible urge to seize a golden opportunity to remove Bishop Reid proved too tempting for those driven by greedy and prideful impulses masquerading as virtue. As the saying goes, pride comes before a fall.

Consider this: Demonstrating forgiveness could have been a powerful testimony to both, the world and the Christian community, elevating the ministry to greater heights along the trajectory at the time. *"By this, everyone will know that you are my disciples, if you love one another."*[74] Bishop Reid: *"I think that in truth, people, out of ignorance and stupidity, do stupid things... I would help them if they really wanted help."* An Elim Pastor expressed sorrow: *"Oh, I wish the clock could be turned back, and things were done properly. Bishop and Ruth should have their property back, their ministry back and his church back."* His reinstatement could have embodied Jesus' message of forgiveness and unity, leaving a lasting global impact.

Instead, the consequence has been a catastrophic downfall of a once-successful ministry. The evidence pointed to the flawed decisions made by those in authority – the blind leading the blind and both tumbling into a ditch. The matter was handled in a cavalier and amateurish manner, making it a laughingstock. An unparalleled ministry in modern times was sold for thirty pieces of silver. This is epitomised in Haman's story – he was hanged on

---

74 (John 13:35)

     CONCLUSION

the gallows he had constructed for Mordechai; drinking poison and hoping for another's demise, an act analogous to shooting oneself in the foot and destined to be recorded in church history as one of the most momentous blunders ever committed by a church leadership.

Decline of Peniel
Fighting God and Mimicking the Called

To sit under this calibre of ministry and then attempt to replace him, hoping to succeed, is incomprehensible. Though acknowledging that God worked through Bishop Reid, support wavered, and the church drifted, unanchored to its foundation and founder. Believing one can lead a God-ordained church without a divine call is a folly akin to the donkey Jesus rode, mistaking the praises for itself. While Bishop Reid's ministry continued to burst with life, what was robbed from him suffered a slow, agonising demise. At his gatherings, the air was electric with excitement, the group buzzing with anticipation. Meanwhile, in Bishop Reid's absence at Peniel, people reported it felt like a funeral service.

Church rebellion mirrors children rationalising knowing better than their parents. People often covet gifts, callings and titles with child-like naivety, thinking money can purchase them, much like Simon the sorcerer: *"Without the Lord building the house, they labour in vain."* Consequently, efforts to replicate what God did through Bishop Reid failed. The attempt to mimic The Father's final speech was laughable. Of course, many can speak and quote Bible verses, but only through the chosen can they impart life.

Three years earlier, Bishop Reid had tackled the matter of church discontent during a GGF event: *"If a church is not giving you what you need, do not cause a schism, don't cause division and don't stay and criticise. Vote with your feet...the one thing you don't do is destabilise the church you're in because there are a lot of people who might be happy with it. Don't become a moaner... because that's not God's will.... Quietly go away, no hard feelings. Find somewhere that will meet the innermost needs of your life."*[75] By June 2010, around 90% of the congregation at the Peniel Church left due to the new leadership. A called man's preaching attracts, while the uncalled, seeking crowds, repels true believers.

Only God holds the complete truth of what transpired. Being a fly on the wall might unveil the puppeteer, whether it be a government entity, individuals, a power-seeking couple, human frailty or a combination of these elements. We do know that God, with foreknowledge, continued to use Bishop Reid, and He will reward each person according to their deeds.

The Future

Like all ministries, Bishop Reid's had casualties. I empathise with the wounded and urge them to seek healing through forgiveness. Across the globe, I hear stones dropping as conviction grips hearts and people obey the Holy Spirit's prompting; defiance ultimately results in self-destruction. After the dust settled, some sought reconciliation. Had more done so earlier, the outcome might have differed.

Nonetheless, Archbishop Idahosa prophesied in 1996 that the work would continue to flourish and not diminish. This plan

---

75 May 4th, 2005

unfolded when, in 2007/8, God revealed His plan for my ministry that included 'dismantling' it. By 2009, circumstances soured for myself and Bishop Reid, and our paths crossed through divine orchestration. Despite his international fame, his availability amazed me. Arguably, the most significant influence on my ministry, he corrected me sternly on our first meeting like a caring father, and for those medicinal words, I am eternally grateful. Our relationship is unforgettable and eternal.

Final Conclusion

The original working title Dr Reid had in mind for this book encapsulates this story: *"Great is thy faithfulness."* God spoke through Archbishop Idahosa about these events in a prophecy. He prepared Dr. Reid for a time of testing, warned Bishop Reid of an insurrection, and told me in 2007/08 to "dismantle" my ministry. At the same time, Reid's ministry was also dismantled, leading our paths to cross. Later, God revealed that in 2023, my ministry would shift gears. Unknown to me at the time, Bishop Reid would go home to be with the Lord in 2023, and I would complete this writing.

Bishop Reid: *"They can't take away what God did ...miracles...words He spoke ...things He built. They might dismantle them...try and destroy them, but they do the work of the devil, [he] came to steal, to kill and to destroy."*

No one anticipated the intensity of the unfolding events, but it is clear that he was unjustly robbed as the founder of a flourishing global ministry.

The lesson is clear. God calls individuals and we have no control over it. Replacing them and building on another man's foundation while expecting God's blessing is naïve. A failure to grasp this reveals a lack of understanding of God's ways and a dull, immature or unregenerate nature. Evading God's correction is futile.

Bishop and Dr Reid dedicated decades to the church; this elderly couple shouldn't have had to battle for housing when those they trusted had promised otherwise. Yet, in their highs and lows, triumphs and trials, they exemplified that what God does counts. His ministry may have appeared like it died, but it has not. His legacy lives on because the most profound stories are not written in ink but etched into the lives they have touched.

From the inception of the church to its takeover, a cocoon phase birthed countless butterflies, now spread worldwide to share what God, through Bishop Reid, instilled in them. His story continues to inspire long after the final chapter. The story does not end; the story continues.

"What we've been through will help people, and it's good for people to see that no matter what happens to you, God always rescues you, pulls you out and dusts you off, setting you back on the path. It's very important that people understand that God's gifts and callings are without repentance. So, He will continue with you and use the person He's called to do what He wants them to do. This is good to me." – Bishop Michael Reid.

His voice must remain heard; the price he paid is a testimony to us all. We will see them again; a day of joyous celebration awaits. He is alive!

Appendix

- Overview: Church History & Achievements
- Supernatural Visitation of 1855
- Extracts from an Interview with Bishop Reid and Dr Reid
- Interview with Claudius Julez Fagan
- Interview with a former Elim and AOG Pastor
- Interview with Everton Morgan
- Interview with Gary
- Interview with John Onifade – Tribunal Hearing
- Miracle Children: Story of Steve and Tracy Smith
- Prophecy For The Body Of Christ

Overview: Church History & Achievements

1965: Became a Christian at meetings in London and moved to Turner's Hall.

1966: Moved to Liverpool, preached at Longcroft with Wally North, and helped at the Queens Road Church with Norman Meeton.

1967-1968: Studied at C.F. Mott Teacher Training College for a year.

1969: Excommunicated from Liverpool's Devonshire Road Christian Fellowship.

1970: Met Ruth, married in Parbold on October 10th, and moved from Liverpool to Burscough in Lancashire.

1971: July – Rachel was born.

1972: November – Matthew was born, and the family moved to Ripon when he was six weeks old.

1973/74: Ian Wilson visited and looked around the bookshop and printing business for one afternoon.

1974: August – Sarah was born.

1975: Moved to Turner's Hall in January, then to Ongar in the summer.

1976: Started a Bible Study in his home in Bowes Drive, Ongar, Essex, with three people – the birth of Peniel.

1976: November 14th – started the church with Trevor Dearing, speaking at David and Gill Green's house in Fyfield.

[Trevor Dearing shifted from Methodist to ordination in the Church of England in 1961. By 1970, he became Vicar of St. Paul's in Hainault, East London, where the small Anglican Church transformed into a revival centre. National media highlighted miraculous healings like restoring hearing and mobility, personal transformations and launching fresh ministries.]

1977: Moved to a large, hired room in the Arts and Activity Centre belonging to Ongar Community Association. They experienced an amazing visitation of God in this room, which birthed the church.

1978: Moved to larger halls in Budworth Hall, also belonging to Ongar Community Association. The numbers steadily increased, fostering tremendous love and cooperation among members. Many physical, spiritual and emotional miracles occurred due to the preached word. The church also ran a public playgroup and managed the entire community centre for Ongar's residents.

1979: Michael and Ruth Reid travelled around the world with the Millers [Ed Miller] for six weeks, as God led them to see what He was doing in every corner of the globe.

During this time, they started a Bible College to educate the church members in the ways of God.

Also, God spoke to Bishop Reid to start a Christian School staffed by church members for the church's children.

1981: Purchased the 49 Coxtie Green Road site to establish a Christian-based school. In April 1981, they found The Bell House.

1982: In January, the Peniel Academy was started.

In May 1982, the purpose-built sports hall was completed. It could accommodate both the church and the school.

They changed the name of the church to Peniel Pentecostal Church.

1984: Received full recognition and approval from the Department of Education and Science for the Peniel Academy.

1984/85: Joined AOG.

1985: Built a purpose-built school block with classrooms, a dining hall and kitchens. The number of children increased as the church membership increased; more and more people were added to the church because of the miracles in their lives.

1985: Met Archbishop Benson Idahaso at AOG Minehead.

1986: The first edition of The Trumpet Call newspaper was published.

1986: Joined Elim.

1988: The late Archbishop Benson Idahosa visited the church for the second time.

February, Ruth's cancer was discovered.

Had meetings set up in Argentina for about two months.

1989: The Peniel Choir was founded.

Set up the publishing company, Sharon Publications (Later called 'Alive U.K.').

October – Interviewed by Demos Shakarian after decades since Reid's conversion to Christ through Demos.

1990: Trumpet Call bookshop opened in Brentwood. Sir Robert Macrindle opened the church's coffee and bookshop in Ongar.

Publication of 'Whose Faith is it Anyway?' was Bishop Michael Reid's first book.

1990: July – Rachel and Philip married.

1991: First visit of Bishop and Dr Reid to the School of Ministry in Benin, Nigeria, at the invitation of the late Archbishop Benson Idahosa.

1992: Began a church in Holland (Rotterdam).

April 1992: Offering taken by Archbishop Benson Idahosa in the church for Michael and Ruth Reid to purchase 53 Coxtie Green Road as a residence for them.

1993: Instituted the Fellowship of Independent Christian Ministries in Britain (became part of the Global Gospel Fellowship), which includes the interdenominational monthly pastors' meeting.

1994: The Peniel Bible College was founded, offering a three-year part-time diploma in theology, structured to give consideration to academic study and practical application of the Word of God to everyday life.

1994: Saw the extension of the church building to nearly double the size as more and more people were being added to the church.

1995: Started a church in Belgium.

Michael Reid was consecrated Bishop by Archbishop Idahosa.

Commenced bi-monthly 'Music and Miracles' meetings in Brentwood and London.

Purchased an additional 29 acres of land for the church and school to accommodate the growth.

1996: Bishop Reid became a member of the International Charismatic Bible Ministry. He was elected European Director of the College of Bishops of the I.C.C.C.

Bishop and Mrs. Reid were introduced to world evangelist T.L. Osborn by Archbishop Benson Idahosa.

1997: Appointed an Associate Regent of Oral Roberts University ('O.R.U.') in Tulsa, Oklahoma.

The Peniel College of Higher Education was affiliated with O.R.U.

1998: A new site, Brizes Park, was purchased to make room for the expansion of the school.

2000: Start of Global Gospel Fellowship (GGF).

2001: The Peniel Academy teams won all eight trophies in the National Schools Table Tennis Championships held at Grantham, Lincolnshire.

2002: TV ministry started.

2002/3: New classroom block for junior and infant school built, having knocked down the old porta cabins.

2006: Affiliation with the University of Wales for Master's and Doctorate degrees.

1994-2007: Seats added to the church to seat approximately 750 people as more and more came in response to the television ministry.

2007: Project completed and paid for to renovate the swimming pool and put an all-weather Perspex cover over it.

2008: His work was stripped from him and gradually dismantled.

2009: James and Bishop Reid met officially for the first time.

Achievements & Academic Success:

1994: Honorary Doctor of Divinity from Christian Faith University, Nigeria.

1998: Earned Master of Arts in Practical Theology from Oral Roberts University, Tulsa, Oklahoma, U.S.A.

2000: Earned Doctor of Ministry from Oral Roberts University, Tulsa, Oklahoma, U.S.A.

2003: Started PhD with Open University, researching 'Oral Roberts whole man ministry.'

2003: Honorary Doctor of Divinity from Oral Roberts University, Tulsa, Oklahoma, U.S.A.

Supernatural Visitation of 1855

"The time has come! Now is the time to leave this country! We must flee to America. All who remain here will perish."

This remarkable 19th-century prophecy led to an intricate series of events that ultimately gave rise to the ministry of Bishop Michael Reid – a story of love, dedication and betrayal.

In 1855, an Armenian boy named Efim Gerasemovitch Klubniken from the Turkish village of Kara Kala became renowned in the region as the 'Boy Prophet'. His family, of Russian descent, were early Pentecostal settlers, choosing to make Kara Kala their permanent home near Mt. Ararat. At eleven, Efim answered the Lord's call to a personal prayer vigil, lasting a week, day and night, during which he was granted a vision that proved a challenge to describe.

Seated within the modest stone cottage in Kara Kala, Efim's gaze fell upon charts and handwritten content in the vision. Promptly, he requested a pen and paper. For the ensuing week, stationed at the rustic plank table used for family meals, he painstakingly drew the intricate forms and patterns of letters and diagrams that unfolded in the vision, despite his inability to read or write. Furthermore, his grandfather tended to complain, hinting that extended periods without food or sleep might lead to hallucinations.

Upon completion, the manuscript was handed to literate individuals within the village. Astonishingly, he had transcribed a set of instructions and warnings using Russian characters. In an unspecified future, as he wrote, dire peril would befall every Christian in Kara Kala. The boy prophesied an impending era of unspeakable tragedy encompassing the entire region, with countless numbers meeting brutal fates. He cautioned that a time would arrive when they must flee to a land across the sea – depicted with meticulous accuracy on a map despite his unfamiliarity with geography books. To the astonishment of the adults, the portrayal showed the remote and unimaginable Atlantic Ocean instead of the nearby seas. The map unmistakably illustrated the eastern coast of the United States

     Appendix

of America. However, the prophecy stated that the refugees shouldn't establish themselves there. Instead, they were to continue their journey to the western coast of the new land. The boy conveyed that God would then bless them, ensuring their descendants became a source of blessings for all nations.

However, most of Kara Kala's residents, including his grandfather, believed that true prophetic abilities had ceased after the completion of the Bible. Many in Kara Kala were sceptical of the young boy's stories and considered the 'miraculous' writing to have a rational explanation. Some speculated that he might have secretly learnt to read and write, orchestrating an elaborate ruse within the village. Others remained convinced of the message's authenticity, returning to the aged pages whenever news of political turmoil reached the serene Ararat hills.

Biblical prophecies often foretold events many years or even centuries in advance. As with many prophecies, the warning held little significance since the Pentecostal experience didn't manifest in Armenia until 25 years after the Pentecostal revival in Russia. Among the initial recipients of the Holy Spirit's Baptism in Armenia was the family of Demos Shakarian.

The Demos Shakarian family comprised a father, a mother and five daughters. During that era, in Armenia, it carried the same stigma for a wife to lack a son as in ancient Israel. On May 25th, 1891, the mother and several other women were sewing in a corner of the one-room farmhouse, her tears mingling with her work due to her longing for a son. During that period, a great-uncle, Magardich Mushegan, who wore a heavy black beard, visited and was engrossed in reading his Bible across the room. Unexpectedly, he stood up, crossed the room and positioned himself before the grieving mother. With a compassionate gaze, he prophesied, *"Sister, God heard your prayer. One year from this day, you will be the mother of a son."* The grandfather smiled, shrugged and marked the date on the calendar. By then, the entire Kara Kala village was aware of the prophecy, and they anxiously awaited the outcome. Exactly one year later, on May 25th, 1892, a son was born and they named him Isaac, signifying his status as a promised son, similar to Abraham's story.

Despite attending Pentecostal worship services, Demos's father hesitated to recognise the boy's prophetic manifestations as divine. Nevertheless, the boy's prophecy was meticulously preserved for 45 years, but its fulfilment remained elusive. At fifty-six, Efim was viewed by some in the community as a misguided prophet.

Around the early 1900s, shortly after the start of the new century, with no prior warning, the Lord directed Efim to alert the Armenians that the moment for the prophecy's realisation had arrived. He proclaimed: *"The time has come! We must flee to America. All who remain here will perish."*

The news spread rapidly in the Armenian Pentecostal community. Those who accepted the message sold everything and set out for America. Efim and his family were among the first to leave. As Pentecostal families left Armenia, non-believers mocked and doubted them. Even some Christians were sceptical, reluctant to believe God could provide specific guidance in the modern era.

The journey was fraught with danger, resulting in some losing their lives. Nonetheless, this steadfast group of believers managed to reach America. They carried the written prophecy with them and safeguarded it within a church they established in Los Angeles, California.

Demos Shakarian senior, moved to America from Armenia in 1905, accompanied by his wife, five daughters and thirteen-year-old son, Isaac. They first arrived in New York and later settled in Los Angeles. The grandfather, seeking affordability, teamed up with two other newcomer families to acquire the square-shaped stucco house at 919 Boston Street in 'The Flats', the most economical area of Los Angeles. God positioned them within a mile and a year of the Azusa Street Holy Spirit outpouring.

Demos, along with his brother-in-law, M. Mushagian, and another Armenian man were walking along San Pedro Street. As they approached Azusa Street, they heard familiar sounds – shouting, singing and praying as they were accustomed to. Upon reaching the former horse barn that had been turned into a mission, they witnessed speaking in tongues. Excitedly, they returned to their community with the remarkable news that God's Spirit was being poured out in America, akin to experiences in Armenia, Russia, the Early Churches and the Upper Room in Jerusalem.

The migration of Armenian Pentecostals to America persisted until 1912, marking the departure of the final Pentecostal family from Kara Kala, where the prophecy had first been revealed. The prophecy given in 1855 and reaffirmed in 1900 was fulfilled in 1914, two years after World War I erupted in 1912, accompanied by Turkey's devastating invasion of Armenia. In a grim display, the Turks initiated the harrowing task of displacing two-thirds of the populace into the Mesopotamian desert. Tragically, over a million people perished in the forced merciless marches, including the complete destruction of Kara Kala, and another half a million were brutally massacred in other villages.

Escaping Armenians recounted tales of remarkable courage, detailing instances where the Turks confined Christians in barns, presenting them with a choice before setting them ablaze: *"If you embrace Mohammed instead of Christ, we'll unseal the doors."* Repeatedly, the Christians courageously embraced death, singing hymns of praise as flames consumed them.

Efim passed away in 1915, in California at the age of seventy-six, less than a year after the prophecy was fulfilled. His funeral in the Los Angeles Flats was the largest ever, with congregations from his Russian-language church and the Gless Street church (Armenian) joining in. Despite objections to Pentecostal practices, Orthodox Armenians and Russians also attended, many having come to America due to his prophecy.

From this family line emerged Demos Shakarian, whose grandfather had adhered to the boy's prophecy. On July 21st, 1913, Demos Shakarian Jr. was born in Downey.

Demos Shakarian founded the Full Gospel Business Men's Fellowship International. In 1965, he arrived in England, where he singled out Michael Reid in a gathering of thousands, and God said: *"Go get that man. I have a work for him to do."*

[Portions based on 'The Happiest People on Earth'. The long-awaited personal story of Demos Shakarian as told to John and ElizabethSherrill, U.S.A. 1975, pages 19-22.]

Extracts from an interview with Bishop Reid and Dr Reid

[Duplicate content found elsewhere in this book has been omitted.]

Bishop: [Explains being confronted about the affair]

"It was at my office…Andrew Love began the meeting by emphasising that whatever was discussed should not go outside that room – it was meant to be kept confidential among all of us. But then Sheila revealed the truth to Ruth, and Ruth was understandably taken aback. She couldn't remember what happened next, to be honest with you."

Ruth: [Ruth explains how Sheila told her] "Even Michael mentioned that she blurted it out, and apparently, I responded, though I don't recall exactly, asking if that was all she had to say."

Bishop: "Yes, you've said everything you needed to say." [...]

Ruth: "Then, either Sam Thorpe or his wife said something… [...]"

Bishop: "[...] thought he would take over the church, and I said, *'No, my wife is quite capable. I'm not well and wouldn't have preached anyway.'* Because to be honest, by the time I had finished the television, I was feeling so sick I needed to go back to bed, which I did. But my wife took the Easter weekend [...]

But what happened was that Andrew told his wife… and she told Belinda, [...] No person stepped down from being a pastor due to the embezzlement. He was one of the ones who covered up the shenanigans with the money, and he had stepped down from running the money because my daughter had gotten involved and told me what was going on."

Ruth: "He also stepped down because he said he had issues."

Bishop: "Oh, he was always on about having issues.... he's brethren and was from Holy Trinity Brompton or [...], but his attitude had been bad for years, and he militated with [...] and [...]. They didn't like how I ran the church because they wanted power. And because I was getting old, they wanted me to retire, which I wasn't going to do. I wouldn't have let any of them run the church because they were incompetent... Besides, they were not called by God to do so."

James: "What happened then?"

Bishop: [Explains how Colin and Andrew told him they'd disliked him for many years.] "I can't remember what it was over."

Ruth: "It was over management."

Bishop: "Yes, over management stuff. He wanted to take control, but I wouldn't let him. Also, he was so irregular at the meetings. He'd go off to watch Arsenal play, come at the beginning of the meeting, and slide out. He would not listen to the preaching or go up for coffee. It was total disrespect."

James: "Colin?"

Bishop: "Yes, the family was a disgrace... his son was always causing trouble at school, and the daughters never respected anyone, including the teachers. So they were a problem at school. When Andrews son was finishing school in the 6th form, Peter Russell told him that it was the greatest day of the school and that they wouldn't be there anymore. And [...] came and demanded that I sack Peter Russell as headmaster... I said, *'No way. Peter is a good headmaster; it's your son that needs correcting.'* The daughters were... rude to the teachers; they respected no one, very much like their mother, who respects no one. That's [...]."

James: "When Peter came and told you to go to Tulsa, was everyone encouraging you or just them?"

Bishop: "No, it was Peter and Carolyn [...]. The interview went on, and we chatted about things and they made notes about everything afterwards. So it was well planned and orchestrated what they were going to do. Then we flew off to Tulsa, and Ian and Carol went with us."

Ruth: [....]

Bishop: "[...] I didn't say I was resigning; I said I was stepping down for a time."

James: "Publicly?"

Bishop: "Yes, to the whole church. [...] Now the board was there. What had happened was that there were factions on the board and factions in the church. So they worked out how to get me out of here forever. [...]"

Bishop/Ruth: [Peter returned and spoke at the church; Ruth was scheduled to speak. [Describes her last sermon about Joseph]

Ruth: [...] "So Peter flew back from Northern Ireland to preach on Sunday, and we flew to Tulsa on the Monday."

Ayo: "... I was there for the Friday meeting. All the families were there, and they came to me and said the board confronted six of them, and Matthew... was there... a lot of people throwing questions, saying he should resign. But Kevin Lee was very supportive, and... he was handling it very well. Matthew got up and said, *'If you want to know what happened, this is what happened.'* At the meeting, it was all hard talk... everyone knew, as Matthew told them. There were a lot of people full of anger.

... started to have meetings with parents, the committed members of the church... at Brizes Park. Peter Linnecar called me and said he wanted to see me and my family, and he came to my home. I asked him what was happening, and he said he would take over until everything was resolved. He left, and before he left, [he/I] said whatever they decide to do, we will support the church. The following day, we had a call that there would be a meeting at Brizes Park, where all the onslaughts took place.

[...] I asked Peter many questions, *'What have you done since you took over?'* He said before Bishop left, he came to see Bishop and Bishop asked Peter when he should be back. Peter said, *'I don't know, just go for now.'* And when he said that I said, *'You have told everyone you have taken the reign and the person you're stepping in for asked you a question: when should he come back?... you didn't answer faithfully by telling Bishop when to return. So I don't see you as a leader.'*

I said, *'I think Bishop shouldn't come back,'* as I was angry, and I asked him for his opinion. Some people thought they were in bondage, and now they were free."

James/Ayo: [...]

Bishop: [Recounts Peter, Carolyn, and Meidre travelling to Tulsa] "I found out she had talked to Sheila and concocted the story, and she was the one who said, *'I will leave the church if Bishop comes back.'* So she was working with Peter and Carolyn, and she was upsetting all the Bible School students, claiming they were all abused, which is why the Bible School was closed. It was a total lie. [...] was very instrumental with [...] and [...] in manipulating the whole circumstances."

[They stayed one day]

James: "How long was that meeting?"

Bishop: "I don't know, a couple of hours... they met me the next day... their whole thing was to take over the church [...] they said we needed to retire, and if we don't, they will sack us. Meidre was her smarmy self... and I told them point-blank... it's totally untrue that I had an affair with [...] And in the tribunal, Meidre said that I had told her privately that I had. [...] I did not speak to her privately. So the whole thing was very sick, and you know they flew back, and within one day of coming back, every book, CD, sign, picture of me, everything was removed."

Ruth: [...]

Bishop: "They never told us they would do that. We had already booked our return tickets, and Meidre knew that. I never asked Peter when I should come back... we were coming back in 3 weeks. [Recounts the

Visit of Tom Matthew regarding threats] Tom Matthew's view was that restoration is the normal thing. But they kept going on, so he told them they had three bases. One was for full restoration back to the position I was before after a certain time, and I can't remember the other 2, but they chose the 3rd option that I should never go back. He also told them that they had a duty of care to look after me and provide a home for me, which they ignored. Their whole strategy was to ban us and not allow us to speak to anyone at church.

[At the airport, John Andabanjo attempted to convince them to return to Tulsa]. I said to him, *'No, this is my home.'* He said it was too dangerous, but I told him, *'No, I am coming home. This is my home.'* He said people would attack me, so I said, *'If they attack me, I will fight back. If they try to kill me, I am not frightened.'* He couldn't persuade me, so we went home. … Kevin had come round, and the day before, John Shelton had got up on Sunday, the day we had come back, and told everyone at church that if they saw me on the church premises, to call Rob Whitaker or whoever it was. We would be forcibly removed from the premises… They cut us off from communication with anyone… […]"

James: "Did you visit the church?"

Bishop: "No. […] However, they had already decided that Peter was going to be their permanent pastor, and no matter what happened, I was never going to go back. So they wouldn't even talk to Billy Burke. […]"

James: […]

Bishop: "[…] But Kevin Lee came round afterwards [with a letter] … he wouldn't stop and talk. He just walked off. I said to him, *'You're a disgrace to Christendom…'* [Letter: an apology to Ruth only] […]"

Ruth: [Police spoke to Peter and Kevin] "…they wouldn't have done that had I not gone to the police, and I made it plain it was a criminal offence."

Bishop: [Hate mail still trickled in]

James: "The instances of individuals standing outside the house?"

Bishop: "That was Kevin Lee and Robby Cleminson. [...] People were afraid to come and visit us because of the intimidation."

James: "On a Sunday?"

Bishop: "Yes... people would come to see us around 11 a.m. because their meeting started at 10.30 a.m. ... standing in the bushes with Robby [...]"

"Robby Cleminson is Meidre's son. This went on for a couple of weeks. Some of the people confronted them. A guy named inaudible, who was here, went out and confronted them and said, *'If you don't like the Bishop, clear off. We are free to visit him, stop trying to intimidate. We are free to visit who we like.'* There was nearly a punch-up, so I complained to the police. Then they lied when they gave evidence to the police, saying that it was us who made the threats, not them. They denied it to the police. The people here got very annoyed and tried to sort it out. [...]"

James: "Share some of the lies they told people."

Bishop: "They had a meeting ... went through our expenses... they lied about the airfare we spent in a year. They added everything together, but I would go with 4-5 people with camera people and everything, and I never flew first class. And if I did, it would be less than the business class. I was very careful with money; I had a medical certificate that my ankles swelled up on long-haul flights. ... Andrew Love suggested that my wife should've gone economy class while I was in business... [...]"

James, Bishop, Ruth: [...]

Ruth: "But he [Peter] did preach when we went away, but in the earlier years, we didn't go away much."

James: "When did they begin discussing your departure?"

Bishop: "... they wanted disciplinary action. They sent me threatening letters. *'We want you out. We'll give you £500,000, but you've got to sign and never say anything negative and go away, and you mustn't start a church within 20 miles.'*"

James: "But what was your understanding before they did that about you staying here?"

Bishop: [Discusses Bell House]

James: "You mentioned something to your son five years earlier?"

Bishop: "Yes, that insurrection, I knew. I told Matthew they were plotting to take over, and I knew that Andrew Love was around Peter, Carolyn and Belinda. Andrew Love did not like me, and I also knew that Colin Cleminson wanted power. ... What they did was they started inviting my son around for dinner ... Andrew kept visiting, so they slowly worked on him to turn my son against me."

James: "Share how Peter Linnecar began working with you."

Bishop: "When he joined the church, he was a teacher but not a good teacher in a comprehensive school in Harlow... his wife was training to be a solicitor. ... for two years, they had tried to set up a church in Harlow with a pastor, Jamie Coleman and Esther Coleman... Peter and Carolyn from Cambridge went to help, but after two years, they had precisely no converts. So they came to the meeting when Trevor Dearing was here years ago in Ongar after the church was already founded and going on, they came to the church and claimed that God met them. So they left Harlow and moved here. At the time, they had no children and Peter could not make enough money to afford to have children as a teacher, so he went out and got a job. I suggested he change his career because if you can't earn enough to live on, so he did. Carolyn ... did her articles and qualified as a solicitor, and Peter went into selling insurance with National Mutual."

James: "So Peter started working and eventually got employed by the church?"

Bishop: "No, he was working for National Mutual, then he went on to work for London Life as he had upset National Mutual...and became branch manager. I had my business... and Peter was doing part-time with Shane Whitaker, and he wanted to ...go full-time with my business. ...as the church grew, I could not spend any time on my business, and at that time, it was making a net profit of about £185,000 a year, and

Peter and Carolyn came in. For a time while I was involved, everything was successful, although I suggested to him that he should sack Shane because Shane told lies to clients. And basically, I didn't trust him and more and more lies came out, and sometimes they were paying about £150,000 to keep from being prosecuted [by] the IFA."

Ruth: "We need to go back to when we moved into this property in 1981."

Bishop: "Yes, we moved to Peniel."

Ruth: [Explain acquiring the initial church property]

Bishop: "Peter and Carolyn …had one-third… should've had a quarter, but I needed someone there."

Ayo: "…Bell House?"

Ruth: "Yes, the Bell House. So they lived upstairs, and we lived downstairs and the old lady Jackie had a separate apartment, too, so it was divided into three. We were great friends; they seemed to be very supportive. Peter helped where he could, but he always had his…job. […]"

Bishop: "But he didn't work in the school."

Ruth: "At that time, we lived in the same house for ten years and never had a fall-out, so it was a good relationship, and it was very convenient that if we ever travelled, Peter and Carolyn looked after our children while we were away, so they were in the upstairs. It was no big deal for our kids for us to go away; they were always staying at the same place, just that Mum and Dad weren't there, so it worked very well."

[Bishop/Ruth describe the acquisition of Testimony House]

James: […]

Bishop: [Elaborates on donating business profits to the church.]

James: "…Peter Linnecar led the business to bankruptcy…?"

Bishop: "Yes, that was years later when I finally resigned as Chairman of one of the companies and my wife as secretary…but stayed as shareholders, but we wouldn't have anything to do with the running of the business because I didn't agree with Peter…he was employing more and more people, and my daughter worked there for a day and, in one day, did what other people spent a week doing. She said, *'Dad, they are just not working.'* The whole thing was run by Peter, but he would never give me information about what was coming in and what was going out. I kept asking, and he wouldn't give it in the end.

The bank came and said, *'Look, things are bad,'* and Peter was going to foreclose on the company, and he called Andrew and me in to help him…Once he got some help, he wouldn't let us know what was going on, was very secretive and very deceptive."

James: "What type of support did you offer him?"

Ruth: "He would come at the end of a meeting and say, *'I need £20,000.'*"

Bishop: "…he would always have a reason, so we took a mortgage on our house. I think it ended up at £60,000. When it was sold, we had to pay off the mortgage, but that money went to McCartney and Dowey, and the salary I was supposed to receive from my company, I paid the tax on it, but I never got a penny, so I never knew what happened to the money."

James: "What are your impressions of […] approach and operational methods?"

Bishop: […]

Ruth: "[…] is very charming."

Bishop: "Conman."

Ruth: "Happy-go-lucky, high-low fellow person."

Bishop: "Blithering idiot."

Ruth: "He has a type of false faith; that's how he got himself into all the debt, losing his sense of reality."

James: "How was he perceived within the church?"

Bishop: "Because of his benevolence and joking, people don't realise what's underneath."

Ayo: "That's true; my impression of […] was a very nice man, trustworthy."

James: "Looking back, do you think he was merely pretending during that period?"

Bishop: "With hindsight, he conned us. If I asked how things were going, he would say, *'Fine,'* but...he was running up big debts, and I never knew.

And with the church, I could never find out whether we could pay."

[Discusses misappropriation of church funds, intervening when his daughter reviewed church accounts]

James: "Three families hold a dominant position?"

Bishop: "Peter Linnecar and his wife Carolyn Linnecar, and Andrew Love, who is Carolyn's brother. The other one is Colin Cleminson, who is part of the Cleminson clan. There are five of them – Carol Veal, Shane Whitaker, Colin Cleminson, and Simon Cleminson and of course, they have children and Robert Cleminson, Meidre's husband. They are all interrelated, and the thing is, Colin Cleminson's daughter married Peter Linnecar's son, so it's all intermarriage interrelated."

Ruth: "Strangely enough, when we heard they were getting married..."

Bishop: "We knew it was trouble."

Ruth: "We just knew inside that it was trouble, but you couldn't do anything. You just felt, *'Oh, that's not a good idea.'*"

Bishop: [...]

James: "They consistently opposed your efforts to do what was right, including your television ministry."

Bishop: "...they didn't like the number of television programmes. [...] Amy Linnecar has married now, but I advised her not to marry the person. It was only when the grandmother inherited a lot of money that they married, and within months, he was up in nightclubs, leaving his wife at home, staying out all night...the whole thing was a mess. I didn't want that to be a mess...same with...Ingrid, Meidre's daughter. She started going out with a South African. I warned them the man wasn't genuine; they wouldn't listen, Rob and Meidre, because he had a nice BMW, was wealthy and had a city job. It wasn't long before he was out in nightclubs and never home at night and was f-ing and blinding his wife because he was so drunk when he did come home, and it ended up with a divorce. Now, I have done everything to protect people. I am not against marriage, not against people falling in love, but if I see someone's a con man, it turned out that the one that Meidre's daughter married had already got a wife and kids back in South Africa, and I told them that before she got married. I told them to search South Africa. I am telling you he's not what you think he is, but they wouldn't listen. So the problem is, people go into disastrous things. Now, I warned them.

They said I ran everything, but actually, Meidre Cleminson ran the office and used to use my name when I knew nothing about it. Sheila Graziona became my PA; she'd use my name in the school, and I knew nothing about it, so decisions were made, and it was, *'Oh, the Bishop said,'* when the Bishop didn't even know."

Ruth: "But you were the leader; why should you run everything? But you were far too busy to run everything."

Bishop: "I never had hands-on control. They said I controlled everything, which is ridiculous. I gave the headmasters and headmistresses full authority...but I was often horrified with some of the things they did. I only found out afterwards.

[...] But what I found was Peter and Carolyn had a problem with table tennis, so their daughter always had an excuse not to play. I didn't realise that, and they undermined the values. [...] undermined the values with his children and [...] with their children. Sometimes, they took a week off here and there, and instead of being in school and class, they pretended they were ill, which was very unsatisfactory. Once you get senior people destabilising, then it spreads."

James: "What motivated you to found the school?"

Bishop: [Explains the importance of discipline standards and values] "...I didn't like mobile phones on the premises, but I found that people like the Linnecars and Loves rebelled against it... it was just not healthy

     APPENDIX

to have them texting each other...during school time...Some of the older pupils began to resent...doing anything."

James/Bishop: [...]

James: "Ayo, share your first-hand experience regarding your children and the school."

Ayo: "I had three children in the school...All my three...went to university. My son had the best results in his class, and my daughter had some of the best results in A-levels. My son... was employed by Deutsche Bank in his final year of his A-levels. He is now one of the credit controllers at Deutsche Bank, and then he became Vice President under the credit section."

Ruth: [...]

James: "Explain the level of parental involvement in the school."

Ruth: "It worked." [Explains how they maintained low fees due to parental assistance in the school].

Bishop: "It was a community school, church members' children. Some people were faithful, and others weren't...as the school got bigger, unfortunately, people came in who didn't want to live by the rules and took advantage. That always happens."

Ruth/James: [...]

James: "How were you able to purchase the school property?"

Bishop: The school grew...and the church grew; we needed another property. Brizes Park was on the market, so by God's grace, we got it. I would say by a miracle...And here is one of the lies Andrew told. We bought that debt-free. Now, when I said that, he got up in one of the church meetings and said we didn't buy it debt-free; we still owed £160,000. No, we bought it debt-free, 20 acres of land plus the buildings and everything, and we had a 2-year option on buying the others. Now we couldn't afford to buy the other land for £109,000-ish. After we bought it six months later, I wasn't a trustee. The trustees decided to buy the land and took a loan to buy the extra land; well, that was them, not me. But we bought the school debt-free. The extra land purchased cost money, and they took a loan months later. That was not me."

Ruth: "The situation with Brizes Park was an absolute miracle; we need to tell that story."

Bishop: [...] "But the problem was and always will be if parents don't have a vision for it, you will lose out." [...]

James: "The Bible School?"

Bishop: "Well, part of the charity was to train people in Biblical things, and it was always my vision to get pastors, educate them and help them... I encouraged people to study. I believe many of the church people took their degrees; it gave them a challenge and educated them. I believe in education and pastors. Many from Africa and all over Europe came, and the interesting thing is they've become very successful pastors, and they loved coming here, especially the Africans. Many of them are grateful for the education they received."

James: "What was their attitude towards the Bible College during your time there?"

Bishop: "Well, the board and Peter did not want it to go on; they felt it took up too much money, and they wanted to use the money for themselves. ...Andrew Love wanted us to stop travelling and ministering around the world because he said it was better to use the airfares on paying Carolyn, as Peter was in debt. He wanted to use the airfares to pay off Peter's debts. I said no way, the church pays Peter's debt."

James: "What set your Bible School apart from others?"

Bishop: "It was a charismatic Bible College, but I ran it and invited people from all over the world to come and speak. Some of them had the best teachings, and they loved my ministry."

Ruth: "...they said, *'Where else can we go to university where the pioneer, the founder, is there and is teaching us?'* They said that you get head knowledge in so many other private colleges, but this man has the experience, and that's what we love."

James/Ruth: [...]

Bishop: "Peter Linnecar refused to talk to them [Bible School student], wouldn't meet them; they wanted to go and see him, but he refused [after closure]."

Ruth: "You had experience with Colin De...[inaudible]."

Bishop: "They still have not given him his results and demanded that he pay. But he said, *'When I get results,'* and he paid £1700 in the end. Then they said it would cost another £40 to get a clerk to tell us your results. It's just negligence, and it's fraud, but that's the way they behaved."

Bishop/Ruth/James: [...]

James: "Tell us about the support you received."

Bishop: "...Billie Burke...came, and they refused to see him."

Ruth: "Even though they knew him, and he had preached at the church several times, he was someone they should've accepted as a friend."

James: "Have you lost friends?"

Ruth: "Have we kept any?"

Bishop: "...they went with their stories...a pack of lies... it's hard then to go and tell the truth because what happens is their prejudice against you. And I was amazed [A] had told a pack of lies out of his prejudice."

Bishop: [...]

James: "Do you have any remarks regarding the tribunal?"

Bishop: "...I sat and listened to Meidre Cleminson lie for a day, and I could not believe the lies that she told... She had been different before, but I sensed the trouble and found her becoming more deceitful, deceptive, and lying...I see the real person now, and she has two faces, and it's a very ugly face. She feels guilty as one of her sons is homosexual and living with a man, which is...contrary to what we believe, and the other son's a ..., Robbie. His businesses always go bust and run up debts, and Ruthie has a mouth full of razor blades. The other daughter got divorced because she got married to a man she was advised not to marry, that turned out foul, so the family is dysfunctional. Her husband didn't come to the church for five years because he was writing his...version of what happened in creation. He kept losing his job, and she was part of a dysfunctional family, but she always blamed her husband."

James/Bishop: [...]

James: "Bishop, to wrap up, let's discuss the rape allegations?"

Bishop: "It's totally false."

James: "Related to the church?"

Bishop: "Yes...They said it happened 31 years ago, apparently."

[Describes the arrival of the police at 4 a.m. and media reports about Bishop]

Ruth/Bishop/James: [...]

[Ruth describes being called to the police station]

James: "You don't have to go in again?"

Ruth: "Not that I know of." [Explains Sarah had made other allegations]

James: "People in the church?"

Ruth: "Yes, I think so; I don't know, that's what I assumed, but I don't know for sure. [...]

Rachel and Phillip initially supported us, but Phillip was made redundant. One of his conditions for receiving a settlement was that he would not speak against the church, and it got too difficult for him, especially because it was a current situation. So they moved away to Chelmsford, as it was an awful situation.

One of the church members even drove at Rachel in the car park when she had Gideon with her and only just stopped in time. So they went to the police over it, and the police gave them blue light protection and told them to move away from the area and not tell anyone where they had gone. They went to Chelmsford and weren't allowed to tell us. Rachel came over one day, and it looked like she wanted a fight because she picked on different things to go to her father with, which she would send him spiralling, and she goaded him, goaded him until he did blow his top. Then Phillip came in and said, *'How dare you treat my wife like this,'* So, at the end, he said to them, *'I don't want to see you in my house again while you're so rude.'* They said, *'Okay, we're not coming back,'* and that's the last we ever saw of them. In the meantime, Rachel, in particular, encouraged Sarah to leave home. So Sarah went up to Scotland for a week's holiday and never told us she was going. On her journey up, she rang and said she was going to Scotland. I was so shocked; I was shaking. Phillip and Rachel came in at that point, and they laughed at me and said, *'That's ridiculous. She's a grown woman; she can go where she likes.'* But it's not like her; she doesn't normally do that kind of thing. She always tells us what she's doing. We've had a good relationship with her. Anyway, when Sarah came back, she left again in about three weeks, and we've never seen her again since."

Bishop: "I'm just amazed at the hatred from Peter, Carolyn and Colin, not from Andrew Love; he's just a hateful person."

Ruth: […]

Bishop: "Carolyn was always bitter, and people didn't like her anyway, and I believe they still don't. They left the church because of her. Richard Cope is an absolute animal, and I couldn't believe Kevin Lee would turn the way he did. The problem is if so many people lie, people believe it… and that's what Peter always did in his business, and so does Carolyn."

James/Ruth: […]

Bishop: "…they…want to take this house, but what I'm shocked at is the treachery of people like Peter, how they can turn. People have come, and you find out their motives, and their reasons are totally false."

Interview: Claudius Julez Fagan

Julian: "I had been going to a heavy-duty Pentecostal Church…the pastors got to know a Bishop, so they started receiving The Trumpet Call newspaper. When I left there, all I remember was picking up this newspaper, and I noticed a church in Essex with a school. …I looked it up on the internet…the second time I came, [Bishop] was preaching.

They were welcoming...but somehow, I had it in my mind that I wanted to hear the Bishop preach...it was exactly what I wanted to hear...at my old church, everything seemed money-oriented and showbiz, like what you see on those Christian channels with all the crazy stuff. But Bishop just gave it to me straight...I thought, *That's it! That's how the Bible is supposed to be preached!* He had this resounding phrase: *'If you don't like what I'm saying, go jump in the lake.'* He wasn't trying to please people or tickle their ears. At my old church, it was all about trying to squeeze money out of people."

James: "Did you witness them collecting offerings?"

Julian: "No, never. Maybe there was one time when they did it for a visiting speaker, but in the eight years I was there, I can count those instances on my hands....Some people tried to insinuate that something dodgy was going on in the church, but I decided to ignore third-party rumours and see or hear for myself if anything seemed off. My wife was sceptical initially...she had also heard these rumours...we both decided to give it a chance. I got baptised in the church after one year."

James: "Did you encounter any negative experiences?"

Julian: "No, I didn't have any bad experiences. I was in the choir and spent some time on the phone team, handling calls."

James: "What were your thoughts about the Bishop?"

Julian: "...he was more focused and wouldn't water down the Bible... The church as a whole had a fantastic culture, and as it grew, it became more diverse with a mix of Black, Asian and Chinese members. It was a blessing to see."

James: "What about the other church leaders?"

Julian: "The church seemed well-organised, and it felt like everyone backed the Bishop. The leadership appeared to be supportive and cohesive."

James: "Explain how you became aware of the news."

Julian: "We received a call from the church office through the answering machine, so I called back. The message said there was a very important meeting, and all church members must attend. Since Bishop had been away on a trip and had food poisoning, we thought it might be related to his health. When we arrived at the meeting, Bishop was sitting in the congregation seat, and about 250-plus people were present. Then, Kevin Lee stood up and said there would be an announcement, but some might feel uncomfortable about it. At that moment, Bishop stood up and said he had sinned and that he and his wife would take some time out."

James: "Did he convey the impression that he intended to return?"

Julian: "Yes, the general impression was that he was just taking some time out and that it was temporary. [Elaborates on the confession.] Looking back, I thought it was just a temporary situation."

James: "Your initial reaction?"

Julian: "...he who is without sin...I believed that if he repented, we should move on."

James: "Were there any other meetings?"

Julian: "...my wife worked at the school...and she would come back and tell me that there were meetings at the school. Peter Linnecar, whom she got the impression was stepping in for a short time, seemed to be present at those meetings."

James: "What was the situation like after Bishop's resignation?"

Julian: "...many people still believed he might return, but there were mixed reactions. [...]"

James: "Did you ever confront Peter about the ongoing situation?"

Julian: "No, we didn't. We left during the Christmas Carol concert in December, and at that time, most people believed Bishop was still in America."

James: "Were you looking for something similar after leaving Bishop's church?"

Julian: "Yes...we looked around for a few months...but we eventually came back to Bishop's church briefly before moving to Seven Kings. However, even after searching, I couldn't find anything like Bishop offered."

James: "Your initial thought upon discovering Bishop's church?"

Julian: "No one I know can open the Bible and make it come alive as Bishop does. When he preaches, there's a sense of connection between him and the words of the Bible, unlike many other preachers who seem detached from the Scripture."

James: "Who did you know in the church?"

Julian: "From my time in the choir, I knew Sheila and thought she and her family were very loyal to Bishop and Mama Ruth. They had a personal connection with them and loved the ministry. Sheila was the main...spokesperson for the church and also the choir mistress. There was a sense of closeness around Bishop and Mama Ruth, and we felt there was a close-knit group around them."

James: "What about Colin?"

Julian: "Colin was the Principal guy leading the praise and worship. I understood that he had been around Bishop since he was a kid and had grown up under his influence. He's still there in the church."

James: "And Andrew Love?"

Julian: "Andrew Love is one of the pastors in the pastoral team."

James: "What are your thoughts on their presence in the church despite being seemingly against Bishop?"

Julian: "It's interesting to see those people who have been seen as part of the inner circle and have been there since the beginning, like Andrew Love, Belinda, Peter, Carolyn, and others, are still there..."

James: "Some are asserting the absence of miracles and their fabrication. Any thoughts?"

Julian: "It's surprising to hear that some are now questioning the authenticity of the miracles. Given the support they had shown to the

Bishop and their involvement in the church, it was unexpected to hear such statements."

James: "Concealing true thoughts while showing loyalty is concerning."

Julian: "...There's something seriously wrong with that...If you don't like something, it's okay to leave, but to stay and pretend to be supportive and then try to get rid of him at the first opportunity is just wrong."

James: "In hindsight, were there any signs predicting this reaction from people?"

Julian: "No, I didn't see any indications. ...we were somewhat on the outskirts...Maybe that's why we were oblivious to what was going on. We genuinely weren't aware of anything undermining him while he was away. Hearing some people saying they felt 'free' now was a shock."

James: "Any final words?"

Julian: [...] "When you first come to the church, you can see God's work physically in the school and the church. It's undeniable that God's hand was in it. So, for them to say they want to put out the founder of the work, it doesn't make sense."

James: "Even someone unsaved can handle the situation better, extending housing and financial support, even assisting in launching a new church. The current actions seem aimed at consistently undermining Bishop and Mamma Ruth."

Julian: "Exactly. It's shocking to see such an intent to scoff at and oppose Bishop and Mamma Ruth. It's as if they are relentless in their efforts to bring them down."

Interview: Former Elim and AOG Pastor

I interviewed a former Elim and AOG Pastor who later became a guest presenter on Revelation TV and had been aware of Bishop Reid for approximately eight years before establishing a personal connection. He attended a leaders' meeting at the invitation of Dr. Chambers, who was unable to attend.

Pastor: "I was pastoring in my...denomination...I noticed a lack of fellowship for ministers there and appreciated the warm welcome and fellowship I found at Bishop's church."

"I had heard of him through the Christian exhibition...However, it was my first time...attending his church when I met him. I regularly attended pastors' meetings and the GGF. I enjoyed meeting prominent ministers like T.L. Osborn, Terry Law, Charles Green, and others...we started attending the 'Music and Miracles' services...the annual carol service and the presentation of 'The Father,' which was great."

James: "Did you personally meet him?"

Pastor: "Yes...Once he understood that I was a pastor, he showed great care and a heart for pastors. He made me feel special and appreciated, and I valued that connection."

James: "How did your fellow Elim pastors respond?"

Pastor: "...they questioned me... *'Oh, you don't go there, do you? You don't support him, do you?'* Being in fellowship with the founder of the work impressed me, especially because he didn't just write books or have ideas; he put his teachings into practice. The excellence of the ministry, the choir, the presentation of everything and the warmth in greeting people all contributed to my desire to be a part of it."

James: "What impression did he portray during the pastors' meetings?"

Pastor: "I knew...that Bishop was a controversial figure. He doesn't beat around the bush and calls a spade a spade. Some of the words he used might not be considered acceptable in the pulpit by some, but I quickly learnt to listen beyond the phrases and hear the heart of the man. So, when I invited friends to the meetings, I warned them that Bishop was different, and they shouldn't be offended by his directness. I asked them to focus on the teaching and understand the heart behind the words."

James: "When did you first learn about the news concerning Bishop?"

Pastor: "...one of the staff members from the church [Shane Whitaker] called me. His tone was shocking, and for a few seconds, I thought Bishop had passed away. After silence, I asked what had happened to Michael (not using the title Bishop). [He] explained that Bishop had confessed to adultery. While it was serious news, I wasn't as affected as I initially thought he had died. I believe that God confronts individuals about their sins, and when there's genuine repentance and a turning away from that sin, forgiveness is available. So, I thought Bishop and Dr Ruth would return after their time in America."

James: "Was that the impression you were receiving?"

Pastor: "Yes, that's the impression I had, but they didn't say that he would be back. [...] My heart was crying out for someone to take authority over this and call these people together to find out what was true and what was not. But in all of this, Bishop's voice had to be heard, and Dr Ruth's voice had to be heard. [...]

...a few weeks after the news of the adultery...I was at my desk, looking at a book, reflecting on what had happened...I felt the Lord very clearly speak to me and say, *'Send them an email.'* My first response was, *They won't read an email from me. Who am I? I'd be wasting my time.'* But the voice came again very clearly...and said, *'Send an email and reach out to them in love.'*

I simply sent them an email saying that the God that forgave King David was their God, and I was praying that the forgiveness King David had, Bishop would have. Then I felt led to say to them that I would be here as a friend for them unconditionally, that whatever happened, whatever else came out, I felt I was on a commission from God to be a friend."

James: "Did you get a response after sending the email?"

Pastor: "I didn't get a response until I got a message saying that Bishop and Ruth were coming to a house in the Brentwood area one Sunday afternoon, and there would be an evangelist from America, Billie Burke...it was an open invitation to go, and I did go. I took my friend...I said, *'Bishop, how are you?'* He replied, *'I'M ALIVE.'* Now, he will never... know how important that sentence was to me because if you think back to the morning, I received that call and thought he had died, my first meeting with him after all this, his first words to me were, *'I'M ALIVE.'* To Bishop, it was just a statement, but it meant a lot to me."

James: "Did you find Bishop's attitude and repentance to be sincere?"

Pastor: "Yes...These few years, I have walked with him closer than ever, and I believe that in Bishop, there is someone who has acknowledged his sin, repented of that sin, and, most importantly, forsaken the sin. He is no longer with the lady concerned or the other allegations that were made. So, I see a man that is transformed, who regrets what happened but cannot live in the regret, but lives in the reconciliation that God gives..."

James: "Your thoughts regarding the way he was treated?"

Pastor: "...many people I thought were for the Bishop were not truly with him. The more I got to know the church, it seemed they were waiting for an opportunity to get rid of him, and unfortunately, Bishop handed them that opportunity on a plate when he said he was stepping down. How I wish he had never uttered those words, but he did. From that moment on, those people took over.

I wish it could all be turned around, and the world could see a group of Christians in that church looking at what they did, considering what they're doing and realising that they will have to answer to God for all of this. Let the world see that the Gospel they preach about God's love, forgiveness, reconciliation and a new start applies to their Bishop, their pastor.

There was no reason why his wife, Dr Reid, could not have carried on as she was a senior pastor, and other pastors could've come alongside her. As I understand it, she was gotten rid of as well and not even allowed to appeal...She would've been a thorn in their side had they allowed her to stay. [...]"

     Appendix

James: "In a five-minute conversation with Peniel, what message would you share?"

Pastor: "I would say, let's start again. Let's look at this whole thing again.

...some of the leaders that are there now said that the Bishop would never come to the church; one was reported as saying, *'Over my dead body.'* I don't want to be vicious, but if God heard that, and He did, God can arrange that if that lady really meant it.

I would say a court be formed, allegations be cleared up, and the lies... and have Bishop and Dr Ruth restored...I would say, *'If you are not happy, let me shake your hand and wish you God bless,'* Let them go, and let's get on with the ministry."

[...]

James: "When you say lack of action..."

Pastor: [He notes that ministers were aware of Bishop's financial troubles but withheld assistance, despite having invested millions in their...ministries.]

James: "How should the ministries Bishop has supported have reacted?"

Pastor: "Together, they could've done so much. They could've helped the man.

[...] I don't believe that [Bishop and Dr Reid] were naïve and were unaware of some people in the church plotting against them...I don't believe they ever conceived the magnitude of the awful thing that's blown up, the hatred, bitterness and the takeover. I don't think they ever conceived that.

What should've happened was that the ministers whom Bishop supported and gave a platform to... were more than happy to be seen with him...made them feel big and...important...they should've come around and supported him, and it could've been done within weeks, not months. The man could've had a building; the man could've had a television ministry...it could've been business as usual while all the other stuff had blown up…All his colleagues and I'm holding up my left hand too, and he was left with less than the digits in my hand, real genuine friends who are ministers with any substance, any size of church ministry."

James: "Prominent ministries have expressed gratitude and pledged support for his new ministry, but very little financial assistance has been provided."

Pastor: "That is it, unfortunately."

James: "Do you have thoughts you'd like to share on this matter?"

Pastor: "…it appears to me that they have written him off. They have continued to focus on the building of their…ministries…and they're forgetting about this brother. I have wept and shared with Bishop. I am not coping well with all that I see happening, and yet I don't see positive action happening to stop all this."

James: "On whose part?"

Pastor: "On the part of those who Bishop believes are close friends… and they are not helping him with a good lawyer. I do believe he may have won the tribunal…I believe John, in his epistles, said, *'Don't love in word only,'* like people would say, *'We're with you, we pray for your ministry, we appreciate your ministry.'* No, it's like putting ice cream in a microwave – it doesn't work."

Interview: Everton Morgan

James: "How long were you in the church?"

Everton: "I went to Peniel College, the Bible School, in 2006…a student of Meidre. I went to the church the same week I started college and said to myself that when I go to church if I hear and see truth, everything I know I will leave at the door. When I went in, I heard the right teaching, and Bishop spoke the truth. I knew I had to be there, so I left all my previous teachings outside the door and said to myself,

'I'm going to start afresh.' ... It was as if God was speaking through him, and I was transformed."

James: "What did you think of the churchgoers?"

Everton: "...very friendly. As I was very outgoing and outspoken, I... would tell you how it was. I realised there were two types of people – those with cliques and those who wanted to be friendly to you."

James: "Cliques?"

Everton: "It was more like family to family. Certain people would stay away from you, even though they would smile at you. But you always had this feeling that they weren't really for you...But that didn't bother me."

James: "What were your thoughts on your tutors, Kent Hodge, Meidre and Dr. Thorpe?"

Everton: "...nice tutors, very supportive of...Bishop and Ruth, especially Meidre. She spoke very highly of him...in class when she was talking about an article from the papers about the Archbishop of York, a black guy and she was saying how this man stood up for the truth. She said, *'Bishop Reid is just like that. He, too, stands up for truth.'* Every time she talked about Bishop, it was always good and not once did she ever talk bad about him. The same with Kent Hodge and Dr Thorpe. They always said Bishop stood for truth."

James: "Did you sense any discontent with Bishop?"

Everton: "They viewed him as a man of God [...]"

James: "Did you consider the church to have exceptional quality?"

Everton: "Absolutely fantastic! It was brilliant. My son said going to this church is like going to a premier match... When I saw that guy, the boxer, he was sitting in front of me, and when we saw his eyes just open, my son's girlfriend...had never been to a church before, burst out crying. ...All the churches I had been to before never had miracles. I've always heard lip talk from pastors, but here, I saw it."

James: "Which days did you attend?"

Everton: "I attended on Mondays, Wednesdays, and Fridays...Sundays. I used to travel from Gillingham...about 35 miles away."

James: "Did you observe the mistreatment of students or within the church?"

Everton: [...] "... When Bishop went abroad, the preaching was totally different. Other people used to preach, and Kent Hodge was the only one that sounded sound. ...they weren't friendly at all when Bishop was not there, and that's what my wife didn't like. [...]"

James: "Did they try to promote negativity in the pulpit?"

Everton: "No, the preaching was very lame, dead and sometimes I couldn't wait for it to finish. You'd go in there around 10 o'clock, and by 11, it would finish."

James: "How did you become aware of the events?"

Everton: "I was at church when someone told me Bishop was sick. I asked, *'Sick from what?'* and they said he had come back from India and hadn't been well for a few weeks. So, I continued going to the church, bored out of my head. When the news...broke, I was surprised how people suddenly changed towards him. [...]"

James: "So, after Bishop went to America for the meeting..."

Everton: "I couldn't go to it as I had to work that day."

James: "What did you hear about the meeting?"

Everton: "All I heard was Bishop went to the church with Ruth and said that he had sinned and asked for forgiveness and would go away for a time of reflection. But others in the church said to me that he stood down. I said, *'Hold on, going away and stepping down are two different things.'* So, I didn't question them anymore."

James: "Did you think he was coming back?"

Everton: "...I honestly thought he had gone away for a time to think and would come back... [He discussed anticipating their return but was surprised by the removal of Bishop's items, including images and the act of turning bags inside out.] I asked, *'What's this for?'* They said, *'We're just having a change around.'*

...all they had in the store was T.L. Osborn's books, Benson Idahosa's books..."

James: "What was the atmosphere like when you returned to the church?"

Everton: "...it was dead... I wasn't happy with what I saw. [...] And then I found out they were saying he was like a tyrant and would keep us down. That was rubbish because what I saw was that they were all over him. Whatever he wanted done, they would...do it...I was very surprised that they could turn from loving a person to hating that person. That's what I didn't understand."

James: "Did you ever confront anyone about it?"

Everton: "Yes ...Kevin Lee. I said to him, *'... if a prophet in the Old Testament had done this, that woman would've been stoned, but you've got that same woman sitting there in the church where Bishop should be?'* She was still going to the church, and I said, *'How can you have a whore in the church and a man of God kicked out?'*"

James: "I didn't know that."

Everton: "Oh yes, she sat in the congregation as normal, and Kevin Lee said, *'Oh no, Everton, we love Bishop; we're just trying to sort things out and don't want to upset anyone.'* I said, *'Bishop isn't welcome, though. If you loved Bishop, he would be here or she would be out as well; that's fair.'* [...]

After the service, I went to Peter on the stage ...He hugged me and said, *'Brother, I will do my best to preach the Word of God.'* I told him I'd see how he does."

James: "Did you communicate with him after that incident?"

Everton: "No, I didn't. I saw him outside after service, and I wanted to speak to him as a friend of mine and his wife had a miscarriage, so I tried to have a word with Peter, but I was totally surprised. He said to me, *'Don't talk to me. I don't have time for you. Please leave me alone.'* I was getting upset, and I was going to say, *'Who do you think you are?'* but I just thought I'd leave it."

James: "Did you confront anyone else?"

Everton: "Yes, I confronted quite a few people...and asked them what was going on. They said, *'Oh, Bishop's done this and that, and he wasn't...a nice man anyway.'* But I told them, *'Hold on, you all thought the world of him before, so why suddenly have you changed?'* They replied, *'Yeah, but you don't know him like we do.'* I said, *'I don't care. At the end of the day, we're all here to help each other.'*"

James: "There was tension following an incident. Please elaborate."

Everton: "... in the canteen. I bought a DVD and played it in the café upstairs...a Pentecostal choir in America, singing in a prison. One of the guys, an elderly gentleman who used to hug me every time he saw me, made a racist remark while we were watching the DVD. My wife was very offended and hurt by it, but I just brushed it off because I know what people are like."

James: "What was the specific remark he made?"

Everton: "I can't remember the exact words, but he was making fun of the black singers in the choir."

James: "What led you to your breaking point?"

Everton: "...I went to the church and asked one of the members who works in the computer office, Anthony Graziano, for some photos of the Bishop. Anthony is related to Sheila; I think she's his cousin. He told me the computers had crashed, and I said that's fine; just let me know when they're recovered. But then, unexpectedly, he told Meidre about it."

James: "And then?"

Everton: "...Meidre called me...saying they needed to talk to me. So, I met with Meidre and Peter Linnecar in the office upstairs. Peter asked me what was going on, and I honestly didn't know why I was being summoned. Then, Meidre brought up the issue with Anthony and the photos. She said he felt intimidated by my request and thought he was going against the church by helping me. I was confused and asked why. I should have asked them instead, to which I explained that Anthony works in the computer office, not them, so that's why I approached him."

James: "How did the conversation unfold after that?"

Everton: "Meidre insisted that if I needed anything, I should ask them first. I apologised and left it at that. But then, Peter questioned me about going to Testimony House, which I understood as Bishop's home. I confirmed that I do go there, and he said I couldn't be attending both Testimony House and the church. I was taken aback and asked why that would be a problem."

James: "What was their reason?"

Everton: "They didn't give me a clear reason. Peter told me that I couldn't be going to Testimony House and coming to the church without [giving me] further explanation. It left me feeling even more confused and frustrated."

James: "How did Bishop react to you attending elsewhere and his gatherings?"

Everton: "Bishop said it was fine. He had no problem. But then Peter said, *'Fine, seeing you're going over there, you are no longer welcome here...'* And I said, *'Pardon?'* He repeated, *'You heard me,'* while putting his hands up. So I responded, *'Look, Peter, you can't stop me from going where I choose.'* Then he threatened, *'Well, if you come here, the police will escort you off this land, and you are now banned from here.'* I was taken aback and said, *'You can't ban me from coming to this church. Since when does someone get banned from going to church?'* He replied, *'Well, I'm sorry, but you aren't welcome here anymore.'*

I then spoke to Meidre and said, *'I'm surprised at you. You used to love Bishop and talk highly of him, always praising him.'* Meidre responded, *'Everton, I do love Bishop, but we have to move on.'* I was frustrated and said, *'I don't care. At the end of the day, you are all two-faced.'* Since then, I haven't been back to the church.

Later, I ran into another member from the church at the petrol station, and she asked, *'Everton, I haven't seen you at the church for a while. What's going on?'* I replied, *'Didn't you know? I've been banned.'* Surprised, She asked, *'Oh no, who banned you?'* I told her, *'Peter Linnecar banned me.'* She reacted, *'Oh no, Peter. He is so nice to do that.'* I retorted, *'If I wasn't banned, where would I be now? I would be in church.'* She admitted, *'Yeah, you've got a point.'*

I also spoke to Kevin's daughter and told her about the situation. She was shocked. I simply said, *'The wolves in sheep's clothing, love.'"*

James: "What did you observe about Peter?"

Everton: "...Peter is like a wolf in sheep's clothing. He puts on a nice facade, but deep down, he doesn't...like people...some individuals didn't seem to like me simply because I was outgoing and made friends with the Bishop.

... Some people felt threatened by me because I wasn't afraid to speak my mind. I didn't tolerate the mistreatment of students...there was a student from Ghana who was struggling because his wife had left him with their daughter, and he was having financial difficulties paying his fees. When he sought help from [?], she treated him terribly, degrading him in the process. I felt that if it were me in his shoes, they wouldn't dare treat me that way, knowing that I understood the system better being born in this country. But because these students were from overseas and unfamiliar with how things worked here, they were taken advantage of.

Similar situations also happened at Brizes Park with Ian Beale. During social events with church members, they park their cars outside Ian's house. I often went there to visit the students as well."

James: "So, where was Ian hosting these dinners?"

Everton: "He would host these dinners in his flat upstairs, which was on the same floor as the student's area at Brizes Park, where the school was located. His part of the floor was blocked off from the rest. My wife and I would come there and prepare meals because we knew some students were not working and had little money. We'd have a big eat-up, and the aroma of the jerk chicken we brought would make Ian comment on how lovely it smelled.

I found it puzzling that he wouldn't invite the students to join these meals either. When I asked some students about it, they said he never did that; he kept them at arm's length and didn't…interact with them except to tell them what they couldn't do. On the other hand, he would have dinner parties with church members.

… Church members would park their cars right in front of the building, but Ian would tell me to park my car on the other side of the field. I stood my ground and refused, stating that if the church members could park there, I could park there, too. The students were surprised I had the audacity to say that to him."

James: "I want to clarify – the students weren't invited to the meals intentionally?"

Everton: "That's right. Back home, we have a saying that a ghost knows who to scare, but I wasn't intimidated by them, especially since I've had a tough life and faced challenging situations. Those middle-class people or those who act like it don't scare me."

James: "What are your feelings regarding Bishop Reid's treatment?"

Everton: "The way Bishop Reid has been treated…opened my eyes to see that those who did this cannot truly be Christians. A genuine Christian is supposed to be patient, forgiving and supportive, especially when someone is down. Instead of offering a helping hand and encouragement, they kept kicking him while he was down. It hurt me deeply to witness that. Bishop Reid and Mamma Ruth are like my parents, and if someone treated my parents like that, I would be devastated."

James: "It's hard to watch unfair treatment, especially among those serving in God's name."

Everton: "Exactly. They are doing God's work, and they deserve better treatment."

James: "Upon discovering the significant value of the church property, how did this change your perspective?"

Everton: "...it made me realise that money was likely a driving factor behind their actions.... their motive wasn't about caring for the man of God or the spiritual work he was doing, but more about acquiring wealth. That realisation was troubling."

James: "It's disheartening to think financial motives may have influenced Bishop Reid and Mamma Ruth's treatment."

Everton: "It was painful to witness such malicious tactics used against them...The whole experience has shaken my faith in those who claim to follow Christ while acting hurtfully and deceitfully."

James: "I understand your scepticism about their sincerity. It's crucial to uphold our values, even with disappointments."

Everton: "You're right. I'll continue to support those who genuinely uphold the true teachings of Christianity and treat others with love, compassion and forgiveness."

James: "Do they continue sending you letters in an attempt to bring you back?"

Everton: "They still emailed me after banning me, but the people who wrote to me did not know I was banned. After all this, I asked Meidre to write a letter to me confirming the ban. I even approached the charity board, and they requested written proof to take action, as they are not allowed to ban people from attending church. However, Meidre would not give it to me each time, and eventually, she told me I was not banned. But I reminded her that she had instructed the ushers to escort me off the premises if I were to come. During the meeting, it seemed they had already decided to ban me. God is watching, as they are hypocrites and racists. My wife had a feeling about them and sensed their true intentions. They only want people there for their money..."

James: "On your first visit, was there a lot of activity and excitement in the air?"

Everton: "Yes, initially, there was a lot of excitement and activity. But after some time, many people left, including those I know who said that Peter, presumably a leader or pastor, had become dull and uninteresting. I discovered that Peter surrounds himself with other pastors, placing them in the forefront while staying in the background, making it difficult for anyone to reach him directly. [...]"

James: "What were your thoughts when people used to attend?"

Everton: "I discovered when I started coming late to the church that some individuals from the church, like Kevin Lee and others, would stand outside Testimony House...and take pictures of people entering the house. This made many people coming to the church feel intimidated. I remember one person saying to me that he felt fearful because they knew where he lived, and he didn't know what they might do...I told him I didn't care about their actions and would come to the house and smile at them. I had nothing to hide from them because my fear was of God, not of man. [...] a car followed me when I came here at night, but I stopped, and the car went away...

...I always confronted them and stayed firm. They didn't like the fact that I was too friendly with Bishop. Once, we were in a class, and when Bishop entered and asked how we were doing, I enthusiastically shouted, *'Oh, Bishop!'* I then asked him if he could be my mentor, to which he responded positively, telling me to keep coming to the church. Others criticised me for speaking to him in such a manner, but I saw him as a man doing God's work. People treated him like he was more than just a man of God. But when everything changed, and they turned on him, they seemed to forget that he was still just a man of God like anyone else."

Interview: Gary

James: "What were your initial thoughts when you arrived?"

Gary: "...I was taken aback in a good way...something happened to me. The preaching was full of life, different from my previous experiences, where I used to fall asleep. Most churches felt like social clubs to me. I went once, then again ...and I found joy again, which I had lost."

James: "So you continued going after that?"

Gary: "Yes, I finished with my ex-girlfriend, quit smoking and felt like God delivered me. I started attending Peniel regularly. I had asked God for a sign ...From then on, every Sunday ...The messages were challenging ... there was always a "wow" factor as I had never heard preaching like that before. It brought life back to me, and I felt alive inside. I observed others around me during the services and often felt they weren't fully engaged or truly listening."

James: "What were your observations about the people around Bishop (presumably the church leader)?"

Gary: "Peter, and possibly Andrew Love, seemed distant and disengaged during Bishop's preaching. When I spoke to these individuals, it felt like they weren't truly born again but rather pretending or not fully embracing their faith. Their lives didn't reflect a genuine Christian commitment."

James: "Did you ever speak to Bishop?"

Gary: "Yes, I patted Bishop on the shoulder once after a service when I went to get tea and said to him, *'Hi brother, if you're frustrated, imagine God's frustration.'* But he responded by saying that God doesn't get frustrated. I agreed with him, but I still felt some frustration in him, considering he had to preach to the same faces week in and week out. He knew this too, as one Sunday morning, he said, *'Trouble with you lot is most of you are religious; you're not listening, you never have life.'* That statement resonated with me."

James: "What year did you start going?"

Gary: "I started attending from 2005 to 2007. I eventually..., not because of the ministry itself, but due to issues with the people there. I couldn't connect with most of them, and it became difficult for me to stay."

James: "Okay, you heard what happened to Bishop. How did you hear about it, and what was your first impression?"

Gary: "... I had already left the church...about two months before the incident occurred. My mother called me one day and mentioned that Bishop Reid had committed adultery. At first, I brushed it off, thinking it couldn't be true. But then I called someone from Peniel... and they confirmed the news. I was genuinely shocked and felt a sense of emptiness inside. I admired Bishop's preaching and felt I had finally found someone who preached the truth with life and sincerity. It was like suddenly losing him, and I couldn't help but feel hurt and emotional...After processing the news, I reminded myself that God is a God of forgiveness and restoration." [Describes how the church lost vitality in the absence of Reid.]

James: "So, this was after everything had happened?"

Gary: "...I honestly told them that I wouldn't be coming back because there was nothing left for me there....one of them agreed with me, saying that they also felt that the church had become more of a social club and had forgotten its true purpose, which was about the ministry."

James: "So, you attended just one service, and that was it?"

Gary: "Yes, that one service was enough for me. After that, I tried to find them, but I knew they had gone to America."

James: "You didn't think they were still here?"

Gary: "No, I had no idea what was happening with them ...I started watching their videos on YouTube, and one day I found out they were back. I was...delighted by the news. I immediately emailed Ruth, expressing my joy at their return. She invited me to their house on Sunday morning, and it was fantastic.... I felt reconnected again. The preaching was the same...When I walked in, I greeted Bishop, and he replied, *"I'm alive."*"

James: "Did you have any bad experiences with people from the church before or after leaving? Did anyone try to call you and get you back?"

Gary: "No, I had a good friend from the church...I called them to meet up, but they asked if there was a particular reason why I wanted to come around. They knew I had been attending Bishop's church, and I told them I wanted to talk about what was going on. We had a conversation on the phone, and they told me they were just listening to what was true, referring to Peniel. I disagreed with them, stating that they were listening to liars because what they were hearing and saying about the situation was exaggerated and not accurate. We had a disagreement, and they just said, *"Take care, might see you and* that was it."

James: "Is there anything else you want to say or share? How do you feel about the way Bishop has been treated?"

Gary: "I'm...disgusted to the core. Like some other people, I became very angry. I was ready to go there, all guns blazing. I was especially upset the night he got arrested by the police at 4 a.m. These people have a lot to answer for, but I trust that God will handle it....and I'm thankful to be where I am now... looking back, I realise that I never really fit into any of the churches I attended in the past. I always felt like the black sheep and was never truly happy with the teachings I received."

James: "Your testimony is powerful because you searched out for Bishop."

Gary: "Yes, I was desperate to find him again because, for me, there was nobody else. I had been to various churches in Kent before coming to Peniel, searching for something more meaningful, but it was all empty, with just some singing and forgettable preaching. For me, this is life; this is great. Since returning to this place, it feels like my life is just beginning, and I've entered a whole new chapter. I come from a background of a lot of hurt and a challenging upbringing, but now I know that I have a future in God. It brings joy to my heart to trust Him and say, *'Thank you, Lord.'*"

Interview: John Onifade – Tribunal Hearing

John: "It was scheduled for five days, from the end of November 2009 to 31st December. Four days were completed, and during the preliminary hearing, Peniel requested two days. However, I refused because starting with two days could lead to a discrimination issue, as traditionally, the respondent should begin. I wanted five days to have enough time to call my witnesses, which I planned to bring between 4 and 6 [witnesses].

During the process leading to the tribunal, I requested the other party's notes of the board meetings. When they sent the notes, crucial parts were blacked out, possibly to hide incriminating evidence. I didn't alert them to this fact. When we reached the tribunal, I asked them to bring the original unredacted documents to compare. My letter to the tribunal expressed my distrust in their conduct and word.

In a tribunal, the bundles of evidence are mainly provided by the Peniel Church since they hold the bulk of the evidence. The tribunal acts as a court of evidence. If a party produces evidence against itself, it becomes clear they have something to hide. In our case, the evidence contradicted their claim that the Bishop was present, revealing that he had already been dismissed before being suspended. Unfortunately, we couldn't call any of our witnesses."

James: "So, out of the five days, how many did you have?"

John: "We were given four days, with one day set aside for the judge to take a holiday. This left us only three days to cross-examine the witnesses from the respondents. Even during the cross-examination, we faced interruptions and pressure from the judge to hurry up."

James: "You mentioned one person who agreed with you, correct?"

John: "Yes, it's interesting because when you are cross-examining somebody, and you have to call into question their integrity, and they have been forced to lie or have not been shown the full facts of the issue, and then when those full facts are brought to them...and they decide to agree with you! It's remarkable. Some of the questions I asked him, no other tribunal I have been to..., has had such responses.

When you are cross-examining someone from the other side, and that person is agreeing with you, what is there to argue?... And you ask the person, *'With the evidence you are seeing, which you have never seen before, would you still have dismissed this person?'* And the person responded, *'No! I wouldn't have advised it.'*

And you ask the person, *'In your...judgement, do you think all the people involved in this issue have been treated equally?'* And the person unequivocally said, *'No!'"*

James: "Who was this person?"

John: "That person was John Shelton; you could see the pain in that man's heart. It's easy to read because he was just brought there to do something against his own judgement.... And when people like that start to agree with you and doubt the people who brought him there, we shouldn't even dwell on it because others would agree that this was fixed.

John was on the board, Chairman of the first hearing of the disciplinary board, and he never saw the letters saying Bishop was not well; he would not have gone ahead in absence with the board."

James: "That's very interesting..."

John: "You have a policy as an employer, and you do not follow your... policy...then there is no case. And the most intriguing part of it was when the Bishop, as the claimant, was on the stand, we looked at the area that he was being accused of breaching. He breached the terms of the policy, and it was the judge himself who brought to our attention that something about sex should not normally be in Christian literature or statements of faith."

James: "And this is in the minutes?"

John: [Describes how Bishop investigated the Statement of Faith, discovered a new clause that had been added, and was subsequently dismissed because of it.]

James: "That's very interesting!"

John: [Explains Peniel's non-denial of adding the new clause.]

"When I got the judgement, I spoke to the Bishop from Cameroon, and in anger, I told him, *'Do not look at me.'* I still feel bitter and wept because I worked hard for that. I told him this is not down to anybody; this is the result of your legal system, your British justice. That was how it was."

 Appendix

Miracle Children: Story of Steve and Tracy Smith

By Steve Smith

My wife and I consulted infertility specialists in the U.S.A., Harley Street (U.K.), and Buckhurst Hill clinics. They confirmed severe tube blockages and deemed conception impossible. Seeking an alternative, we visited Professor Robert Winston, a fertility pioneer with over 40 years of experience. He enrolled my wife on an 18 to 24-month waiting list. In the meantime, Bishop Reid prayed for us and told us he saw us with children, so we waited, but nothing happened.

About 6 months later, the clinic called to inform us that we could start the treatment. We viewed it as a divine intervention that placed us at the top of the list for a 3-month treatment.

We were instructed to wait for my wife's third menstrual cycle, then contact the clinic for egg removal, initiating the treatment. Despite the due date being Friday, there was no progress. Following a series of uneventful days, she reached out to the clinic on the next Friday, being reassured to wait. After another cycle, she was advised to visit for a check-up if there were no changes by Monday. On that Monday, during the check-up, it was discovered that the reason for the delay in starting the treatment was due to her being pregnant already!

Three specialists had all concluded that she couldn't conceive, a diagnosis affirmed by Professor Winston. She was even undergoing treatment to prevent egg production. However, it seemed God defied their assessments remarkably, acting through Bishop Reid. On the day he prayed for us, he explicitly stated, *"I see you with one child, then another, and eventually six,"* using those exact words. Aaron was born on January 2nd, 1996 and Jordan was born in July 1998, both outstanding individuals.

Nevertheless, the Bishop's words were striking. He mentioned one child, then another – an unusual phrasing. We soon had two children, just as he had said. I had complete faith that we'd have six had I not opted for a vasectomy to eliminate any risk.

I witnessed many miracles at Peniel, affirming the Bishop's divine call. We were long-time attendees, who brought many others to the church and cherished Ruth.

Excerpts from 'PROPHECY FOR THE BODY OF CHRIST.'
By Bishop Michael Reid
[Recorded on Sunday September 12th, 2010]

I want to tell you something that's going to happen. He's going to choose very specific people to do specific tasks, and it's going be those who are prepared to give up their… ambition, their…plans, their… desires, and yield to him. That's going to demand forgetting the past, forgetting what you know and going for the future. Those will be choice vessels. God always chooses choice vessels. It doesn't take many people for God to move.

God spoke to me; I've seen angelic visitations. I know when God comes. I know when He's ready to come. I know when He can just blow very gently, and a mighty wind comes through the place. I know when He can transform people, I know when His power is exhibited, and I know His keeping power. I know His purpose, and I saw it far off. I went up into heaven and saw as it were the beginning of time, and I heard the very Word of God as He sent it forth from His heart in all creation, and I heard Him speak. I was there and beheld what He said, and I saw that as He spoke the Word, the thing came to life, for He spoke it from the end of eternity, the beginning of eternity, the very centre of eternity. He just spoke the Word, and that which was nothing became something; out of nought, He spoke everything.

I beheld, and He spoke to the winds. He spoke the winds to blow, and they blew across the face of the deep, and He […] everything by His Word. I saw it in the […] I wondered. He divided night and day, He divided the sea and the land, and then He spoke every being in the

 APPENDIX

creation, every form, every flower, every plan, everything came from His heart. He saw it, beheld it and spoke it. I marvelled at the wonder of my God and what He said.

Then I saw His plan from all eternity to bring it back, fallen man to the place where He desired him to be, and I saw He raised up [...] people of the family. I saw and beheld. I beheld one like the Son of man. I know when I beheld Him, I saw He was the Risen one. His hair was as white as snow. His eyes were like a flaming fire. As I looked upon His face, I saw it as the bright sunshine. The glory of God was all around. When I saw and looked up into His eyes, I saw the burning love of God come forth. I was in His arms. He held me so close. I beheld Him, the Son of Man, the Son of God. He spoke to me. He sent me. He told me the things to come and the things that have been. He showed me from creation to eternity that I might know from whence I came and where I go. He showed me the steps everyone, and He declared it.

From this day, He's beginning in the Earth a new thing. I heard the winds blow, I saw His Word, and I saw everything become a very substance, and when He spoke, it was as though a substance came from His mouth as the faith of that Word created. He's come to establish, He's come to cast down. He's come to make plain, He's come. It was like a bright light that came from His mouth, and I saw in that light a sword, and that sword went forth, it cut down, it cleared out, yet it created, it established, it brought forth a people.

I began to look and see from all corners of the Earth a people arise; they were dressed in white robes, they had within their hand a palm, they waved, they shouted, they sang, the lion of the Tribe of Judah has prevailed. They gazed upon Him. They gave all glory unto Him. I looked, and there was a throne set up in the heavens, one like unto the Son of man sat upon the throne. He looked, and it pleased His heart that what was being established was always in His purpose. The people came; they came like a multitude from the north to south, east, and the [west]. He'd established His purpose in the Earth.

Then I saw the cherubim. The cherubim [...] who control all the seasons on the Earth, they blew with a mighty sound. When they blew with a trumpet, there was one like unto the Son of man who began to descend. When He came, I saw the multitudes caught up as a cloud to Him ever to be with Him. Then I saw the City, that great City, come down out of heaven from God. I saw the heavens rolled up as a scroll. I saw the Earth burned with unquenchable fire. Lo and behold, I saw a new Heaven and a new Earth. The Lord established His people on the new Earth. The Bride of Christ came down adorned with such beauty. They came down to Earth and I beheld him from all eternity. His purpose was accomplished. I wondered, and I say, Lord, how long? He said it's not for you to know, but it shall be even as I declared it. It shall be, but hear the sound of the wind, see the signs in the heaven and the signs on the Earth, for it declares the time is sure, the time is near. It shall come. It shall be. Nothing shall stop it [speaks in tongues].

[...] Oh Lord Jesus, no Jesus [...] pay and He would say to thee, I have seen the cry [...] and I have seen that which thou hast had within. For so long for thou has prayed unto me and said, "O Lord, how long can this go on and what shall be. Where can I find this light? Where can I find this light? Where can I find that which I seek?" And the Lord would say to thee, "My child, their assault, that which is true and now has heard many things and many times thou has tested it and found it not so but this day, hear, for love has come to thee, not the love of man but the love of thy God."

Into the depths I saw, and there shall be a liberating, the chains shall fall. There shall be a change in the very depths of our soul. For that which thou has so shall be in thee from this moment. There will be a release. You shall find an easy place of rest for your soul. Father, I just thank you that your Word is always true Lord. I just thank you that you're a God of love, Lord we thy people, those called by thy name [...] just want to please and delight thy heart, Lord. We're not seeking to be anything but what you want to make us. We're not seeking to do anything but what you desire. Lord, we have nothing without you.

 APPENDIX

Lord, I just pray for each one here and everyone that hears this message. Lord, let them know that we've come to fulfil only your will. Lord, let every heart rest in confidence that you will accomplish that which you've set about to do. Nothing, nothing shall [thwart] your purpose. Lord, bless each one and let your healing power flow to each one this day, Lord. Let us hear the wonderful things you have planned. Show us, Lord, teach us, Lord, we submit to you. We [are] prepared for anything to delight you. We pray in Jesus' precious, the most wonderful name, amen, amen.

Glory to God. Lord, let life and light flow. Let your Word be heard again in this land, Lord. Release your Word in a new way, Lord. Let every one who hears know there's a God in heaven who can keep us in the lion's den, who can shut the mouth of lions. Lord, every single one who hears, Lord, open their ears, those inward ears, O Lord. Open the spiritual eyes to see, for truly it's a time and a time and a half when your Word will go forth with tremendous power, for you've sent your angels. They have gone carrying the gifts you gave them, and from the four corners of the Earth, the sound of your voice has come. Your voice will be heard as never before. The Word that burns like a fire will go forth and burn up the dross. Those that are raised up to hear shall hear. They shall be transformed by the power of that Word.

No longer will there be hesitation, no longer will it be a time for the future, and for it is the time, a time and a half. I saw the angels that bear the Word. I saw those that heard. I saw a mighty fire begin to kindle. I gazed and wondered at it. I heard the voice of many waters. I heard the declaration of the King of kings. I saw the cherubim speaking, for I saw in their hands the power of life. I heard as it were thunder across the heavens. I beheld thunder and lightning and a still, small voice. I saw those that were precious for the Lamb; those were a peculiar treasure and on fire, but the fire did not burn them. The fire did not hurt them; the fire cleansed them. The fire quickens. The fire was life and light and power.

Stay updated on new books about Bishop Michael Reid by
registering your email at www.globalgospelfellowship.net

Connect with us on social media too!

Ways of God Ministries